EUGENICS

and

EDUCATION

in

AMERICA

Complicated Conversation

A Book Series of Curriculum Studies

William F. Pinar
General Editor

Vol. 18

PETER LANG
New York • Washington, D.C./Baltimore • Bern
Frankfurt am Main • Berlin • Brussels • Vienna • Oxford

Ann Gibson Winfield

EUGENICS
and
EDUCATION
in
AMERICA

Institutionalized Racism and
the Implications of History,
Ideology, and Memory

PETER LANG
New York • Washington, D.C./Baltimore • Bern
Frankfurt am Main • Berlin • Brussels • Vienna • Oxford

Library of Congress Cataloging-in-Publication Data

Winfield, Ann Gibson.
Eugenics and education in America: institutionalized racism and the implications
of history, ideology, and memory / Ann Gibson Winfield.
p. cm. — (Complicated conversation: a book series of curriculum studies; vol. 18)
Includes bibliographical references and index.
1. Racism in education—United States. 2. Eugenics—Social aspects—
United States. 3. Discrimination in education—United States. 4. Racism—
United States—History—20th century. I. Title.
LC212.2.W56   371.82900973—dc22   2006022457
ISBN 978-0-8204-8146-3
ISSN 1534-2816

Bibliographic information published by **Die Deutsche Bibliothek.**
Die Deutsche Bibliothek lists this publication in the "Deutsche
Nationalbibliografie"; detailed bibliographic data is available
on the Internet at http://dnb.ddb.de/.

© 2007 Peter Lang Publishing, Inc., New York
29 Broadway, 18th floor, New York, NY 10006
www.peterlang.com

Printed in the United States of America

This book is dedicated to my son Lucian and to school children everywhere who have been sorted, tracked, and pushed out through no fault of their own to the detriment of us all.

Contents

Foreword

As finite beings in an infinite and expanding universe, our understanding of the world is necessarily contingent, partial, and incomplete, and yet we live for the most part as if our everyday assumptions, biases, myths, and common sense are simply and entirely true. To say that we are—each and all of us—blind to our own blind spots is a tautology. To take that tautology as a provocation, as a point of departure toward upending our own orthodoxy requires curiosity and courage. Ann Winfield has an abundance of both—a lively and exquisite mind combined with a willingness to relentlessly poke around in the dark. The result is a work of power and importance—breathtaking in its reach and surprising on almost every page. Here she interrogates—through the lens of a movement and an ideology that dominated our culture for much of the twentieth century—the story of democracy, freedom, and exalted forward progress that we Americans love to tell ourselves. Written out of the official story as quackery and the handiwork of a few nutcases, Winfield demonstrates beyond doubt that eugenics was not only respectable, mainstream science but also that its major tenets were wellsprings in the formation of American public schools with echoes in the every day practices of today. Formed in the crucible of white supremacy and rigid hierarchies of human value, American schools have never adequately faced that living heritage.

We no longer talk of "miscegenation" or "imbeciles," of course, and we are likely to look upon forced sterilization and race-based marriage laws as archaic. But Winfield undermines any sense of smug superiority we might grant ourselves by drawing a direct line from those repulsive labels and practices to our own obsessions with "standards" and "accountability," test scores and grades. White supremacy surely changes its spots but it remains durable and dominant.

Education, of course, is never entirely neutral—it always has a value, a position, a politics. Education—teaching and schooling—either reinforces or challenges the existing social order. For humanists and democratic educators, the largest, most generous purpose of education is always human enlightenment and human liberation, and the driving principle is the unity of all humanity. We embrace the conviction that every human being is of incalculable value, entitled to decent standards concerning freedom and justice and education, and that any violations, deliberate or inadvertent, must be fought against, testified to, and resisted.

The unity of human beings is based both upon a recognition of differences as well as a consciousness of our interdependence. People are different—distinct capacities, unique needs—and we are, at the same time, entirely connected. In today's world, where we seem to know the price of everything and the value of nothing, the knowledge we lack includes an acknowledgment of the reality of our wild diversity—something that just *is*—and at the same time an acceptance of our deep connectedness. The knowledge we desperately need now is a knowledge based upon recognition, upon unity and solidarity.

The relationship between education and freedom is deep, intrinsic, and profound—they are essentially the same thing. Both concern themselves with the fullest expression of human development. To the extent that people reflect upon their lives and become more conscious of themselves as actors in the world, they insert themselves as subjects in history, constructors of the human world, and they enact and express themselves, then, as free human beings.

The aim of humanistic educators is to organize schools in such a way that every member can develop and use all of his or her capacities and powers without infringing upon the basic conditions or rights of others. The classroom becomes an association in which the free development of each is the condition for the free development of all.

To be a good teacher in this context means above all to have an abiding faith in all students, to believe in the possibility that every person can create things and is capable of both individual and social transformation. Education becomes a form of reinventing, re-creating, and rewriting, and this is a task that can be accomplished only by free subjects, never by inert objects. Education, then, is a dialogical process in which everyone participates actively as equals—a turbulent, raucous, unpredictable, and participatory affair. The goal of dialogue in this context is critical thinking and action—knowledge emerges from the continual interaction of reflection and action.

In democratic schools, an emphasis on the needs and interests of the student is co-primary with faith in a kind of robust public that can be created in classrooms, as well as in the larger society. To be exclusively child centered, to the extent that the needs of the group are ignored or erased, is to develop a kind of fatalistic narcissism; to honor the group while ignoring the needs of the individual is to destroy any possibility of freedom. This is the meaning of community, the creation of places where people are held together because they are working along common lines in a common spirit with common aims. These are places of energy and excitement, unlike the sites of coercion and containment that are all-too-familiar in schools: the difference is motive, spirit, and atmosphere. These qualities are found when people move from being passive recipients to choosing themselves as authors, actors, builders, and makers within a social surround.

When the aim of education is the absorption of facts, learning becomes exclusively and exhaustively selfish, and there is no obvious social motive for learning. The measure of success is always a competitive one—it is about comparing results and sorting people into winners and losers. People are turned against one another, and every difference becomes a potential deficit. Getting ahead of others is the primary goal in such places, and mutual assistance, which can be so natural, is severely restricted or banned. On the other hand, where active work is the order of the day, helping others is not a form of charity, something that impoverishes both recipient and benefactor. Rather a spirit of open communication, interchange and analysis become commonplace. Of course in these places there is a certain natural disorder, a certain amount of anarchy and chaos as there is in any busy workshop. But there is a deeper discipline, the discipline of getting things done and learning through life, and there is an appreciation of knowledge as an inherently public good—something that can be reproduced at little or no cost, and (unlike commodities), when it's given away, no one has any less of it. In a rational society, knowledge would be shared without any reservation or restriction whatsoever.

Schools serve societies—in many ways all schools are microcosms of the societies in which they are embedded—and they are both mirror and window onto the social reality. If one understands the schools, one can see the whole of society; if one fully grasps the intricacies of society, one will know something true about the schools. In a totalitarian society, for example, schools would be built for obedience and conformity; in a kingdom, the schools would teach fealty. But in an authentic democracy we would expect to find schools defined by a spirit of cooperation, inclusion, and full participation, places that honor diversity while building unity. Schools in a democracy would resist the over-specialization of human activity— the separation of the intellectual from the manual, the head from the hand, the heart and the head, the creative and the functional—as a distortion. The goal of democratic schools would be the fluidity of function, the variation of work and capacity, the mobilization of intelligence and creativity and initiative and work in all directions.

The education we are used to is only a caricature—it is not authentically or primarily about full human development. Why, for example, is education thought of as only kindergarten through 12th grade, or kindergarten through university? Why does education occur only early in life? Why is there a point in our lives when we feel we no longer need education? Why again, is there a hierarchy of teacher over student? Why are there grades and grade levels? Why is there attendance? Why is being on time so valuable? Why indeed do we think of a productive and a service sector in our society, with education designated a service activity? Why is education separate from production?

Eugenics and Education will change the way you think about curriculum and teaching, school reform, educational policy and practice, and even the current debates concerning immigration and marriage. This is essential reading for anyone who hopes to understand the sorry state of our schools today, and the deep changes we must undertake to improve them. After seeing the world through Ann Winfield's eyes, when you hear the terms "gifted and talented" or "at risk" you're likely to wince. Good.

William Ayers
Distinguished Professor of Education
at the University of Illinois, Chicago
Author of *To Teach* and *Teaching Toward Freedom*

Acknowledgements

This work has come about as the result of a great many factors, not the least of which are the people in my life who deserve my deepest thanks. I am most appreciative of the support and input of my dissertation committee Paul Bitting, Ken Brinson, and Peter Hessling and especially to my comrade, friend, mentor, and committee chair Anna Wilson all of whom inspired and incited my courage, reigned in my purple pomposity, and provided a wholly meaningful graduate experience. Deep appreciation and thanks go to my colleagues at Roger Williams University who have graciously shared their knowledge and experience and have eased my transition into academia tremendously. Particular thanks go to Bruce Marlowe for his editing prowess and pithy commentary on the manuscript both of which served to transition this work from its origin as a lumbering dissertation. William Pinar has provided much, through both his scholarship and support as has the work of William Ayers, William Watkins, and Maxine Greene. Each has shaped my thinking in important and powerful ways. My son, Lucian, has tolerated me and infused my life with joy, humor, pre-teen (and now teen) perspective, and Spongebob philosophy. Finally, my academic accomplishment rests squarely on the shoulders of my family who have supported me in all ways. Thank you for the love, politics, and perspective, without which none of this would have been possible.

Introduction

Adolf Hitler had a model for his program of racial purification: the eugenics movement in the United States. In 1924, the movement was in full swing, reflected by the passage of a number of laws having to do with immigration, mandatory sterilization, and anti-miscegenation, all designed to protect white Americans from a perceived threat: mongrelization at the hands of throngs of millions of immigrants. When Hitler published *Mein Kampf* in 1924, it was the U.S. Immigration Restriction Act of 1924 that served as a model for his plan to create a Nordic white race, beginning a relationship that has eluded the national consciousness since. For the first six decades of the twentieth century, political and social discourse in the United States was dominated by an ideology that relegated the vast majority of the human race to imbecility, declaring that only those of Nordic ancestry were worthy of survival. During this period, hundreds of thousands of Americans were denied the right to reproduce as a result of forced sterilization, marriage restriction, and institutionalization. From New England to California, a war was waged upon entire ethnic groups, the urban poor, rural "white trash," the sexually deviant, Blacks, Jews, Native Americans, Asians, Latino/as, the deaf, blind, epileptic, alcoholic, petty criminals, the mentally ill, and anyone who did not fit with the pseudoscientifically established blonde, blue-eyed "norm" represented by the eugenically glorified "superior" Nordic race (Black 2003).

Eugenics, both the ideology and the movement that propelled it into a dominant cultural norm, was an early twentieth-century iteration of a strain of a deeply held philosophical maxim in Western thought. The intentional weeding out of the human population of those deemed weak or malformed can be traced to ancient Sparta and is also evident in the writings of Aristotle and Plato. Indeed the revered idealized states depicted in *Politics* and the *Republic* provide the state with the power to strictly regulate procreation based on perceived mental or physical "fitness." Hierarchical models of human worth can be traced throughout intellectual history.

During the latter years of the nineteenth century, Social Darwinism and the application of a *survival of the fittest* mandate to social theory and policy began to sour in the minds of an increasingly Progressive public sentiment.

Due to the seductive nature of ideology, and an especially visceral recognition of fundamental precepts defining human worth and ability, this public distaste was merely a bump in the road for racialized scientism—one of many. Racist ideological structure has, in its American iteration, existed virtually unscathed for the past two centuries weathering public argument over Imperialism, the civil rights movement, school desegregation in the 1950s, 1960s, and 1970s, the Bell Curve wars in the 1980s, The Human Genome Project, and school resegregation in the 1990s. Definitions of human worth and ability have changed their tone, and changed their language—instead of "morons" and "idiots" we now talk about "at risk" children—but the core has not been altered. This book traces those fundamental precepts regarding human worth and ability from Puritan imperatives through Social Darwinism and ultimately to the eugenics movement in the United States. The historical context leading up to and including the eugenics movement had, and continues to have, profound implications for the establishment of our system modern education.

The efforts to eliminate non-white segments of the population was not the work of some extremist sect in America. Indeed, this war was waged by venerated professors, ivy league universities, wealthy philanthropists and industrialists, educators, armies of social workers and medical professionals, and government officials of all stripes. Cloaked in a mantle of respectable science, eugenics relied heavily on a pre-existing stream of historical consciousness comprised of base racism, ethnic hatred, and academic elitism. The ultimate eugenic purpose was clear: the prevention of what Franklin Roosevelt called "race suicide" and the creation (within three generations) of a superior Nordic race. It was within this ideological context that our modern form of schooling in the United States was conceived and formed; a fact that historical accountings of education have, for the most part, so far failed to acknowledge.

Ashley Montague, the American geneticist who exposed the fallacies of Nazi race hygiene and so-called scientific racism throughout his career, wrote in 1945 that

> no activity of man, whether it be the making of a book, the contraction of a muscle, the manufacture of a brick, the expression of an idea, or the writing of a work such as this, can be fully understood without a knowledge of the history of that activity insofar as it has been socially determined. For, obviously, any neglect to take into consideration the relations of the social framework can only lead to a defective understanding of such events. (1945, p. 62)

So it is with the institution of education in America. The history of education, from the ubiquitous mentions of the Old Deluder Stan Act of 1647 and Horace Mann"s common-school movement, to the factory model of schooling and the Committee of Ten, has so far failed to heed Montague"s warning. The so-called Fathers of Curriculum, including John Franklin Bobbitt, W. W. Charters, G. Stanley Hall, Edward L. Thorndike were all enamored of eugenic ideology and their work in the field of education reflects their hierarchical conception of the human race. The unique blending in America of history, ideology, and memory during the first three decades of the twentieth century ensured that schooling in America has been defined and organized according to a racialized scientism that has sorted children ever since.

The eugenics movement in America has impacted not only education, but also societal institutions in general. Myriad patterns of thought, policy considerations, forms of social dialogue, and multiple political, social, philosophical, and ideological trends within modern culture can be traced to the undercurrent of racialized scientism represented by eugenic ideology. Eugenics has been dangerously dismissed as an unfortunate, pseudo-scientific blip in the grand expedition that is American Progress. This is an extremely dangerous stance for a number of reasons. First, that the eugenics movement was a reiteration of older, similarly dismissed conceptions of human society (Great Chain of Being theory and Social Darwinism being two examples) indicates that there is something at work beyond misguided, haphazard, historical repetition. To ignore the operation of socially propagated ideological streams in our own lives is to submit ourselves to past mandate. Second, our persistent dismissal of eugenics as a miscreant child along an otherwise exalted national unfolding leads to an inability to uncover the ways that both national and individual identity are confined by ideologies from the past. That identifiable, ideological strains of thought persist throughout human history suggests that there must be a mechanism by which it travels. I will argue that ideological constructs, like racism, persist by means of collective memory, both familial and institutional.

Scholars have long been aware that ideological structures and patterns of thought persist through generations, but it is relatively recently that the phrase "collective memory" has been used to describe the process. In order to understand the ways in which institutionalized racism operates, it is helpful to think of individual memory as reliant on a collective context. We learn to make sense of the world through our interactions with institutions like family, church, and school, and it is in these places that memories from the past are operationalized in the present. Collective memory provides the model to which individual memory is bound to conform and, furthermore, the capacity of collective memory to endure depends on the social power of the group that holds it.

Our own apparent blindness to, or denial of, the effect of eugenic ideology on the foundations of education in America exists in direct proportion to the degree to which this ideology is operationalized within individuals and society. In other words, we cannot see it because it seems normal to us, a natural explanation of things; it is the stuff of assumptions. "Why, of course," we think, "there are some among our children who are gifted, and others who are inherently 'at risk' by virtue of their family heritage." "After all, the tests prove it, right?" Indeed, we dismiss historical introspection at our own peril, particularly given our current (continuing) preoccupation with a quest for genetic perfection (and an increasingly alarming arsenal of medical advances to achieve this quest), not to mention our insistence that reliable and valid measurement of human ability and worth is possible. Once we know, we are obligated to protect our children from being subjected to the miscalculations of those who have come before.

While the core of this book establishes the relationship between eugenics and education specifically, it is also about the deeper ideological roots that direct Western thinking altogether. Furthermore, the use of concepts like collective memory and historically directed popular culture theory provide a model for investigating the relationship between ideology and culture generally. The operation of ideology within social discourse, and its manifestation within collective memory, is revealed through those popular cultural artifacts used by society to make sense of itself. Textbooks, pamphlets, state fairs, lecture circuits, conferences, institutions, books, magazines, films, posters, and the detritus of a paper-driven society provide a rich source of insight into the popular culture of the early twentieth century and it is to these sources that I have turned in order to investigate the interrelationship between eugenics and education. Beginning with Puritan forms of social discourse through the Great Chain of Being theory, Social Darwinism, and the development of the Progressive movement, this book proceeds to outline the eugenics movement in terms of its structure, philosophy, and influence, revealing a deeply intertwined relationship between eugenic ideology and the educational philosophy that defines our current system.

History, ideology, and memory are the three fundamental societal elements that contribute to current patterns of thought, policy considerations, and the multiple political, social, philosophical, and ideological trends within modern culture. Chapter One briefly examines these elements and outlines the rest of the book. I introduce eugenic ideology, outline the movement and its historical context, introduce the concept of collective memory and my uses of popular, material, and media culture theory.

Using an anthropological perspective to examine the theoretical literature on the concept of memory, Chapter Two describes the relationship between memory and specific social contexts such as family, social class, and schooling. Following recent scholarship in the discipline of history regarding the relationship between the past and the present, I will show that history is not simply a recording of the past in a linear chronology, but instead, history continues to exist in the present because of the role of collective memory and our interaction with our cultural environment.

Analysis of artifacts and objects of culture and their role in the formation and validation of belief and power systems reveal how eugenicists could so successfully disseminate their beliefs. Chapter Three examines media, material, and popular culture theory and focuses these investigative tools on an historical era. The most prominent public figures of the time, from scientists to philanthropists and politicians, eugenicists were successful at shaping governmental policy on issues of sterilization, immigration, and marriage laws. Through their use of grassroots organizing techniques, education, and popular culture venues, eugenicists were also successful in creating widespread public acceptance within an otherwise Progressive political climate and a sense of national unity around their policies.

Chapter Four is concerned with prior forms of race theory as well as those patterns of cognition unique to the United States that helped shape the dialogue around race. This chapter examines the fundamental constructs of positivism, and those foundational scientific theories, ideologies, and philosophies upon which so much of modern science still relies including the "Great Chain of Being" theory, Naturalism, Darwin, and Social Darwinism. Finally, Chapter Four introduces the Progressive context within which the translation of Social Darwinism to eugenic ideology emerged.

During the first three decades of the twentieth century a prodigious group of scientists, politicians, and philanthropists waged a vicious campaign against those peoples considered defective and feebleminded. Chapter Five concentrates on the rise of eugenic ideology in the United States. The movement is presented within the historical and social context of immigration, poverty, crime, and dependency. The success of the eugenics movement, examined in Chapter Six, can be traced, in part, through the passage of widespread mandatory sterilization legislation, Supreme Court rulings, immigration policy, and marriage restrictions.

Chapter Seven explores how the "Fathers of Curriculum," namely Thorndike, Bobbitt, and Hall among others, inserted their beliefs about race, degeneracy, and ability into their theories of education. Chapter Seven also examines the many ways educational history has traditionally articulated this period including humanism, mental discipline, developmentalists, child study, and social efficiency educators. Using North Carolina Department of Public Instruction data gathered from the North Carolina State Archives, Chapter Eight examines the translation of eugenic ideology into popular conceptions of schooling through the mid-1950s.

The legacy of eugenics in terms of the descriptors and classifications used by schools appeared well in to the 1950s in North Carolina and was roused to the surface largely in response to the national push for desegregation that culminated in the United States Supreme Court ruling *Brown v. Board of Education.*

Finally, Chapter Nine concludes the book by tying the previous eight chapters together and superimposing them upon the present time. Hailed as a progressive solution to social ills, leaders associated with the eugenics movement successfully lobbied for, and largely directed, social policy in many fields that continue to define common notions of human worth and ability. I use the theory of collective memory along with popular/media/material culture theory to describe the trajectory of racist ideology, manifest in many forms both prior to and following the eugenics movement, through the generations. In schools all across the country students are being required to participate in a century-long national experiment whose intentions towards them are questionable at best, and downright malicious at worst.

Just hearing the word *test* can make most of us lapse into a memory-induced mini-coma replete with glazed eyes, sweaty palms, and a tight stomach. If our discomfiture comes not from embedded memory of our own experience, then another likely source is the humdrum of the discourse. The same old words are repeated over and over, about something you *think* you are supposed to believe in, something you *think* sounds good, but you just are not sure. And those memories, ever persistent, are always there. Some people call the current debate over high-stakes testing rhetoric, some call it sound reasoning. Whatever they call it, it is sweeping the nation essentially unabated. Many of us are too busy stuck in the quagmire with our own children, hoping they will get through the fourth grade writing test, or the dreaded end-of-grade test, and not crack under the pressure. I have seen the discomfiture in my own son, and although I fundamentally disagree with the methodology of our schools in sorting and tracking students, I am embarrassed to admit that I have pushed him to do well on the tests and more, to care about them.

Investigation into the form and function of ideologies such as eugenics in modern society is a convoluted business. Conduits of influence extend across a broad spectrum, delineations blur, strength waxes and wanes. However, nothing compares to a distillate understanding of who we are, and why we think the way we do, than a concentrated exegesis of present and past ideological structures and their flow through time and populous. Further, exposure of ideological form and function lends itself to change and possibility by providing not only the tools to dismantle the shackles of the past, but also by revealing the true nature of the shackles themselves. This book is about ideology, it is about memory, it is about us. The ideology? Eugenics. The memory? Human worth and ability as defined by race and class. Us? Every person educated in the United States.

1

Ideology, Tools, and Perspective

During the first half of the twentieth century the operational ideology in America was eugenics. This was an ideology wherein the so-called well born, representing the "superior stock" of the nation, felt themselves to be under imminent threat of "race suicide" from abundantly fertile throngs of "unfit" and "feebleminded" poor, non-white, non-Protestant segments of the population. This book is about us. Privilege and ancestry aside, we are all bounded by the same ideological substrate, infused in collective memory, signifying everything. We are in an era of profound vehemence on the part of ideologues who promote *standards* and *accountability* as representative of the nation's best hope for progress. Given this, it behooves us, as both educators and citizens, to examine critically the roots of this ideological mandate. Eugenic ideology, persistent for over a century in the American psyche, provides an invisible substrate for commonly held assumptions about ability and human worth.

As an iteration of an intellectual tradition far older than the historical blip that is America, eugenic ideology traces a path in America from the latter decades of the nineteenth century through the *Brown v. Board of Education* (1954) federal mandate to desegregate the nation's public school system and into present-day problems such as resegregation, the achievement gap, astronomical dropout rates for all but middle and upper-middle class white students, to name a few. For the purpose of this inquiry, I concentrate specifically on the way in which eugenics and social engineering were advanced in the schools due, in part, to the unique blend of supposed scientific legitimacy and ideology employed by eugenicists. Using Geertz' (1973) description of the form and function of *cultural systems*, the unique blend of science and ideology that was the American eugenics movement constitutes an imminently enduring cultural system. Geertz describes the role of science within cultural systems as providing a diagnostic and critical dimension, while ideology, on the other hand, provides a justificatory, apologetic dimension. We will see that early twentieth century eugenicists were quite proficient in formulating a cultural system that, were it not for the deeds of Adolf Hitler, might have result- ed in an America that looks very different from its current state. Before we dismiss the effects of eugenic ideology altogether, it is important to understand that there was no great repudiation of the underlying ideas of racial purification in America. Rather, the movement went underground, while the infrastructure that was already in operation in the form of our great institutions continued to operate as if noth- ing had happened. Ideology, according to Geertz (1973), refers to the part of culture which is actively concerned with the establishment and defense of patterns of belief and value. "A political ideology," according to Freeden (2003),

> is a set of values, opinions, and ideas that 1) exhibit a recurring pattern; 2) are held by significant groups; 3) compete over providing and controlling plans for public policy; and 4) do so with the aim of justifying, contesting, or changing the social and political arrangements and processes of a political community. (p. 32)

We will see that eugenics satisfies this definition in important and ultimately dele- terious ways.

The implications for our society of eugenic ideology acting in the capacity described by Geertz and Freeden are grave. Historical data show that, in fact, eugenic ideology was successful in establishing and defending patterns of belief and value that defined racial and class inequities in terms of heredity and innate abi- lity. By undertaking an historical analysis, my purpose is to reveal the ways that social and political ideologies of the past, like eugenics, have been preserved through col- lective memory and, thus, have the potential to be manifest in social policies of the present. Specifically, I seek to understand the historical connection between edu- cation and eugenic ideology using a framework that defines history not as an accounting of past events, but instead as a phenomenon that occurs as a function of collective memory.

Beginning with ideological constructs that exist within memory in the present, I argue that it is possible to follow the pathways by which these doctrines travel from Puritanism in America and the intellectual history that preceded its arrival. Referencing the present ideological agenda, Smith (2003) describes a bifurcation within America's publicly mediated account of identity and aims, and the escalat- ing global perception that a dangerous exclusionary ideological agenda is at work. In Smith's view, the cold war has been replaced by a war on human diversity, religious freedom, free speech, and the "relentless logic of the new Caesars" (p. 489). Smith (2003) argues, for example, that the Bush/Rumsfeld/Cheney-led "war on terror" is an example of a thinly veiled intensification of long-standing global impe rial aims on the part of the United States. It is here, Smith (2003) explains, that the line between knowledge and misrepresentation has become completely blurred and in which thinly veiled doctrines are imbued with the power to influence the production of social policy.

It might be noted that a great deal of valuable time and attention is spent on this already, but rarely do we trace such doctrines backwards through time. What Smith is talking about is evidence of the same core ideological structures at work in the present. Meanwhile, education is, as it has always been, co-opted by this ideological substrate, dressed in a Progressive rhetoric of equal opportunity while functioning as a mode of governmental control by helping to construct what Graham (1991) calls *governable subjects*. Education, formed as a discrete area of academic inquiry within the same period of history dominated by eugenic ideology, carries a legacy informed and created by eugenic ideology, which has defined, sorted, and categorized students on the basis of a heretofore unexamined yardstick of "scientific" racialism.

Put another way, we share a collective memory in America that shapes, frames, and defines our thinking about race, ability, and human worth. This shared framework extends into virtually all public perception and debate and is shared to the extent that it transcends rhetorical labels of progressive versus conservative, (although of course, unique variations occur along racial, class, and gendered lines). Racist ideology, traceable to biblical and Greco-Roman traditions, came to America with the Puritans and was cemented in the modern era by eighteenth-and nineteenth-century advances in science and the paradigmatic dominance of positivism. The division of human beings into a racialized hierarchy of ability and worth subsumes the common parameters of intelligence and ability and extends to cultural constructs of all kinds including economic, religious, and political groupings, as well as foreign and domestic policy. Scientific approaches and explanations of human difference are embedded within social discourse as a function of collective memory.

Identity politics aside, each individual bears responsibility for an engagement with internalized ideological structure within his or her own psyche. Nevertheless, it is from a perspective of hope that I offer this book. Despite often overwhelming evidence to the contrary (the war on terror, the standards and accountability movements that so characterize education in the present, and the increasingly successful right-wing conservative agenda in American politics are examples), it has been argued that contemporary North American dominant culture is experiencing increasingly desperate, and ultimately dangerous, times. Desperate because fundamental flaws in the Western philosophical canon are being challenged by the forces of globalization (Stolke, 1995; Smith, 2003; Carlson, 2003) and dangerous because epistemological shifts over the past half-century have begun to reveal the soft underbelly of the larger imperial aims within the American worldview. On every front, from federal education policy to the so-called war on terror, dominant American culture is infused with fear as the deep etchings of scientific racialism echo falsely. The political right is strong and vibrant, but references to "the bedrock values of our nation" make me deeply uneasy. Assumptions about race, ability, and human worth, provided in their modern form by race theorists from the nineteenth century, entered into the public vernacular and, subsequently, into the collective memory of our nation during the first three decades of the twentieth century, and they have not left. In order to conceive of a global future that is free of erroneous divisions we must dismantle the internalized and often unconscious constructs that have shaped the debate thus far.

Eugenics has been variously described as "an ideal, a doctrine, a science (applied human genetics), a set of practices (ranging from birth control to euthanasia), and as a social movement" (Paul, 1998, p. 95). Ideology, on the other hand, "names the structure of situations in such a way that the attitude contained toward them is one of commitment" (Geertz, 1973, p. 231). Both eugenics and ideology define a structure by which to understand the world. Ideology, though, is more seductive. Ideology has a way of sneaking in the back door, whether manifest as a policy directive or a rock concert, it is, as Geertz said, "ornate, vivid, [and] deliberately suggestive" (Geertz, 1973, p. 231). Ideology seduces us "by objectifying moral sentiment through the same devices that science shuns, [and in so doing] it seeks to motivate action" (p. 231). Eugenics is an ideology, replete with imperatives that spawned deep commitment among its followers and motivated action within a multitude of human activities in America[1] and beyond. As an ideology, eugenics operated in myriad ways to construct definitions of race, ability, and degeneracy that are uniquely American.

This chapter briefly defines eugenic ideology and then provides an introduction to the rest of the book by introducing the major elements of my argument. I demonstrate that we are not only influenced by and the product of our history but that we and our policies are the living manifestations of that history.

What Is Eugenics?

In 1883, Sir Francis Galton,[2] an English mathematician, coined the term *eugenics* (Galton, 1904, p. 35) as a way to describe the process of improving the "stock" of human populations. Galton (1904) was specifically concerned with the preservation of superior "stock" and offered the following definition:

> Eugenics is the science which deals with all influences that improve the inborn qualities of a race; also with those that develop them to the utmost advantage. (p. 35)

From its inception, then, eugenics was not solely concerned with heredity but rather, it was concerned with what to do with the results of heredity. Eugenic ideology relied on the premise that human worth was the function of a hierarchical system based, in part, on race and class. In the early twentieth century, the United States was becoming increasingly both urban and industrial (Zinn, 1980; Cremin, 1988; Kliebard, 1997; Stoskopf, 1999) and it was during this period that the eugenics movement flourished.

Fear of the "Other"

A number of factors contributed to both the success of the movement as a whole and the degree to which eugenic ideology infiltrated institutional development during the height of the movement in the 1920s and 1930s. At the turn of the twentieth century, America was experiencing an enormous influx of immigrants and public alarm was on the rise. The common perception of these immigrants held that they were very different from their Northern European predecessors. Cubberley (1934) echoed the widespread view among eugenicists that these Eastern European immigrants were "of a very different sort" and were "largely illiterate, docile, [and] often lacking in initiative" (p. 485). Furthermore, the estimated 2 million immigrants who entered the country between 1906 and 1910 were deemed to be "wholly without Anglo-Saxon conceptions of righteousness, liberty, law, order, public decency, and government" (p. 486). "Their coming," Cubberley (1904) continued, "has served to dilute tremendously our national stock and to weaken and corrupt our political life" (p. 486).

This trend, as well as changes brought about by the Industrial Revolution[3] and shifts in the demographic landscape, gave rise to a large, poverty-stricken underclass concentrated in American cities. The turn of the century saw an intellectual transformation from the premises of Social Darwinism[4] to eugenics as many people in intellectual circles began to call into question, on moral grounds, the assumptions and results of Social Darwinism. The Progressive movement, formed from charitable roots and a desire to achieve societal betterment, was provided a nurturing environment by America's Puritan legacy. Puritan inclinations regarding salvation, the idea that America represented an exalted position as a "city on the hill" and was God's chosen place (McKnight, 2003) were instrumental in establishing a level of comfort with the imperatives defined by eugenic ideology. It is precisely at the confluence of these contextual elements, Puritan inclinations, Social Darwinism, and the Progressive movement that the eugenics movement was able to define itself (and everybody else) such that acceptance of eugenic assumptions occurred practically unchallenged for decades. Eugenicists did this by positing solutions to social problems and reinterpreting Social Darwinism in Progressive language, and in so doing they were able to appeal to a broad audience of Progressive psychologists, anthropologists, theologians, and educators.

Further fueling European American[5] middle and upper class fears during this period was an increasing level of militancy among the ranks of labor; socialism and anarchism reached a peak of popularity during the 1920s and 1930s as did the organizations of Progressive women fighting for suffrage and workers' rights (Zinn, 1980; Lemann, 1991; Takaki, 1993). Finally, Americans were feverish in their efforts to pursue an enlightenment-induced path towards societal and national progress. Ideas about the scientific method and objectivity were seen to be imbued with reason and so, with a scientifically justified racist foundation, eugenicists found a ripe environment to embed racist ideological hierarchy into the American mindset.

The Dilution of Genetic "Stock"

Eugenicists argued that the human gene pool was in danger of being weakened in terms of intelligence, strength, and ability through miscegenation and "wanton breeding" by "inferior" peoples (Galton, 1898; Thorndike, 1903; Shannon, 1904/1915; Pearson, 1909; Davenport, 1911; Goddard, 1911; Grant, 1916; Robinson, 1916; Popenoe, 1918; Stoddard, 1920, 1922; Wiggam, 1924; Hollingworth, 1929; Cubberley, 1934; Holmes, 1936; Hooten, 1939). For example, John Franklin Bobbitt, author of *The Curriculum* (1918) and currently hailed as a "Father of Education," was a eugenicist and believed that prosperity and progress were possible only if strict and unrelenting care was taken to control the spread of "inferior blood" and "worm eaten stock" (Bobbitt, 1923, p. 385). In contrast to Social Darwinists who eschewed charity and schools of any kind—believing that they interfered with natural selection—eugenicists believed that social ills would not fix themselves and that social progress required government intervention (Shannon, 1915; Popenoe, 1924; Holmes, 1936; Scheinfeld, 1939). Eugenicists believed that what they viewed as the biologically superior classes were destined, by virtue of their genetic makeup, to occupy the pinnacle of human civilization. Popular opinion supported the notion that the process of evolution would simply be too slow to adequately handle the needs of civilized society. Lynn (2001) contends that eugenics was supported by most scientists and social scientists up until the 1960s.

Over the course of the first four decades of the twentieth century, through legislative mandate, government successfully 'helped' nature along and defended civilization from what many eugenic popularizers referred to as *the rising tide of feeblemindedness* (Goddard, 1911; Stoddard, 1920; Wiggam, 1922; Sanger, 1924). Neither Darwinian thought nor its new cloak of eugenics did much to transform what was known as the "Great Chain of Being" theory popular in Victorian scientific circles (Tucker, 1994). Contemporaries of Darwin saw the Nordic race as occupying the position of the top link in the chain, with gradations down towards the African peoples whose position was just slightly above that of the ape (Hooten, 1937). This view held that non-white people were essentially living fossils and that while they might be able to achieve some progress over time, so too would whites, thereby maintaining the hierarchical status quo (Pickens, 1968). Eugenicists and Progressive conservatives were highly critical of social welfare programs that threatened to interfere with the forces of natural selection by aiding in the survival of the unfit.

Immune to Invalidation

One common inaccuracy regarding the eugenics movement holds that once its self-proclaimed scientific legitimacy in the form of Mendelian genetics was disproved, eugenics was discredited and denounced by society at large. Not only is this characterization wholly inaccurate, it is dangerous for its capacity to blind us to the deep and abiding impact of eugenic ideology on American culture. While it is true that the scientific validity of many of the claims made by eugenicists were called into question as early as the 1910s (Paul, 1998), this did little to dispel the movement's momentum garnered by the movement's initial campaign tactics.

Despite its questionable standing as a science, the pervasiveness of support for eugenics was clear, ranging from the nation's best-known scientists, to corporate philanthropists, to legislators, high-ranking court justices, and presidents (Kevles, 1985; Stoskopf, 1999; Black, 2003). Although a great deal of prestige was garnered by the sheer proliferation of high-profile support, the eugenics movement took nothing for granted and eugenic proponents were expert in their manipulation of various forms of popular culture to spread their ideology.

Dissemination Campaign

Leading eugenicists during the 1910s and 1920s were highly cognizant of the power of dissemination. Efforts to reach audiences beyond literate intellectuals often appealed to the public sense of civic duty and promoted the notion that it was no less than a moral obligation to engage in measures that would ensure the betterment of society. For example, The American Eugenics Society charged their Popular Education Committee with the task of sponsoring Fitter Families Contests at state fairs throughout the country (Haller, 1963; Kevles, 1985; Hasian, 1996; Selden, 1999). During the 1920s, these contests "graded" families, suggested possibilities for successful mating, and in so doing created a culture of fear and competition (a culture still in evidence today) in which families competed to secure genetic stature within their communities. Eugenicists believed they were engaged in a scientific practice that could ultimately identify the potential parents of a more eugenic future (Selden, 1999). Winners of the Fitter Families Contests were presented with a medal that proclaimed "Yea, I Have a Goodly Heritage" and were often frontpage material in local newspapers (Selden, 1999). In classrooms, at state fairs, in auditoriums and church basements, education of the public was a place where the struggle to contend with society's ills was finally a hands-on activity. Education of all types offered the opportunity to enhance natural law by furthering, as well as possible, the "blood wisdom" (Wiggam, 1924, p. 42) of inferior peoples. Further, education enabled each individual to reach whatever limited potential they might have.

In 1925, the American Eugenics Society charged its Committee on Formal Education with the task of advancing eugenic teaching in the schools (Paul, 1998). In addition to advocating for the biological sciences as the most promising avenue through which heredity and hygiene were taught, the committee also pushed for the use of mental tests so as to reinforce the perceived scientific nature of the information and thus counter charges of "pseudoscience." The provision of an important role for mental tests in American education privileged eugenic ideology in three important ways, according to Selden (1999). First, the key eugenic assumption that intelligence was hereditary could be more forcibly argued with tests as evidence. Second, a certain degree of legitimacy was afforded through the mere act of test administration, and third, the professional status garnered by test administrators, enhanced further if tests were administered in public schools, provided opportunities for dissemination (Selden, 1999). Given the corner on the multi-billion dollar textbook, test administration/scoring/analysis market of corporate giants like McGraw-Hill in the present, it is incumbent upon educators (who are under mandate to deliver the system) to understand the assumptions contained therein (Kohn, 2002).

While the connection between eugenics and the field of education has been acknowledged by a number of scholars, the extent to which eugenic ideology is part of the foundational substrate of public education in America is left entirely out of educational histories past and present. Historical accounts of education generally either fail to mention eugenics altogether or they provide only a cursory mention, although, to be fair, many of the eugenic mandates for education are presented as the work of social efficiency educators. In any event, until Selden's (1999) book *Inheriting Shame*, virtually no direct address of the impact of eugenics on education had been made.

Sterilization of the Unfit

In 1907, Indiana passed the first compulsory sterilization law for persons determined to be "unfit" (Carlson, 2001). Largely as a result of the work of one Charles Davenport, who established the Eugenics Record Office in Cold Spring Harbor, New York, and was secretary of the eugenics wing of the American Breeders Association, involuntary sterilization laws were passed in over 30 states governing the reproduction of "defective strains" within the general human population (Kevles, 1985; Carlson, 2001; Black, 2003). It has been reported that Harry Laughlin, a chief proponent of sterilization of the "unfit," was awarded a gold medal by the Nazis who subsequently used his model eugenic sterilization law in Germany (Kevles, 1985; Carlson, 2001; Black, 2003). Those considered "defective" were people who were blind, deaf, epileptic, "feebleminded," paupers, alcoholics, prison inmates, institutional populations, unmarried mothers, and children thought to be sexually deviant due to masturbation (Carlson, 2001). Many state sterilization laws followed the (1927) U.S. Supreme Court decision known as *Buck v. Bell*. U.S. Supreme Court Justice Oliver Wendell Holmes affirmed the judgment of the lower courts against Carrie Buck whom he described as "a feebleminded White woman . . . the daughter of a feebleminded mother in the same institution, and the mother of an illegitimate feebleminded child" (Holmes, 1926). Writing the majority opinion, Holmes wrote:

> it is for the best interests of the patients and of society that the inmate under [the superintendent of a State Colony] care should be sexually sterilized, he may have the operation performed upon any patient afflicted with hereditary forms of insanity, imbecility, &c [*sic*]. (Holmes, 1926)

Thereafter, sterilization became a major front in the war against the "rising tide of feeblemindedness" from Delaware to California. States proudly published their statistics, a practice that continued, in some cases, into the mid-1970s.

Progressive Roots

An examination of historical literature (Link, 1955; Hofstadter, 1963; Pickens, 1968; Selden, 1999) regarding the Progressive movement reveals a clear consensus about the level of complexity among the ideologies, actions, and motivations of the times. Despite this, one finds an alarmingly consistent portrait of the period. Generally, the Progressive movement is considered to be an amalgamation of extraordinarily activist constituent movements whose intent was to address fears of communism and socialism, to engage in labor union busting, promote birth control, prohibition, immigration restriction, racial segregation, super-patriotism, fundamentalism, and finally to achieve the application of a business model efficiency to government and education (Hofstadter, 1963; Pickens, 1968). What is missing from the literature is a reflection of the degree to which eugenic ideology was intertwined with almost every issue. Selden (1999) contended that "the continuing belief on the part of many of today's educators that Progressivism was a period of solely liberal motives, actions, and consequences seriously limits our critical abilities" (p. 26).

For example, Margaret Sanger (1922), known primarily for her work in the area of birth control, was an early supporter of eugenics and worried about the "blind and haphazard consequence of uncontrolled instinct" (p. 99). Sanger expressed the common eugenic fear that:

> Everywhere we see poverty and large families going hand in hand. Those least fit to carry on the race are increasing most rapidly. People who cannot support their own offspring are encouraged by Church and State to produce large families. Many of the children thus begotten are diseased or feeble-minded; many become criminals. The burden of supporting these unwanted types has to be bourne by the healthy elements of the nation. Funds that should be used to raise the standard of our civilization are diverted to the maintenance of those who should have never been born. (p. 100)

I contend that much will be gained by engaging in a re-examination of our assumptions about motivations where Progressive issues are concerned. It is to the severe detriment of valuable introspection that we should assume that the Progressive movement was one of wholly uplifting, emancipatory intentions. The extension applies to the motivation behind early theorizing about education as well.

Eugenics and Education: The "Fathers" of Curriculum

The field of education regards John Franklin Bobbitt, G. Stanley Hall, and E. L. Thorndike, among others, as the "Fathers of Curriculum." Given this designation, it is imperative that we examine the impact of their self identification as eugenicists on the development of curriculum theory and resulting practice in schools. Furthermore, the fact that many current practices, particularly testing, were developed and formed within the same set of societal influences suggests that the connection is not just theoretical, but contextually required.

Eugenic ideology was an integral part of many of the educational reform movements of the 1910s and 1920s and guided innovations in teacher training, curriculum development, school organization, and especially testing. During this period, the first *Intelligence Quotient*[6] tests were being developed and tested on World War I recruits, a fact that had significant ramifications for education, immigration, and the formation of attitudes about ability (Lemann, 1999). Testing offered a "scientific" legitimacy that began to permeate the fields of both education and psychology. Other trends in education such as the measurement of ability, the provision of special services for the gifted, vocational education, and the preoccupation with test scores as an ultimate measure of innate ability can be traced back to the period of time that had as its intellectual foundation a deeply rooted belief in innate inequalities that must be addressed by schools (Bobbitt, 1918; Popenoe, 1924; Curti, 1959; Cremin, 1961).

Testing as a Tool

Given education's current reliance on testing and its results, an understanding of the context and assumptions that guided the development of testing as an educational tool is crucial. Testing became a standard bearer for what Lemann (1999) describes as the "Puritan attraction to improvement of the human state through system and order" (p. 18). Mental testing was attractive in part because it promised the ability to "quickly, almost miraculously, measure the innate capacity of the brain" (p. 18). Since the innate capacity of the brain was believed to be inherited, and since furthermore, many believed the world's darker-skinned races were inferior in intelligence than lighter-skinned ones, testing provided the moral equivalent to absolution when it came to access to education and, by extension, wealth and power (Lemann, 1999).

Why it Matters

The field of education is an infinitely appropriate window through which to inquire about society. Schooling, more than any other of our social institutions, constructs the link to history for the people of the United States by providing the perspective, sense of importance, and "spin." Contained within the daily occurrences of schooling we find a reflection of both the very best and the very worst of what we have been and who we are. Indeed, school experience is filled with the individual concerns of many teachers and administrators for the welfare of children. However, school is also filled with race, class, and gender disparities, and often provides unacknowledged reification of societal values (Curti, 1959; Tyack, 1974; Farber, 1994; Apple, 1997, 2001; Kliebard, 1997; Lemann, 1999).

Dewey (1936) argued that an intelligent theory of education must first determine the causes of conflict among participants in schools, and resist adhering to one side or another. Such a theory must attempt to proceed from a level of understanding that is deeper and more inclusive than the past half-century of multicultural education has proven to be. To proceed towards Dewey's conception would require three things: (a) an investigation into the causes of conflict among theorists and practitioners, (b) a persistent reconnoitering that reveals the cause of achievement gaps; and finally, (c) a close inspection of those latent assumptions about race, class, and ability that contribute to formulating the conception of curriculum currently in use. An oft-cited argument contends that because we have all experienced education first hand, we are a nation of opinionated education experts. Rather than bemoan this state of affairs, it may be useful for us to harness this phenomenon by attempting to reveal the source of our "expertise." Perhaps it is the nature of our collective culture that we rely on boundaries to structure our navigation of the present without requiring consciousness of the historical substance of those structures. Such is the danger, and the limiting nature of the term "context." By failing to take into account the residual effects of historical moments on our action in the present, we are indeed ignoring the foundational substance of our present reality.

How it Matters

Often, memory is experienced as elusive, cursory, embedded—a source of both joy and despair. What is memory and how does it function? What are the implications of memory in the collective sense for the conception and establishment of education policy? If we are interested in context, then by necessity we must be interested in the function of memory because it is at the juncture of memory and context that individuals both recognize and construct reality. I begin with the concept of memory because it is at the center of this book. The concept of collective memory is distinct from individual memory in terms of substance, rather than manifestation. Memory in the collective sense refers to patterns of social distribution wherein sets of memories regarding major cultural moments, for instance, slavery, or the civil war, manifest themselves into an individual understanding of the world.

Collective memory challenges democracy by requiring of us that we acknowledge that our thoughts and actions in the present are not wholly autonomous from the past. Recognition of the extent to which structures and boundaries of collective memory provide the intellectual foundation for present-day paradigms is essential for critical thought about society, each other, and ourselves. Thus, the examination of contextual influences of educational policy, as originally conceived, is useful for revealing how social ideologies from the past might be evident in policy today. Such an examination provides a context wherein we can begin to understand mitigating factors beyond our own, seemingly independent, actions. Furthermore, memory as an investigative tool provides possibilities for understanding the long-standing and deeply held intellectual assumptions that drive present behavior. The role of collective memory in education has the potential to reveal the extent to which what we say that we do is congruent with what we actually do.

Due primarily to limitations in methodology brought about by a limited scope of relevant artifacts, as well as our long history of historical misrepresentation, the use of historical context itself as a tool for understanding the present is a severely underutilized resource (Connerton, 1989; Hutton, 1993; Sturken, 1997; Bal, 1999; Simon, 2000). Societal change, rapid or slow, tends to subsume individuals into the moment. History is often deemed irrelevant at best, and deficient at worst, for providing insight into the present. Nonetheless, history provides a fundamental means for understanding the present in a way that reaches beyond rhetoric and resistance to change. In fact, because of the role of collective memory, there is no human activity that does not derive substantial meaning from an inextricable relationship with its own history. Education is no exception. An inquiry into the historical context of education must include the advent of testing, in conjunction with the rise of scientific determinism, social engineering, and eugenics.

The aim of this research is to understand the means by which the social ideology of eugenics is not only embedded in the collective memory of the nation, but also is manifest within, and thus perpetuated by, the institution of education in this country. As Selden (1999) put it, the relationship between education and eugenics was (and is) surprising both "for its breadth and depth of engagement [and] for the lack of recognition and understanding that we have of it as practicing educators" (p. xiv).

Role of Collective Memory

Collective memory offers an ability to trace the means by which social ideologies such as eugenics persist over time. Specifically, I concentrate on the scholarship of Maurice Halbwachs (1952/1992), who argued that individuals acquire, locate, and recall their memories purely as a result of their membership in particular social groups. While Halbwachs identified class, family, and religion as the three primary groups in which collective memory is formed, I would expand this to include other social institutions. For example, institutions such as schools work not only to provide an additional translation of memories, which stem from class, family, and religion, but are also a source of memories themselves.

The subject of memory, recently rediscovered in the disciplines of history, sociology, and anthropology, has significant implications for education. Authority and autonomy, reproduction, and reconstruction are all subjects inherently embedded within the concept of memory and its function in society both historically and in the present. Following critical theory, I work under the assumption that (a) history is not linear, (b) concepts such as "the past" are misleading and entrenched in specific dominant cultural approaches which seek to define the present by controlling how we think of the past, and that (c) history can be reconceptualized through the notion of collective memory as it exists in the popular cultural portrayal of life. Eugenic ideology and policy, vastly popular during the first three decades of the twentieth century, is not a historical relic existing solely in the past. Instead, eugenic ideology continues its influence by means of the social frameworks that support collective memory and consequently informs, guides, and continues to provide the force behind present-day policy. The emphasis of eugenics on defining race and ability as a genetically endowed natural hierarchy has worked its way directly into current conceptions of the role of schools, and the ability of the students that fill those schools. In addition to the direct translation of eugenic ideology into curriculum form and practice, eugenics has become a part of our national collective memory, regardless of individual perspective.

2

Memory, History, and Culture

> History as the artificial extension of the social memory . . . is an art of long
> standing, necessarily so since it springs instinctively from the impulse to enlarge
> the range of experience; and however camouflaged by the disfiguring jargon of
> science, it is still in essence what it has always been. History in this sense is story.
> —*Carl L. Becker*
> *Everyman His Own Historian*

There is, of course, an extent to which we are all simultaneously ignorant of, and responsible for, the abuses of history. To borrow from Benjamin (1939), we cannot "but contemplate with horror" the results of an ideology that relegated the vast majority of the human race to imbecility. What is less clear is how the victors might owe their existence to the "anonymous forced labor" of the victors' contemporaries. I argue that it is collective memory, along with the power of popular culture, that has ensured the unwitting allegiance of educators and social workers alike to perpetuate eugenic imperatives. Prior to an exploration of memory, let us look more deeply at the concept of ideology in general so that we can understand the complexity of just what is being perpetuated *by* memory.

Ideology is not as Michael Freeden (2003) points out, the enemy. Indeed, ideologies have gotten a bum rap, perceived by many to be "ideational straightjackets" (p. 3) that require debunking, a source of perpetual distrust and suspicion. It is not ideologies themselves that represent misuse, it is how they are wielded, and by whom. Freeden describes a Marxist co-optation of the way ideology is perceived in society, resulting in an over-reliance on the notion of absolute truth. Pursuant to this over-reliance is what I would call the most dangerous result; the assumption that "ideology is dispensable; it is a pathological product of historical circumstances" (p. 8) bound to wither away when those circumstances improve.

In this way, ideology is generally regarded as an oppressive smokescreen covering an inevitable truth which is always available for conclusive excavation. The danger inherent in this Marxist conception, Freeden argues, is that ideology comes to be regarded as something to be disposed of as quickly as possible, resulting in a dramatic loss of introspection. Ideologies exist in complex permutations and a sore injustice occurs when we dismiss and disregard without first understanding ideological variants and operators in society. In other words, a large number of concrete ideologies are in operation at any one time during a given period of history and it is the "shared features [that] provide immensely significant aids to making sense of the political world" (p. 9). In the case of education, it is the unique combination of eugenics, Progressivism, a Puritan-inspired form of social dialogue, and the pre-existing hierarchical, racial streams of thought that we need to examine for their "shared features." It is dangerous to imbue societal change with an ameliorative power it does not have. Any tendency we have to dismiss ideological beliefs that we have determined are flawed, without first excavating the various places they exist both within ourselves and within the institutions around us, serves to compound and perpetuate that ideology in the present.

There are positive aspects to the Marxist co-optation as well. For instance, according to Freeden, "we have picked up . . . the significance of social and historical circumstances in molding political (and other) ideas" (p. 10) and furthermore, we understand that ideas and ideologies are the product of groups. Ideologies, Freeden tells us,

> are endowed with crucial political functions . . . order the social world, direct it towards certain activities, and legitimate or delegitimate its practices. Ideologies exercise power, at the very least by creating a framework within which decisions can be taken and make sense. (p. 11)

These are key aspects to consider as we move through an examination of the impact of eugenic ideology on society and schools.

Finally, Freeden argues that the Marxian method has taught us to acknowledge that ideologies are not always what they seem. "If we wish to understand ideologies," Freeden explains, "we have to accept that they contain levels of meaning that are hidden from their consumers and, frequently, from their producers as well" (p. 11). This inquiry, then, follows Freeden's proscription that we engage in the "enterprise of decoding, of identifying structures, contexts, and motives that are not readily visible" (p. 11).

Memory and History

In his examination of the writing of history, Certeau (1988) points out that there is no assumption more ubiquitous that the differentiation between the *present* and the *past*. We seem to regard our history, Certeau tells us, with a dual sense of indebtedness and rejection creating "a rift between the *discourse* and the *body* (the social body)" (p. 2). Furthermore, as a result of this rupture between past and present, the content of history has been organized around the relations between labor and nature providing an immediacy of perception, a profound absence of context both historically and in the present moment. As Certeau put it, history

> assumes a gap to exist between the silent opacity of the "reality" that it seeks to express and the place where it produces its own speech, protected by the distance established between itself and its object (*Gegen-stand*). The violence of the body reaches the written page only through absence, through the intermediary of documents that the historian has been able to see on the sands from which a presence has since been washed away, and through a murmur that lets us hear—but from afar—the unknown immensity that seduces and menaces our knowledge. (Certeau, 1988, p. 3)

This unknown immensity is the place that holds the connection between the past and the present. It is what Carl Becker called "story," or history as the artificial extension of social memory. Whether we have an inkling of the unknown immensity of the historically silenced or not, we are menaced by it nevertheless, both internally and externally. Although history has the value of a scientific model in its deliverance of parameters and definitions, history, in Certeau's estimation, provides a "*modus operandi* that fabricates 'scenarios' capable of organizing practices into a currently intelligible discourse"—namely, the task of "the making of history" (p. 6).

My investigation regarding the role and implications of memory relies on a critical approach to history that redefines and alters traditional approaches to historical investigation. First, history is much more than a linear amalgamation of facts and events. Rather, history contains social constructions developed from the remnants and mergings of older ideologies and collective memories. History does not exist outside of the cultural milieu and is not immune to the suppositions and hypotheses of the people who live that history. Renditions of history are used, defined, refined, and forgotten according to power differentials and contextual pressures that require of history that it be malleable. Such is the case with eugenics and its influence on education. Historians of education have placed eugenics on the back steps. History has been used to recast educational reform within the contexts of economy, science, and globalization leaving out the fundamental inequities regarding race and ability that so characterized turn-of-the-century America.

Second, unexamined concepts such as "the past" are misleading and entrenched in specific dominant cultural approaches which seek to define the present by controlling how we think of the past. Our national love affair with heritage (Lowenthal, 1996), often provides a rendition of history that attempts to cast the past in a light most becoming to our needs in the present. Finally, history can be and is redefined or reconceptualized while versions of ourselves in the media are ubiquitous and provide a lasting basis from which we create social constructions of the past. The addition of the concept of memory takes nothing away from the exceedingly useful reinterpretations of historiography described by Certeau and others. Memory deepens this reconceptualization of history by providing a language through which we can discuss and access the "unknown immensity."

Memory

As Seixas (2004) explains, memory studies have significantly challenged and enriched historiography by altering the way we conceive of the past. Memory provides access to beliefs and practices outside the purview of historians and challenges Certeaus' "currently intelligible discourse" by broadening the spectrum of what we listen to from the past, and where. Memory, in the collective sense, is rooted in the work of French philosopher Maurice Halbwachs (1952/1992). Later, more modern iterations of his theory (Lowenthal, 1985; Connerton, 1989; Nora, 1989; Coontz, 1992; LeGoff, 1992; Lowenthal, 1996; Sturken, 1997; Bal, 1999; Roberts-Miller, 1999; Simon, 2000; Morris, 2001; Huyssen, 2003; Zerubavel, 2003; Seixas, 2004) have solidified the notion that the study of memory has decidedly arrived. Memory allows scholars to examine

> the structures that enable societies to hand down beliefs about the past from one generation to the next, the purposes for which those beliefs are mobilized, their nature and shape, and the ways that they change over time. (Seixas, 2004, p. 5)

As such, it is through memory that we can begin to see the presence of intellectual history within every aspect of our social and individual lives. There are, of course, and infinite number of threads, or trajectories, available for fruitful examination, but I am interested specifically in the shaping of our notions of ability and worth in the present, as defined and institutionalized by eugenic ideology during the unfolding of our modern form of education.

We can tell, Zerubavel (2003) points out, that memory is not just a simple reproduction of the past by virtue of the fact that as individuals, we do not remember every single thing that ever happened to us. Far from being random, however, memory is "patterned in a highly structured manner that both shapes and distorts what we actually come to retain from the past" (p. 11). Like Halbwachs, Zerbavel regards these patterns as unmistakably social, identifying a number of plotlines along which we "habitually reduce highly complex sequences to inevitably simplistic, one-dimensional vision of the past" (p. 13). Plotlines exist within historical narratives which define concepts upon which we are highly dependent; notions of progress, individual ability, national unity, and democracy are all examples of collective understandings. While plotlines provide the stuff of memory, power differentials in society ensure that details may differ depending on perspective. Nevertheless, a collective core from which we all draw remains intact, acting, often invisibly, to direct thinking in the present.

Sustaining Social Contexts

Anticipating Foucault's post-modern thinking on the subject of collective memory Halbwachs argued that memory was only able to endure within sustaining social contexts. He discussed a reduction of idealized images into *imago*, which provide the conceptual schemes into which individual memories come to be located. The reason, Halbwachs (1952/1992) argued, for this reliance of memory on collective context is that even individual memories are woven into an understanding of the past that is socially acquired.

According to Halbwachs, the structure of collective memory provides the model to which individual memory is bound to conform and, furthermore, that the capacity of collective memory to endure depends on the social power of the group that holds it. As Morris (2001) notes, historians and novelists are not immune to the politics of memory, indeed it is "the powerful [who] shape memory for public consumption" (p. 15). This topic brings about the concept of the role of historical "distance," or what Phillips (2004) calls "distance-constructions" (p. 89) wherein both the reader and the writer of history play a role in the act of constructing distance. Distance then, is a term that can be directed, as Phillips argues, "to a history's *ideological* implication as well as its *affective* coloration, its *cognitive* assumptions as well as its *formal* traits (p. 89; emphasis in original). In the case of eugenics, distance is encompassed by memory, directed internally towards significant dimensions of engagement and disengagement with the past.

It is precisely Halbwachs' argument about the social contexts of collective memory that historians have recently found useful in their reconsideration of the connections between memory and history (Hutton, 1993). Working at a time when the boundaries around the discipline of history were tightly guarded, Halbwachs (and nearly everyone at the time) was highly enamored of the promise of positivist science for scholarship in the twentieth century (1993). It is important to note, therefore, that Halbwachs himself did not necessarily intend for the nature of his discoveries to be used in the way they are being used today. Nevertheless, by expanding on Halbwachs' limiting belief that history began where memory left off, scholars have used Halbwachs' theory to come to conclusions that have proven to be highly useful tools in understanding the present.

Perhaps the most enduring notion that has emerged from Halbwachs work is his notion of *cadres sociaux* or social frameworks. Halbwachs envisioned collective memory as an elaborate network comprised of social mores, values, and ideals. Individual imagination is bounded by the attitudes of the social groups to which we belong, and the very survival of our individual memories depends on their situatedness within the shared social frameworks of our group. Halbwachs explained his analysis with the observation that

> modern societies pretend to respect the individual personality. Provided that individuals perform their essential duties, they are free to live and to think as it pleases them, to form their opinions as they wish. Society seems to stop at the threshold of interior life. But it well knows that even then it leaves them alone only in appearance—it is perhaps at the moment when the individual appears to care very little about society that he develops in himself to the fullest the qualities of a social being. (1952, p. 50)

In other words, as members of society, when we believe we are free to have control over our own thoughts and actions, we are less likely to question the impetus behind those thought and actions.

Memory Within the Family

How does collective memory operate within and between social spheres? To answer to this question, Halbwachs' theory regarding the function of family, kinship, and social class is helpful. For Halbwachs, family was an institution wherein our positions were bound not by personal feelings, but by "rules and customs independent of us that existed before us" (1952, p. 55). What dominated as an operating feeling in families though, was a feeling of kinship, rather than the patterns and structures of individual kinship patterns which vary from culture to culture. Put another way, these feelings can only be explained by the family, and arise within the family, but are not a function of the teaching of any individual. Rather, these feelings are derived from a "general conception" of the family. While individual families retain memories which are specific, and revealed to them alone,

> they are at the same time models, examples, and elements of teaching. They express the general attitude of the group; they not only reproduce its history but also define its nature and its qualities and its weaknesses. When we say "In our family we have long life spans," or "we are proud," or "we do not strive to get rich," we speak of a physical or moral quality which is supposed to be inherent in the group, and which passes from the group to its members . . . the various elements of this type that are retained from the past provide a framework for family memory, which it tries to preserve intact, and which, so to speak, is the traditional armor of the family. (Halbwachs, 1952, p. 59)

So strongly did Halbwachs feel about the influence of family, he claimed there was "no object upon which we reflect that cannot serve as a point of departure, through an association of ideas, to retrieve some thought which immerses us again, in the distant or recent past, in the circle of our family" (1952, p. 61). It is through this kind of internal and often unconscious attachment to the past, through social frameworks such as kinship, that we begin to see how the model might be used to track the political significance of ideological constructs like eugenics. According to Hutton (1993), historians are then able to track the way representations of collective memory change over time. However, Halbwachs spoke of the oppositions in society to change such as distortion of the past or a limiting of the field of memory altogether. For example, in the case of eugenics there is strong evidence to suggest that society has both distorted the past and limited the field of memory. The social frameworks supporting the eugenics movement have not been altered and continue to be passed down in families. This would explain why the scientific debunking of eugenics as a result of advances in genetic theory have had little relevance to its perseverance in collective memory.

Memory and Social Class

For Halbwachs, social class was another sphere in which collective memory operated to connect the past and the present. Again, the idea that tradition and our continued attachment to the repetition of specific rites, formulas, and symbols has, in fact, enabled past ideologies to persist through successive periods of social evolution. Particularly interesting is Halbwachs' argument that some social classes have a more highly developed collective memory than others. I argue that access to manipulations of collective memory is a function of power and control more than some inherent factor of class but regardless, there is much to be gleaned from his model. Halbwachs contended that "two nobles who meet each other for the first time should be able, after exchanging just a few remarks, to recognize themselves as two members of the same extended family that establishes their kinship link or alliance" (1952, p. 128). Indeed, there is ample evidence for a conception of society that engages in a continual reading of these social framework texts as we interact with our fellow human beings. These texts operate not only in and through, for example, clothing rituals and speech patterns, but also through economic status, political affiliation, and skin color.

Manipulation of Memory

Other features of Halbwachs' theory include questions about how memory functions in society and how it can be manipulated. For example, in his discussion of the French nobility, Halbwachs believed that at some point, it became

> necessary for society to reorganize and to modify to some degree the social frameworks of its memory. Society could do this in two ways. First, it could deliberately distort the past . . . but society could also avert its attention from whatever was not proximate in time and thereby limit the field of its memory entirely to the last generations. (1952, p. 135)

In other words, collective memory, as conceived by Halbwachs, functioned with a life of its own. It is unlikely that collective memory is vulnerable to the actions of an individual group. Nevertheless, some groups may have an inordinate amount of influence, depending on their standing in society. Indeed, whether a society is

> directed toward the past or toward what is a continuation of the past in the present, it participates in present-day functions only to the extent that it is important to adapt these functions to traditions and to ensure the continuity of social life throughout their transformation. (1952, p. 129)

That society participates in present-day functions only to the extent they help to preserve traditions has strong implications for the function of collective memory in the preservation of eugenic ideology. We are only able, according to this definition, to make use of what we are given. However, the caveat is that we must desire to ensure the continuity of social life. If we have determined that such a continuity is antithetical to our beliefs and intentions, then perhaps we can be freed from the restriction of collective memory.

The Role of Virtue

Finally, Halbwachs (1952) made an interesting point concerning the role of "virtue" as an operating concept in society. He referred to the way certain virtues such as economy, honesty, and austerity made the transition from commonly accepted qualities to ones which rank highly in the scale of social values.

> It was acknowledged that, in the wealthy classes more than in other classes, is to be found mastery of self, a spirit of sacrifice, a firm disposition to live up to one's ideas, a sharper sense of honesty and probity, more loyalty and fidelity in friendship, more stable virtues, and an irreproachable moral purity. Poverty became equivalent to immorality, and the legislation concerning the poor treated beggars like culprits. These ideas, preserved in collective memory, became grounded in the experience of the virtues—or at least in the manifestation of virtue—of the wealthy. (p. 150)

Like family, social class offers individuals an armor. It is through the specific mechanisms of collective memory that ideas of the past are continually folded in to conceptions of the present.

Types of Memory: Personal, Cognitive, and Habit

How then can we integrate this theoretical conception of collective memory with our individual working understanding? Probably one of the most difficult tasks we can set for ourselves is that of extracting memory out of the things we do every day. In fact, it cannot be done. Memory is an intimate part of everything we do from the lowly washing of our face, to reading, understanding, and the creation of meaning. So is it the case that memory provides societies and cultures with the framework within which individual interact with the world around them.

Connerton (1989) distinguishes among three types of memory: *personal, cognitive*, and *habit* memory. *Personal* memories are those that are a direct result of one's own life history and are distinguished by their reliance on the past, as experienced and interpreted by individuals, as the primary source of individual conception of self. Personal memories do not exist independent of the social contexts in which they are formed but instead are the product of those contexts. This concept supports a constructionist ontology in that it distinguishes between the creation and construction of meaning. Personal memories are important for understanding how ideologies such as eugenics can become part of an individual's worldview. Additionally, personal memories ensure that a persistent reckoning with the past occurs as part of identity formation. This speaks to the relationship between the individual and society by revealing a constant negotiation between the individual, societal norms, expectations, and values.

Cognitive memory claims are those that are involved with recalling the meaning of words, or directions to our place of work. According to Connerton (1989), *cognitive* memory claims are also concerned with "mathematical equations, or truths of logic" (p. 22), which implies they are strongly implicated in structuring the way we think altogether. Paradigmatic forms such as positivism and naturalism, both of which contributed to the acceptance of eugenic ideology, are implicated in this form of memory. Connerton explained that "What this type of remembering requires, [is] not that the object of memory be something that is past, but that the person who remembers that thing must have met, experienced, or learned of it in the past" (p. 23). Schools, too, are implicated in this type of memory for it is there that we formally learn whatever society deems fit to teach at any given time.

Finally, *habit* memory "consists simply in our having the capacity to reproduce a certain performance" (Connerton, 1989, p. 24). Examples of habit memory include reading, writing, or riding a bicycle and are distinguished by the fact that performance is often the only evidence of the fact that we do indeed remember. This type of performative memory is far removed from conscious cognition and as such, it is very much like a habit performed regularly but thought about rarely. Of the three types of memory, it is *habit memory*, according to Connerton, that has been accorded the least attention. In his discussion of social memory, Connerton focused on this third type. I contend, however, that it is a combination of all three types of memory which is at work in the collective. It is precisely this combination which serves to keep ideologies alive in individual thought and action whether one is aware of it or not.

In addition to these three classes of memory, much has been offered by cognitive and experimental psychology, surrounding the concept of "encoding" and work regarding the nature of the psychoanalytic relationship. Morris (2001) offers an exceptional analysis of what she calls "post-Freudian" interpretation wherein the "complexities and ambiguities of self" replace the Freudian "reification of self"

(p. 28). Morris outlines psychoanalysis as

> a form of hermeneutics that offers insights helpful for understanding the ways
> in which we might psychologically frame memories, especially when these
> memories are repressed. (2001, p. 25)

Although Morris is specifically referring to repressed memories of the Holocaust, her keen insight into the value of deconstructing the way in which we frame memories as a "clue to our own resistances and limitations" (p. 25) applies to memories of all types. Connerton (1989) contended that the task of the psychoanalyst is to uncover individual inclinations to maintain a "narrative discontinuity" (p. 26) in which significant portions of the past become blocked out of individual consciousness. Within such a scenario, memory is defined as the capability of forming "meaningful narrative sequences" (p. 26). Here we begin to see the importance of taking all three classes of memory into account when inquiring into collective activity. According to Connerton (1989),

> Experimental psychologists, on the other hand, have shown that literal recall is
> very rare and unimportant, remembering being not a matter of reproduction but
> of construction; it is the construction of a "schema," a coding, which enables us
> to distinguish and, therefore, to recall. (p. 27)

This coding may be divided into three dimensions: semantic, verbal, and visual. Cognitive psychologists identify the semantic code as the key to the whole operation of memory, or a "mental map acquired in childhood" (p. 28) and, as such, it is a code that is shared collectively. Furthermore, these mental maps vary from culture to culture and by acknowledging this, cognitive psychologists are "admitting the possible application of their findings to socially variable object-domains" (p. 28). Despite the significance of this new possibility, the primary concern of researchers in this area has been to locate those "fundamental structures" with a universalistic application, or, put another way, "mental faculties that are essential to human nature" (p. 28). What makes this both interesting and significant is that it offers a jumping off point for the inquiry into the intersecting space between collective memory and the function of history.

History and Memory

The following discussion of history takes as its starting point identifiable limitations in historiography and juxtaposes them with what we have learned so far about the function of collective memory. Lowenthal (1985) argued that there is a significant distinction between memory and history. In his view, history differs from memory not only in how knowledge of the past is assigned, but also in how it is validated, transmitted, preserved, and altered. Furthermore, history and memory may be distinguishable not as types of knowledge but in the attitudes people hold towards that knowledge (Lowenthal, 1985). This view implies that veracity, in the case of either history or memory, is irrelevant. Whether or not a theory has been proven, or makes sense, is not a prerequisite to its establishment and veracity in the public mind.

Historian Carl Becker (1935) defined history simply as the "memory of things said and done" (p. 239). In making a definitive connection between history and memory, Becker connotes that history itself is an illusion, and so too is the present. Becker claimed that because history does not exist for us in the present, we create history by dipping in to the past and by believing that recent events belong solely to our immediate perceptions. Thus, as we attempt to prepare for what is to come in life, we necessarily draw not only on the past, but also on a concomitant anticipation of the future.

In fact, according to Becker, "the more of the past that we draw into the specious present, the more an hypothetical, patterned future is likely to crowd into [our awareness in the present] also" (1935, p. 241). Essentially, Becker argued that the work of historians was necessarily corrupted, from our standard of objectivity and "truth" by virtue of the fact that memory of the past is inscribed into present perception. It is the function of historians, as it was for bards, storytellers, and priests throughout history

> not to create, but to preserve and perpetuate the social traditions; to harmonize, as well as ignorance and prejudice permit, the actual and the remembered series of events. (Becker, 1935, p. 247)

Acting as an artificial extension of memory, history becomes a convenient blend of reality and fantasy in its distinction of fact and interpretation. Despite this, we nevertheless rely on the idea that what we know of history is a valid representation.

One immediate connection we can make between the theories of Halbwachs and the practice of historians concerns autonomy and the notion of independence of thought. Halbwachs (1952) believed that society pretends to allow for independent thought, but in actuality, such independence is impossible due to the workings of collective memory. Connerton (1989) added that the reason historians continue to question the statements of their informants is not because they question the veracity of the statements, but because of a fear that face value acceptance amounts to an abandonment of their autonomy as practicing historians. We need to believe, these theorists are saying, that we are in control of what we think and what we do. However, the evidence is mounting that there are considerable obstacles to autonomy when it comes to our formation of values, attitudes, and measurements of worth. Autonomy eludes us even as we decide that we have rejected the past while determining that we have discovered anew how best to live.

> A particularly extreme case of such interaction occurs when a state apparatus is used in a systematic way to deprive its citizens of their memory. All totalinarianisms behave in this way; the mental enslavement of the subjects of a totalitarian regime begins when their memories are taken away. (Connerton, 1989, p. 14)

Connerton (1989) described the futility of autonomy in terms of a state apparatus depriving its citizens of their memories. Furthermore, he claimed that all totalitarianisms rely on the mental enslavement of subjects through memory deprivation. This may sound rather extreme, but it is important to realize that actions in the present that preserve and promote oppression from the past are, in effect, paramount to depriving non-dominant group members from the influence, and thus the capacities therein, of their own collective memories.

Pierre Nora (1989) has done extensive investigation into the representations of the French national memory. While traditional historiography is concerned with a search for common origins, Nora followed Halbwachs' (1952) model and identified the myriad branches of tradition that collectively make up the memory of the nation. Nora's model focuses on the centrality of memory in the formation of identity in the present, a concept that has enormous possibility for further research. In order to disclose discordant traditions Nora's analysis proceeds from the present into the past and relies on the assumption that the past can be, and is, represented in alternative ways. Nora believed that history is anchored in tradition and, using a wide range of archaeological, geographical, iconographic, and historiographic sources, Nora demonstrates that memory is inherently political (Hutton, 1993).

Nora (1989) described *lieux de memoire*, or sites of memory, which originate with the sense that there is no spontaneous memory, that we must "deliberately create archives, maintain anniversaries, organize celebrations, pronounce eulogies, and notarize bills because such activities no longer occur naturally" (p. 12). For Nora (1989), memory and history are in fundamental opposition because memory is in a state of permanent evolution, while history is concerned with the reconstruction of what is no longer. Further, Nora claimed the relationship between memory and history to be inherently impossible because "history is perpetually suspicious of memory and its true mission is to destroy it" (1989, p. 9).

The role of memory in the production and preservation of cultural knowledge is an area of inquiry that has only just begun. The potential inherent in such a line of inquiry for an increased understanding of how political ideologies from the past continue to operate in the present must not be underestimated. By examining Halbwachs' conception of social frameworks, and Nora's sites of collective memory, we see they may be regarded as tools for an understanding of the present. Inquiries into the role of memory have made significant strides beyond what was previously the domain of cognitive and experimental psychology, and have expanded to the point where scholars have begun to theorize about the cultural locations where memory operates most fundamentally.

Perhaps one of the most promising lines of inquiry that could potentially be paired with collective memory is that of material and popular culture which is explored in the following chapter. Material and popular culture studies, concerned as they are with cultural expression as it is represented in non-traditional forms, offer us a window into collective memory because so often expression of collective memory is generated by unconscious, rather than conscious, forms of cognition. If we desire to create change and achieve understanding in the present, then we are urgently required, by the very fact of its existence, to include the legacy of the past as it is manifested in collective memory. The ramifications of pursuing such a line of inquiry reach far beyond education policy to virtually every social institution in existence today. Institutional policies that impact, regulate, and legitimate medicine, law, social policy, politics, the economy, religion, education, and many other social institutions do so by drawing on the rich historical legacies contained in their institutional collective memories.

Constructionism and Constructivism

Finally, it is important to consider, in paradigmatic terms, the social dimension of meaning as it concerns constructions of race and ability in education in the United States. Crotty (1998) distinguishes between *constructivism* and *constructionism* by explaining that the former comprises an individualistic understanding of the latter. Crotty found it useful to reserve the term *constructivism* to describe those epistemological considerations focusing exclusively on individual meaning making. *Constructionism*, on the other hand, refers to the collective generation and transmission of meaning. My concern for the perpetuation of ideology and its subsequent effect on the social institution of education compels me to employ the constructionist paradigm for its collective implications. This is not to say, however, there is no role for the constructivist paradigm; indeed, individual experience and subsequent construction of meaning is imperative for an understanding of this inquiry on a personal level. I, as researcher and author of this inquiry, certainly employ a constructivist paradigm every time I consider the path of racism through history and its manifestation within myself. Nevertheless, constructionism, focused as it is on the social dimension of meaning making, is more appropriate and specific to this inquiry as a whole.

Another important component of the distinction between constructivism and constructionism warrants discussion. Inherent within constructivist ontology is the provision of validity for individual conceptions of the world. This provision is essential for criticality which might call into question those constructed meanings bequeathed to us by culture. Constructionism, on the other hand, is wholly concerned with

> the hold our culture has on us: it shapes the way in which we see things (even the way we feel things!) and gives us a quite definite view of the world . . . on these terms, it can be said that constructivism tends to resist the critical spirit, while constructionism tends to foster it. (Crotty, 1998, p. 58)

A critical perspective is essential to this inquiry to the extent that such a perspective emphasizes the potential to identify societally generated meanings that favor hegemonic interests. When we are talking about the hierarchical racial assumptions held by individuals in positions of power during the height of the eugenics movement, arbitrary assignation of meaning becomes problematic. Not that individual meaning is arbitrary, rather, that it requires the added revelation that collective understanding offers. While I certainly condone the validation of multiple voices through an acknowledgment that individuals construct meaning uniquely, I find it necessary that such an ontology take into account power differentials in society.

As do all self-respecting paradigms, constructionism contains a specific set of assumptions that comprise a fundamental belief system concerning order, knowledge, and ways of knowing. Constructionist ontology assumes that there is no universal, knowable reality. Unlike objectivism, constructionism assumes that truth and meaning reside in consciousness independent of objects and institutions. Thus, constructionism

> is the view that *all knowledge, and therefore all meaningful reality as such, is contingent upon human practices, being constructed in and out of interaction between human beings and their world, and developed and transmitted within an essentially social context.* (Crotty, 1998, p. 42; emphasis in original)

From the constructionist perspective, meaning can be described as neither "objective" nor "subjective." Instead, making meaning from this perspective takes into account the social origin and institutional embeddedness of the human practices therein (Crotty, 1998).

Though subjective epistemology exists most strongly in structuralist, post-structuralist, and post-modernist thought, there is an important distinction regarding the subjective within the constructivist paradigm. According to Crotty (1998), human beings do not create meaning, they *construct* it because they utilize the world around them. This notion of utilization of a collectively generated social sphere to construct meaning is important because it acknowledges the ability of ideologies to traverse generations. These generational abilities form and inform our mediations with societal structures and ideologies. Furthermore, constructionism holds that although the world, and the objects in the world, are meaningless without the presence of experience, they are nevertheless complicit in the generation of meaning (Crotty, 1998). This expiates the relationship between memory and history, individual and collective, by explaining that we *must* use the artifacts of culture to create meaning. Furthermore, meaning comes not from just our conception of artifacts themselves, but is also the product of our interaction with them. In this way, constructionism mirrors the concept of intentionality in the sense not of purpose or deliberation but of "referentiality, relatedness, directedness, 'aboutness' " (p. 44).

This paradigmatic framework is essential for two reasons. First, social ideologies like eugenics are not historical relics but instead travel through generations by means of collective memory because people create meaning by relying on external cues taken from cultural artifacts. These artifacts, once embedded in collective memory, exist irrespective of public awareness and opinion and are capable of persisting within collective memory without the necessity of individual awareness. Second, the establishment of a connection between individual, collective, and institutional memory relies on the notion that meaning is constructed, not created, and that it relies on the past to do so.

3

Popular, Media, and Material Culture

Certainly, ideas and philosophies pass down through generations of individuals. Although historical events, ideologies, and phenomena are passed to younger generations consistently through family influence, they persist within culture in ways other than familial or institutional as well. Forms of popular culture, including news media, academic and trade writing, and other forms of distribution such as pamphlets, posters, and displays enter into the formation of cultural memory in many ways including forms of social dialogue, rhetorical form, paradigmatic influence, and by means of interaction with all kinds of social institutions such as the judicial system, the medical establishment, religious organizations, and, especially, education. In addition to their function within collective memory, these forms of communication make their way into curriculum and pedagogy. Of parti-cular importance to this process is the role of language. Language exists within an ideologically imposed social sphere. The form of public dialogue, including the details of habits and commonalities of expression, is instrumental in the transmission of ideology from popular culture to collective memory.

Popular culture, media culture, and material culture investigations provide insight into cultural constructions both past and present. Following Prown (2001), I use these terms to indicate the practice of investigation itself, rather than the artifacts which are the objects of study. An exploration of the theoretical underpinnings of such investigations enables us to locate the intersection, as discussed previously, between individuals and the cultural context with which they interact. In particular, the scope of cultural context can be expanded through the utilization of popular, material, and media culture studies directed towards historical pursuit. Cultural studies can aid in identifying the historical beliefs that contribute to the construction of values, ideas, attitudes, and assumptions. Material culture, media culture, and popular culture have much to offer in terms of understanding how cultural knowledge is transmitted and received, and what that may mean for education policy.

Material culture, media culture, and popular culture investigations hold in common an attempt to glean information about society and its cultural practices by means of artifacts produced by that society. While material culture is primarily concerned with objects, functional or otherwise, media and popular culture have tended to investigate media in its various forms, primarily music, television, and film (Daspit and Weaver, 1999). My focus here is not the analysis of the artifacts themselves, but rather the form that analysis takes, and how we might project that form onto certain more traditional artifacts, such as written material and documents, and analyze them in a new way. Another commonality with material, media, and popular culture investigations is that they are relatively new fields, having emerged in the 1970s and taken considerable form and shape only during the 1980s and 1990s. Given both the newness of the field and its focus on contemporary society, any theorizing regarding this subject must necessarily be comprised of a language of possibilities rather than conclusions. Certain areas of social science are emerging from a positivistic shell. While leaps of faith might seem frightening and untenable as a basis for theorizing, we can only continue towards what seems like understanding in new ways if we are comfortable with the notion of uncertainty.

Artifacts and Objects

By expanding our definition of what constitutes popular and media culture, and by distancing the theory's reliance on technological forms of transmission, we will find that the ways in which people interact with their social environment are more constant than the newness of what we experience today would lead us to believe. If we assume that meaning and identity are socially constructed, and that part of the human condition is to seek out sources that generate this meaning and identity, then it makes sense that the underlying cultural processes through which this process occurs would have been present in society long before people began to theorize about them. This section is concerned with an expansion of those things we consider to be artifacts that individuals use to construct meaning. As Farber (1994) explained,

> it is necessary to examine factors that contribute to the impoverishment of discourse about, and erosion of trust in, the institutions of modern society,

including formal education. To do so requires inquiry concerning the way that views are formed, at various levels of engagement and interaction, about the central institutions of modern life. The quality of discourse about schooling is contingent upon how schooling is understood, the ways in which the multifarious meanings schooling has for diverse people are formed and modified over time. (Farber, Provenzo, and Holm, 1994, p. 7)

Thus, views do not form within a vacuum but at or near the boundaries between the individual and his or her societal context. These intersections are a function of identity and are not defined by any particular institution, nor are they the exclusive domain of academic, public, or personal ideologies. Rather, they form as a result of various levels of engagement and interaction with a vast array of modern (in the relative sense) institutions. Today, such institutions include television, music, movies, theatre, etc. A century ago, those communicative institutions included books, journals, pamphlets, displays, and lectures. The utilization of recently developed theoretical frameworks for an investigation of prior forms of popular culture contribute a great deal of insight into society past, and present.

The ideas of a great many thinkers (see, e.g., Nora, 1989; Coontz, 1992; Farber, 1994; Strinati, 1995; Lowenthal, 1996; Sturken, 1997; Brunner, 1998; Bal, 1999; Daspit, 1999) from a wide range of fields have led us to begin today, to learn about ourselves from the self-study of our own culture. I imagine that such thinkers face a conundrum when considering how to proceed. In other words, how does one seek to understand something when to ask the questions in the first place may represent an adherence to a specific way of thinking? Part of the solution to the problem will come from an increasing willingness on the part of social scientists to adjust their line of inquiry away from the confines of positivism and objectivity. As the constructionist paradigm shows, objectivism and subjectivism are subsumed under the imperative of societal meaning making. Any attempt at a search for "universal truth" about the connection between eugenics and education would be inaccurate, nevertheless there are implications for the creation of my own reality, even as I attempt to decipher it.

Artifacts and Beliefs

Schlereth (1980) situated his work as part of a new history (at the time) which emphasized an intellectual and philosophical approach to the past, rather than a linear, fact-based approach. In the 1970s, anthropologists and archaeologists first used the term *material culture* to describe those artifacts produced by culture

(Schlereth, 1980). Akin to the constructionist distinction between meaning that is constructed rather than created, the concept of *production* requires us to regard artifacts as products of culture, rather than culture itself. Schlereth (1980) emphasized the need to examine artifacts of material culture within their own "cultural history context" (p. 3) so as to separate, as well as possible, the cultural bias of the investigator from the cultural bias of the creators and users of the artifact. While material culture investigations hold investigative possibility for many fields of inquiry, they are probably best thought of as a branch of cultural history or cultural anthropology (Prown, 2001).

The apparent discontinuity between the "baseness" of those things generally considered *materials* of a culture, and the loftiness of the term culture itself has engendered a debate within the field that also extends into the media and popular culture arena. The debate centers mainly around how best to make sure investigations do not unwittingly give advantage to cultural forms traditionally regarded as "pure" in some sense such as theatre, art, and certain kinds of music. This debate over "high" and "low" culture speaks to how the term "culture" was traditionally defined as a pursuit of the economically and intellectually advantaged classes. Material culture investigations offer a connection to the belief systems that produced particular artifacts of material culture. In the case of eugenics, the artifacts are multitudinous and intimately connected to the institutions and groups over which they had the most influence. One common association between cultural belief and artifact has to do with attached *value* (Prown, 2001). Produced by eugenicists, the artifacts used in this investigation were imbued with *scientific* language so as to appeal to the cultural perception of *value* at the time.

Schlereth (1980) and Prown (1982/2001) contend that material culture artifacts have the special advantage of providing a voice for the majority of people who may not be literate or, more generally, for those groups, individuals, and events that have been omitted from the sanctioned version of history found in school curricula. Thus, a cultural history approach that utilizes material culture artifacts chooses to be concerned with the experience of those Americans who do not fall under the generally accepted rubric of the intellectual elite. In other words, through this type of investigation we have the opportunity to get a closer reading of the experience and beliefs of a broader spectrum of Americans than we do through other approaches. For example, in the case of eugenics, debate centered on the process of societal improvement, but did little to question the fundamental racial assumptions that extended beyond the eugenics movement itself. Due to the concerted efforts of eugenicists to disseminate their information well outside academic boundaries, there is much to be learned through an examination of material culture artifacts about how people generally considered voiceless interacted with and consumed eugenic ideology.

Another unique quality of material culture investigations concerns investigator bias. There has long been a debate about the degree to which investigators are entrenched within their own cultural biases, and whether or not this is surmountable. While investigators can do their best to be aware of the problem, and through that awareness, avoid bias as much as possible, material culture artifacts provide investigators with a much more substantial opportunity to avoid their own bias. When individuals interact with the artifacts of material culture, they operate not with their minds, the seat of cultural bias, but rather they operate through their admittedly biased senses (Prown, 1982/2001). By utilizing this type of investigation I refer not the end product of culture, but a glimpse of those manifestations of thought and belief that were responsible for the generation of the end product.

Prown (1982/2001) reminded us that some cultural assumptions are so generally accepted that they cannot necessarily be detected in *what* a society expresses, but may be more observable in *the way* they are expressed, or what Prown would call their "*style* of expression" (p. 52). Style is evident in all forms of cultural expression be they verbal, behavioral, or material. Material culture is potentially more "truthful" than other forms because of its relative immunity to "cultural spin" (Prown, 1982/2001, p. 74). In fact, artifacts may be regarded as embodiments of mental structures, and in addition to revealing patterns of belief unfettered by self-consciousness, they also reveal the connection between thought and action as it occurred during the past.

Shaping Perception

Both popular and media culture theory are concerned with a social analysis that draws its data from outside of academic pursuits. Instead, popular and media culture theory rely on what have variously been called "texts" or artifacts produced by the culture for its own information and entertainment (Farber, 1994). In general, both popular and media culture studies investigate the content of radio, film, television, music, and print media for the collective implications they have for creating and maintaining power differentials, identities, and political ideologies. Because of their focus on technology-based forms of communication, theories of popular and media culture have tended to direct their analysis towards contemporary society and have not used their ideas to engender any theories regarding popular culture as it occurred prior to the present technological era. According to

Strinati (1995), the distortion and domination of the public at the hands of cultural production has had a long history but in the latter decades of the twentieth century those theories were revised and are now concerned with the present.

Popular culture has a significant impact on the shaping of perception and on creating and maintaining cultural knowledge. In his book on the rhetorical dimensions of popular culture, Brummett (1991) described it this way:

> If culture means those objects and events that nurture, shape, and sustain people, then popular culture must be those artifacts that are most actively involved in winning the favor of the public and thus in shaping the public in particular ways. Popular culture is the cutting edge of culture's instruments that shape people into what they are. (p. xvi)

The term popular, by definition, implies a level of public acceptance and, more importantly, recognition. Thus, Brummett argued that artifacts defined as part of popular culture represent most directly the intersection between individuals and their culture. Whether or not an individual "likes" or "dislikes" certain elements of popular culture is, for the purpose of this inquiry, irrelevant. The very fact of a certain level of saturation implied by the use of the term "popular" ensures that the public is exposed to, and therefore has within their frame of reference, artifacts generated by culture. The significance of popular culture for a historical investigation is that theories about race and worth existed within a number of different popular cultural artifacts and forms. During the first decades of the twentieth century there was a prolific and active lecture circuit drawing hundreds of people in venues accessible to people from all social strata. The demographic context of the period combined with pre-existing conceptions of race and worth ensured that there was a great deal of fear surrounding non-white people and those deemed "unfit." Popular culture is often popular precisely because it speaks to particular psychological needs within a society; threats of "race suicide," mentally unfit parents, and prolific breeding among the poor and foreign born provided an especially eager audience for eugenic popularizers.

Mass Culture

Perhaps the most enduring legacy to come out of early critical theory, especially the Frankfurt school, regarding the impact of popular culture is the debate over the notion of "mass culture," and whether or not the public is wholly dominated by, or engages in resistance through, popular culture (Connerton, 1989; Farber, 1994;

Daspit and Weaver, 1999; Popkewitz, 2001). Let us look briefly now at mass culture theory to see why, despite years of rejection, some theorists set aside their reservations, and are now considering a revived potential for mass culture theory.

Mass culture theory, as described by Strinati (1995), argues that industrialization and urbanization caused society to devolve in a number of ways. The impact of industrialization and urbanization created a citizenry whose interactions were highly formal and contractual. Furthermore, the rise of industrialization and urbanization were accompanied by a decline in mediating social organizations, and a decline in what Strinati called a "moral order" (p. 7). In turn, Strinati argued, this formal and contractual nature of human interaction caused people to turn to "surrogate and fake moralities" (p. 7) making them more vulnerable to manipulation by media and popular culture. Strinati further contended that

> it is clear that mass culture theory can and has accommodated the idea that democracy and education have been harmful developments because they have contributed to the pathological constitution of a mass society. (1995, p. 7)

Another feature of mass culture is that by creating its own emotional and sentimental responses, it actually denies the effort of thinking and in so doing becomes instrumental in defining social reality (Strinati, 1995). Kellner (1995) rejected the "mass culture" hypothesis as being both "monolithic and homogenous" (p. 33) in its erection of a binary opposition between "high" and "low" forms of culture and its assumption that the masses are empty vessels at the mercy of dominating forces. Reservations about mass culture theory over the previous half a century center around a charge of elitism which dissenters say is inherent in mass culture theory. Particularly problematic is mass culture theory's general orientation towards the audience which it sees as a

> passive, supine, undemanding, vulnerable, manipulable, exploitable and sentimental mass, resistant to intellectual challenge and stimulation, easy prey to consumerism and advertising and the dreams and fantasies they have to sell, unconsciously afflicted with bad taste, and robotic in its devotion to the repetitive formulas of mass culture. (Strinati, 1995, p. 48)

Not only is the whole idea of a mass audience as preposterous today as it was when the theory was first formulated, according to Strinati, but it is clearly impossible as evidenced by the simple variation of social context and social location of consumers. While charges of elitism regarding mass culture theory have come primarily from popular culture theorists, these theorists have, themselves, tended to speak on behalf of the audience. What is called for in this situation is not so much a complete reversal, wherein the audience is now as, or more, powerful than the producers of popular culture, but rather a recognition that a more balanced view of things is in order.

Daspit and Weaver (1999) attempted to achieve this more balanced approach by calling for a de-centering of popular culture analysis that works to encourage alternative readings of popular culture texts, "readings that flow within, or alongside, our own narratives" (p. xxi). In any event, assuming a constructionist ontology, there is a clear lack of delineation between wholly empowered individuals and the impact of social norms and beliefs on questions of worth and value. Whether or not the public is passive and undemanding or an active agent in the incorporation of cultural beliefs, the notion that such beliefs are generated by the collective rather than the individual is necessary for the incorporation of mass culture theory into an exacting account of the influence of history on the present.

Myths and Symbols

Apparently, Strinati is correct when he suggests that mass culture theory is still alive and well. Indeed, despite the misgivings regarding the monolithic role of the audience, there may be much we can still use within mass culture theory. Consider the following quotation from Kellner who, we recall, rejected mass culture theory:

> Media culture helps shape the prevalent view of the world and its deepest values: it defines what is considered good or bad, positive or negative, moral or evil. Media stories and images provide the symbols, myths, and resources which help constitute a common culture for the majority of individuals in many parts of the world today. (Kellner, 1995, p. 1)

It would certainly be an understatement to say that times have changed, yet, in terms of the manner in which cultural beliefs are transmitted and received, they have. Media culture is concerned with not the fact of this change, but the manner in which it affects our lives. So pervasive is media culture, according to Kellner (1995), that in addition to the shaping of political views and social behaviors, media culture provides the "materials out of which people forge their very identities" (p. 1). The identity factor has dramatic ramifications for the social construction of race, gender, ability, and worth.

In addition to its role in the formation of identity, media culture is most often associated with a profit-driven, industrial model of mass production with appeals to mass audiences and adherence to formulas, codes, and rules (Kellner, 1995). The extent to which contemporary media culture and, I argue, past forms of media culture (which were less technical but equally as communicative) have supplied such formulas, codes, and rules represents a profound and unrecognized source of cultural pedagogy (Kellner, 1995).

Media culture, as a significant site of contestation for competing political ideologies, has further potential for influence. That the public is colonized by these struggles and ultimately induced to identify with dominant social and political ideologies speaks to the power of media culture to inform. Mirroring arguments about "high" and "low" forms of culture, one finds within media culture investigations a similar debate as to whether media culture is solely a source of domination or whether it provides resources for resistance as well. What is required here is an analysis which contextualizes specific media culture phenomena within contemporary society. If society represents a terrain of domination and resistance, then what we glean from media content must be derived from many angles, and must include the material culture artifacts associated with it. Kellner suggested that media cultural texts are

> complex artifacts that embody social and political discourses whose analysis and interpretation require methods of reading and critique that articulate their embeddedness in the political economy, social relations, and the political environment within which they are produced, circulated, and received. (Kellner, 1995, p. 4)

Since the embedded forms of circulation and receipt of media change over time, contemporary interpretations are likely to both act upon and be transformed by these changes. What results from this interaction between interpretation and change is a kind of continuity over time such that belief systems of the past are able to, in a sense, reinvent themselves so that they adapt to the present context.

Cultural Transmission

According to Kellner (1995), Jean Baudrillard was "arguably the most important and provocative media culture theorist of the 1970s and early 1980s" (p. 297). Baudrillard's "delirious postmodern funhouse" (p. 297) theorized a post-modern society "organized around simulation, in which models, codes, communication, information, and the media were demiruges of a radical break with modern societies" (Kellner, 1995, p. 297). Baudrillard (1994) believed that "in its reality, as much as in its mode of production, culture is subject to the same demand to be 'up to date' as are material goods" (p. 66). Meaning, as in the meaning behind a Van Gogh painting, has been co-opted and becomes now cyclical, dependent on the same forms of communication a society relies upon to dictate the length of skirts or the right hairstyle. Furthermore, the religious and sacrificial ceremonies found throughout human history no longer occur through a symbolic medium, but rather a technical, or electronic, one (Baudrillard, 1994, p. 68).

Media and culture theories imply the satisfaction of some kind of need on the part of both the consumers and producers of popular culture texts. Baudrillard (1994) identifies this need, contending that culture is subject to the same demands as material goods in its *need* to be "up to date," but he falls short of identifying the need of the audience. Popular culture texts may indeed become popular because of their ability to reintroduce messages, such as that of progress and achievement that emerge from the intellectual past.

Pierre Bordieu (1990) is another example of a major theoretical voice concerned with the role of culture in the reproduction of social structures. Especially, he is concerned with

> the way in which unequal power structures, *unrecognized as such and thus accepted as legitimate*, are embedded in the system of classifications used to describe and discuss everyday life—as well as cultural practices—and in the ways of perceiving reality that are taken for granted by members of society. (Bordieu, 1983/1993, p. 2; emphasis mine)

Interestingly, dominant ideologies elicit the support of the audience even when presented in such a way that they are not recognized as being dominant. This brings to mind Strinati's (1995) discussion of the elitist arguments against mass culture theory. Strinati notes that popular culture has "always been a problem for 'other people,' be they intellectuals, political leaders, or moral and social reformers" (p. 40) who, as a matter of opinion, believe that the consumers of popular culture "should ideally be occupied with something more enlightening or worthwhile than popular culture" (p. 40). I contend that this elitist stance on the part of these "other people" is actually replicated in the various forms of popular culture where adherents to certain alternative music forms, political alliances, alternative films, etc., are every bit as disdainful of those who do not share their tastes as elites are of popular culture in general. With this we begin to see how, for instance, people who considered themselves to be part of the Progressive movement in the 1920s and 1930s could ally themselves with a movement as exclusionary as eugenics. What becomes even more significant than the content of various forms of popular culture, is the way in which they are communicated, or, as Prown (2001) would say, the *style* in which they are imparted.

Meaning Emerges

Baudrillard (1994) wrote that "to dissimulate is to feign not to have what one has. To simulate is to feign to have what one hasn't" (p. 176). Baudrillard argued that the validity of the distinction between idea and thing, object and representation, has eroded and in its place are simulacra (simulations) which have no reality but their own as their referent. For Baudrillard, the television newscast is there not for its ability to report the news, but for its ability to narrate. Baudrillard charted simulacra as it progresses from what he calls the "Utopian" (p. 173) principle of equivalence between "the sign and the real" (p. 173) to that of pure simulation:

These would be the successive phases of the image:

- It is the reflection of a basic reality.
- It masks and perverts a basic reality.
- It masks the *absence* of a basic reality.
- It bears no relation to any reality whatever: it is its own pure simulacrum (Baudrillard, 1994, p. 173; emphasis in original).

Again, we are back to the conclusion that content, though certainly not irrelevant, is secondary to the form and style of transmission. That simulacra potentially carry as much weight as any proffered reality speaks to the power inherent in cultural transmission itself, be it at the behest of dominance or resistance. In addition, it becomes clear that popular culture alone is inadequate to provide structure of meaning. Meaning emerges when popular culture texts interact with cultural knowledge that is already present.

Verbal Influence

Having examined the possible applications of the methodologies of material, media, and popular culture to the investigation of conceptions of schooling, I now turn to the subject which binds them all together, that of rhetoric. Brummett (1991) wrote that rhetoric has historically been described as "the art of verbal influence" (p. xi). In his examination of the rhetorical dimensions of popular culture, Brummett claims that public discourse has taken on a different form in the past century. From "a distinct historical practice carried out during concentrated periods of speaking and listening, or reading and writing," (p. xii) rhetoric has dissipated out into a cacophony of popular culture venues. Brummett explains that

> When we consider the rhetoric of popular culture, then, we are considering how artifacts work to influence us and to make us who we are, and how cultures symbolically nurture and engender their members. I argue that rhetoric is a dimension of all cultural artifacts rather than a discrete set of objects or actions. (1991, p. xi)

This is not only an expansion of the definition of rhetoric, but it is also an expansion of the definition of an artifact, as the use of rhetoric itself becomes an object of examination.

As to the use of rhetoric in the past, while Brummett's description of rhetoric occurring "in halls or parks to hear speakers debate for an hour" (p. xii) there were simultaneous variations being carried on through countless outlets of popular dissemination. Like theories of popular culture, the uses of rhetoric have the potential to be re-examined as tools to investigate the past as well as the present and there is the possibility that rhetoric functions to incur memory, and is then reflected by popular culture.

It behooves us, as inquirers into the function of culture in education policy and practice, to utilize popular culture theory and to apply it backwards in time. In addition, we need to expand the scope of what we accept as popular culture artifacts. Due to the fact that these theories have been solely concerned with interpreting the present, their gaze necessarily relies on those things that have been produced in the present and did not exist a century ago. In addition to considering the ephemera such as pamphlets, flyers, and state fair displays, which at present skirt the edges of material culture and traditional historiographic data, I propose that we consider broadening our horizons even further.

If we think of school documents themselves as popular culture artifacts, along with the academic writing that supported and maintained pedagogical theory and practice, we substantially broaden our window of inquiry. Further, if we add to our analysis the concept of collective memory, and its function in intertwining the present with the past, we have deepened our analysis of the past in a way that we can utilize our knowledge to inquire into the present.

Reflecting the earlier arguments about elitism, Brummett provided the *Oxford English Dictionary* definition of culture:

> The tracing, development and refinement of minds, tastes, and manners; the condition of being thus trained and defined; the intellectual side of civilization. (*Oxford English Dictionary*; quoted in Brummett, 1991, p. xv)

Brummett observed that the clearly elitist meaning in this definition reflects the assumption of hierarchy commonly accepted in traditional academia and many popular culture theories as well (1991, p. xv). Further, this conceptual framework requires of people that they "assume that a given cultural artifact has some stable or objective nature that is good or bad" (p. xv) and that its meaning is stable as well. Rejecting the assumption that there is a distinction between reality and symbols of reality, Brummett contended that "to experience is to craft symbolically, that things are what we make them because we manipulate strategies of understanding and meaning, that is, we act rhetorically (1991, p. xvii). Indeed, Brummett distinguished between concrete and abstract symbolic construction. The former operates at a cognitive level while the latter operates at the level of everyday experience and practice, and "it is how we construct the latter that culture is made flesh" (p. xvii). I suggest that what Brummett is talking about is not that distant from the concept of collective memory. In this sense, culture loses its elitist veneer and becomes "specific artifacts (objects, actions, and events) coalescing into a whole way of life and springing from, or being grounded in, groups of people" (p. xviii).

Though Prown (2000) is talking about material culture objects, he adds to this argument with his observation that it is not only unrealistic, but also unrealizable for any producer of popular culture artifacts to either intend or assume that their purpose be understood by all recipients equally. But, more importantly, it is nevertheless the case that "every maker must have that purpose, even unconsciously, in order to make" (p. 92). Furthermore, he says that an artifact is a sign that conveys "meaning, a mode of communication, a form of language [and may] communicate a specific meaning outside of itself" (p. 92). It is imperative that we include in our quest for understanding not only artifacts themselves, but also the cultural knowledge that is already present for the producers and receivers of that knowledge.

Finally, Prown noted that particular cultural artifacts may trigger a wide range of emotional responses and it is the degree to which these responses are shared that is significant. Prown further argued that even though he himself has emphasized the importance of "striving to achieve objectivity and to maintain scientific method as an ideal," that the common practice of disregarding one's own deductions actually works to inhibit the process and is more appropriately approached with "vigilance, not martial law" (p. 82). Indeed, subjective assumptions, such as those contained in eugenic ideology, that go unrecognized for the longest time are "often the most deeply rooted cultural assumptions" (p. 82). Investigators who work with, and accept, their emotional reactions to the artifacts with which they work have a unique opportunity to reveal the shared cultural knowledge that originally went into their production.

Collective memory is helpful in providing a framework with which to understand the penetration and perpetuation of ideology within culture and is also useful for our understanding of the way history intersects with individuals and the present. Theories of popular, media, and material culture, on the other hand, hold enormous possibility for examining historical data. This is especially true when an expanded definition of what constitutes popular and media culture is included, along with a distancing of the theory's reliance on technological forms of transmission. Certain aspects of mass culture theory, such as the formal and contractual nature of interpersonal relationships, the role of industrialization and urbanization, and the dependence on surrogate and fake moralities, offer further avenues of inquiry into the production of cultural knowledge. Finally, historical investigations into popular conceptions of education would benefit from drawing on theories of collective memory, the role of rhetoric, and the application of post-modern inquiry methods. Collective memory theory, along with rhetorical analysis, goes a long way towards providing the mechanistic infrastructure by means of which political ideologies and cultural knowledge travel. It is this last point in particular that is in urgent need of expansion as an argument for if we can establish a mechanism of operation, we have a new lens through which to interpret our data.

4

Early Race Theory: From Science to Civic Virtue

Puritan ideology, early race theory, positivism, and naturalism are all elements of the environment into which Darwin's theory of evolution, and later Social Darwinism were introduced. It is important to understand that the American experiment has always been superimposed upon a much older ideological grid which continues to serve as an infrastructure for the way we think about broad, guiding principles such as democracy, freedom, success, and each other. There are, of course, many ways in which we might approach an inquiry into the effects of ideological osmosis and many profound thinkers precede me. In this instance, however, I am interested in discovering a very specific thread of ideological transmission, one that attempts to get at the roots of institutional and societal racism. The application of heredity and evolution to social problems did not arise out of a vacuum. Indeed, previously conceived systems of hierarchy and worth such as Positivism, Great Chain of Being, and Naturalism all led to post-Darwinian concepts such as "survival of the fittest" and the "White Man's Burden." It is here, at the nexus of these ideas, that eugenic ideology emerged, first conceived by Sir Francis Galton and subsequently taken up by Karl Pearson and various facets of Progressive America.

Great Chain of Being

Scholars (Link, 1955; Pickens, 1968; Tucker, 1994; Numbers, 1999) have long pointed out the role of Greek philosopher Aristotle in providing the foundation for the way race and hierarchy have been viewed through time. It was Aristotle who first arranged all animals into a single, graded scale that placed humans at the top as the most perfect iteration. By the late nineteenth century, the idea that inequality was the basis of natural order, known as the *great chain of being*, was part of the common lexicon. Particularly important for the present inquiry is the basic premise of the great chain of being concept, which ascribed hierarchical rank to every form of life. This hierarchy, in turn, provided an enduring structure establishing biological variety as synonymous with natural inequality (Tucker, 1994). It was a small step, contended Tucker (1994), to apply the hierarchical order to human beings,

> a step that seemed only natural to Europeans as they came into increasing contact with people of color from newly discovered lands. The hints of relative racial merit contained in the scientific tradition, with its attachment of personal traits and esthetic judgments to skin color, soon merged with the assumptions of the great chain, and the creation of a vertical ordering of the races became an accepted task of science. (p. 10)

European Americans, using this analysis, placed peoples with darker skin somewhere between humans and other animals. The conclusion that "on the basis of anatomical and physiological evidence . . . blacks were a completely separate species, intermediate between Whites and apes," was first proffered by English physician and surgeon Charles White in 1799 (quoted in Tucker, 1994, p. 10). Not only did White propound one of the most egregious examples of inhumanity in the guise of science, he compounded it by declaring a lack of malice towards blacks in which his only purpose was "to investigate the truth, and to discover what are the established laws of nature" (quoted in Tucker, 1994, p. 10). According to Tucker, White fervently proclaimed that he had no desire to see blacks oppressed just because they were a "separate species, of greater biological proximity to anthropoids than to Europeans" (p. 10), and he hoped that nothing he said would "give the smallest countenance to the pernicious practice of enslaving mankind" (quoted in Tucker, 1994, p. 10). Here we have not only a foundation of the application of great Chain of Being theory to a hierarchical sorting of human beings by race, but also the foundation of the "doing it for their own good" maxim and, I suppose White would add, the good of all humanity, a precedent that remained clearly delineated for the next two centuries.

From Religion to Biology

The desire to explain, justify, and forecast social affairs led to the development of a rich history of ideas many of which continue to build and rely on their previous incarnations. Prior to the introduction of the concept of evolution, racial ranking occurred in two modes known as *monogenism* and *polygenism* (Gould, 1996). Monogenism upheld the religious notion that all peoples emerged from the single creation of Adam and Eve, while polygenism abandoned scripture, considering it allegorical and held that human races were separate biological species. Both modes of racial ranking enjoyed heated debate, especially in the south where the defenders of slavery were forced to contend with a difficult quandary between science and religion. In the south, Gould contended, degeneration of blacks "under the curse of Ham was an old and eminently functional standby" (p. 102), which rendered science in opposition to the status quo. The American debate over polygeny, according to Gould,

> may represent the last time that arguments in the scientific mode did not form a first line of defense for the status quo and the unalterable quality of human difference. (1996, p. 104)

It was the unique combination of the unquestioned propriety of racial ranking among white leaders in the eighteenth and nineteenth centuries, along with Puritan ideology and the infusion of the positivist paradigm into scientific intent and methodology that provided the structure and method for the intelligentsia of the mid-to-late nineteenth century.

Puritan Legacy

The translation of racial hierarchy by Puritan settlers in America has had profound ramifications for the way we think about schools. From the very beginning of Western European presence in America, an enduring faith has held that the institution of education embodies the greatest promise for the salvation of social ills and inadequacies. According to McKnight (2003), this persistent cultural construct has been carried forth by means of the Puritan provision of the "rhetorical and institutional means of perpetuating this symbolic narrative" (p. 3). The provision, however, was not just one of content but also of form. McKnight describes how the *crisis sermon*, also known as the *jeremiad*, was written and spoken by reverends and teachers and usually concerned both sacred and mundane matters. Furthermore, McKnight argues, "the institution of schooling . . . whose pedagogical methods mirrored the jeremiad form" (p. 3) was considered by the Puritans to act as a moral and intellectual mold through which individuals were brought in to the "corporate fold" (p. 3). As Kellner (1994) pointed out, educational ideologies reflect and configure expectations about education which in turn strongly influence education. This places added emphasis on the importance of an investigation into what those expectations were and how they were formed.

The jeremiad form is far more insidious than simple denouncement/solution, and for Roberts-Miller (1999) the implications speak to "our cultural and pedagogical inabilities to create a public sphere in which argument is a form of *inquiry*" (p.1; emphasis in original). Roberts-Miller argued that the Puritan public sphere was authoritarian and democratic, hegemonic and individualistic, creating a paradox that has regulated public discourse ever since. Political social discourse takes the form of a contest, or game, in which both sides enter committed to an ideology that is both abstract yet specific. Social discourse thus conceived requires of its participants adherence to an argument coupled with a specific plan to win. The result is a form of argument that is entered upon not to *discover* one's viewpoint but rather to ensure that others come to share it. This form views change and indecision as a sign of "deep moral weakness or evil" (p. x) wherein

> [s]hifting one's thesis is almost always interpreted by people who ascribe to this view as some kind of sloppiness as best and stupidity at worst. Often the speaker behaves as some kind of Old Testament prophet, not only damning the opposition (as fools if not sinners) but also presenting his or her own case as though it were self-evident to all right-minded people.

Puritan rhetoric then creates a style that is opposed to cognition by presenting opposing arguments as illegitimate while it also epitomizes the Puritan conception of difference.

Apparently, Americans learned early and well the lesson of categorizing, and thus altering, historical events so that they would not interfere with current conceptions of freedom and democracy, the "real" American ideals. McKnight (2003) argues that historians of education failed to recognize the influence of Puritan ideology and its persistence into the present due largely to a "linguistic secularization that became fully privileged during the 1800s" (p. 3). I argue that they also fail to recognize the influence of a science-as-savior mentality that permeated the nineteenth and twentieth centuries.

The influence of Puritan ideology provides two important components for the current inquiry. First, a precedent is set for the process by which ideologies persist through generations by illustrating that something as seemingly innocuous as a form of communication, the *jeremiad*, can act as a boundary which shapes how we identify, analyze, and solve problems. Second, the specific content of Puritan ideology provides a backdrop for eugenics in terms of the intent and form of eugenic programs that were designed to solve society's problems through "human betterment" and improvement of racial "stock" (Wiggam, 1924).

Myth of Errand and Progress

The most resilient Puritan symbol depicts America as a "city upon a hill" whose inhabitants are engaged in an "errand into the wilderness" and, according to McKnight (2003), it is the jeremiad form, the crisis sermon, that proclaims, defines, and interprets current events, fitting them into the desired depiction. Crisis sermons are ubiquitous and provide a form of communication we recognize and respond to, indeed, perhaps require in order to make sense of another Puritan legacy, the conception that the world is in a state of chaos.

According to McKnight (2003), following the Protestant Reformation with the new emphasis on written text, education for the Puritans became the path towards morality within a context of depravity. The Puritan worldview held that although all things were naturally depraved and in need of purification, this presence of evil ought to be regarded as an opportunity and means to place emphasis on moral dilemmas. Thus, the *errand*, to deliver our enlightened countenance to the rest of the world, became a moral imperative, necessary for individual and societal progress. The symbol of the errand, and the form of its communication, the jeremiad, are crucial for understanding the relationship between eugenics and education. Puritan ideology regarding the form and function of education helps to explain the collective memory link between the perceived ameliorative qualities of education and the moral certainty expressed by practitioner and policy maker alike.

McKnight (2003) rejects the common historical treatment of the Puritans as people concerned solely with theological truth and autocratic government and claims instead that the Puritans provided the symbolic narrative that continues to govern conceptions of education. During the nineteenth and twentieth centuries, the symbolic narrative, previously well developed into a sacred sense of history by the Puritans, shifted towards a secular, technological understanding. Initially, this shift came about as a result of the Romantic era wherein, it was thought, literary technique provided access to universal truths obscured by history. By the late nineteenth century, the notion of progress so long connected to the pursuit of theological truth was altered largely by the newly emerging professional historian class. The shift realigned progress to conform to imperatives drawn from the natural sciences, specifically Darwin's theory of evolution, as a way to explain why America's identity and destiny were special.

Darwin to Compte: Science and Race Unite

The philosophy of naturalism was a solid philosophical root shared by eugenics and Progressive political theory. Key components of naturalism including such concepts as economy in nature, the Great Chain of Being theory, teleology (the notion that the fact or character of being is directed towards an end or shaped by a purpose) were critical to the application of eugenic ideology to social institutions. By projecting their class prejudices as objective laws of nature and civilization, scientists, educators, and social leaders demonstrated their distrust of democracy and projected their alarm regarding an increasingly diverse, urban, and industrial America.

Link (1955) contended that naturalism, as articulated by the leading French naturalist Emile Zola, never truly took hold in America because of the proscription to describe natural phenomena in a manner completely removed from emotion and morality. America may not have been ready to leave behind its moral convictions when it came to addressing societal problems, but naturalism had much to offer and the acceptance of the structural elements of naturalism provided a resilient infrastructure that persists to this day and is used by both the social and natural sciences. Key to the interdependence of science and the legacy of Puritan morality was the orchestration produced by this notion of natural hierarchy with the American intolerance for leaving out compassion and morality as components of analysis.

While American scientists embraced the idea of objectivity, they were less than diligent in their efforts to evaluate the morally presumptive direction of their investigations. The combination of science and morality afforded the perfect vehicle for new theories about education. Additionally, this particularly American version of naturalism provided the backdrop for the impact of Darwin's *On the Origin of Species* (1858) and the subsequent translation of the theory of evolution into a scientific justification for societal inequities.

Darwin

Gould (1996) begins and ends his book *The Mismeasure of Man* with a phrase from the slavery chapter in the *Voyage of the Beagle*: "If the misery of our poor be caused not by the laws of nature, but by our institutions, great is our sin" (Darwin, 1845). What Gould wants us to understand has been uttered by others as well (Hofstadter, 1944; Degler, 1991; Hasian, 1996): that during the eighteenth and nineteenth centuries, leading Western thinkers did not question racial hierarchical assumptions. The motivation for this shortsightedness was not because they were callous and uncaring, but, worse, because the conventional rankings, resulting from unexamined presuppositions used by scientists, arose from a shared social belief that at no time questioned racial difference.

Given the epic proportions of his influence, the intentions and motivations of Darwin have been explored by a range of scholars (see, e.g., Link, 1955; Degler, 1991; Tucker, 1994; Gould, 1996; Hasian, 1996; Numbers, 1999) and conclusions vary. As we can see from the above quote, Darwin was complicated and sensitive in ways not generally discussed. Despite the fact that Darwin did "construct a rationale for a shared uncertainty," the later emphasis drawn from evolutionary theory that inequality was born of biological rather than social constructs was inadequate to provide a definitive conclusion as to Darwin's underlying beliefs (Gould, 1996, p. 418). The point is underscored by the fact that Darwin continues with the declaration, "It makes one's blood boil, yet heart tremble, to think that we Englishmen and our American descendants, with their boastful cry of liberty, have been and are so guilty" (Darwin, 1845).

According to Degler (1991), although Darwin's opponents based their opposition to the theory of evolution on the supposition that morality was a uniquely human quality, Darwin himself was deeply concerned with morality as well as biology. If Darwin could demonstrate that moral consciousness was rooted in man's animal ancestry, then his objection to the inherent self-interest in the uniquely American utilitarian principle of happiness must be superceded by an emphasis on the good of the group.

Positivism

French philosopher Auguste Comte, founder of positivism, developed the idea that the goal of knowledge was to describe experienced phenomena, not to question whether it exists. Comte (1907) believed the solution to persistent social problems existed within a hierarchical framework and applied the methods of observation and experimentation to create the science of sociology. Indelibly etching Puritan form upon social scientific inquiry, Comte wrote,

> the science of society . . . supplies the only logical scientific link by which all our varied observations of phenomena can be brought into one consistent whole. (1907, p. 2)

In this way, arguments about social phenomena adhered to a form that de-legitimized the observations and perspectives of anyone who was not part of the scientific establishment. Voice became privileged, and an era of boundaried, class- and race-based inquiry ensued.

Comte's goal was to address the "great crisis of modern history" (p. 1) which emerged from the Age of Enlightenment by first acknowledging

> how hopeless is the task of reconstructing political institutions without the previous remodeling of opinion and life. To form then a satisfactory synthesis of all human conceptions is the most urgent of our social wants: and it is needed equally for the sake of order and of Progress . . . A new moral power will arise spontaneously throughout the West, which, as its influence increases, will lay down a definite basis for the reorganization of society. (1907, p. 1)

That a philosopher could be so certain of the future implications of his ideas, and especially that he could be so accurate, is not so much surprising as it is impressive. Nevertheless, Comte suffered from no illusion that his philosophy would be usurped before it could accomplish his vision that positivism

> will offer a general system of education for the adoption of all civilized nations, and by this means will supply in every department of public and private life fixed principles of judgment and conduct. Thus the intellectual movement and the social crisis will be brought continually into close connection with each other. (1907, p. 3)

The synthesis of "all human conceptions" was not, for Comte, an objective matter. Positivism, a paradigm that has dominated Western thought, inquiry, and action for over a century, epitomizes the dual ideas of progress and errand. Positivism set the task of becoming "more perfect" (p. 6) on generations of aspiring investigators.

Further integrating the new conception of science to hierarchical racial constructs, Comte (1907) wrote that social regeneration would at first be limited to the "great family" (p. 6) of Western nations and would afterwards extend, in accordance with definite laws, to the rest of the white race. Through the work of Comte and others (Spencer, 1857; Galton, 1889; Loeb, 1900; Galton, 1901; Pearson, 1901; Hollingworth, 1914) racism was established as a fundamental component of one of the most influential paradigmatic shifts in history and provided a nourishing petri dish for the development of ever more insidious forms of racial ideology.

Social Darwinism

William Graham Sumner (1914) is credited with the first use of the term "*Social Darwinism.*" Sumner, an American sociologist, political economist, and prominent

Yale professor (Hofstadter, 1944; Link, 1955; Montague, 1974) was considered to be the American counterpart of Herbert Spencer, and he used the law of evolution to defend radical *laissez-faire* economics. Sumner argued that

> the struggle for existence is aimed against nature. It is from her niggardly hand that we have to wrest the satisfactions for our needs, but our fellowmen are our competitors for the meager supple. Competition, therefore, is a law of nature. . . . We shall favor the survival of the unfittest, and we shall accomplish this by destroying liberty. Let it be understood that we cannot go outside of this alternative: Liberty, inequality, survival of the fittest; not-liberty, equality, survival of the unfittest. The former carries society forward and favors all its best members; the latter carries society downwards and favors all its worst members. (1914, p. 398)

Sumner provided a fundamental link between *liberty* and *fitness*, a link that was to serve as a rallying point for decades to come. Social Darwinism and later eugenics are used extensively to justify and moralize the maintenance of the status quo for European Americans economically as well as ideologically.

From 1899 until his death in 1910, Sumner was a vice president of the Anti-Imperialist League which was formed to protest direct territorial imperialism (Curtis, 1981). Sumner (1914) emphasized a version of economic individualism that glorified acquisition so as to articulate a Progressive relationship with Social Darwinism. In so doing, he set the stage for an argument that persists today; material success is evidence of a superior capacity for "labor and self-denial" which are virtues ordained by "God and Nature" (p. 343). As for the other side of the equation, the exploited have only themselves to blame for their exploitation due to their unrestrained indulgence in "vulgar enjoyments" and spendthrift natures (p. 346). What Sumner achieved was a recasting of civic virtue. No longer was civic virtue defined as an active concern for the social good. Instead, civic virtue opposed any infringement upon individual freedom and the laws of nature. This new, peculiarly American version of Social Darwinism provided the ideal condition for yet another recasting of civic virtue by eugenicists with their promotion of "racial purification-as-moral-duty."

"Survival of the Fittest"

The key phrase that defined Social Darwinism—*survival of the fittest*—was coined by English philosopher Herbert Spencer who argued vociferously that government and social institutions should not regulate the "natural processes" that occur within the social order (Degler, 1991). A British philosopher and sociologist, Spencer wrote about evolution and progress in 1857, two years prior to the publication of Darwin's *Origin of Species*. However, it was Darwin's (1859) work that propelled Spencer's ideas into the ideology of Social Darwinism.

Like Sumner, Spencer (1857) veered away from evolutionary theory's emphasis on perpetuation of species and took a decidedly more individualistic stance arguing that individual freedom superceded community and therefore governmental regulation retarded progress. In the Spencerian view, progress was vague to the point of erroneousness and was based on a teleological conception that was no longer relevant. To rectify this, Spencer suggests a recasting of the notion of progress so that it

> consists in the produce of greater quantity and variety of articles for the satisfaction of men's wants; in the increasing security of person and property; in the widening freedom of action enjoyed whereas, rightly understood, social progress consists in those changes of structure in the social organism which have entailed these consequences. (Spencer, 1857, p. 445)

Spencer (1857) was one of the first to argue for the separation of a definition of progress from a requisite furthering of "human happiness," a definition that he deemed inadequate because such conceptions are thought to be progress "simply *because* they tend to heighten human happiness" (p. 455; emphasis in original). Anticipating the eugenicists argument, and somewhat in opposition to his own emphasis on the individual, Spencer called instead for a definition of progress that inquired into the nature of change irrespective of human interest.

Tucker (1994) expressed the modern interpretation that Social Darwinism is "a mixture of oversimplified biology and opportunistic politics that arose as the dominant sociological thought of the late nineteenth century" (p. 26). About Spencer and his phrase "survival of the fittest" Tucker has this to say:

> Herbert Spencer, the major exponent of Social Darwinism, preferred to stress the "survival of the fittest," an inappropriate use of the superlative that converted the subtle dynamic suggested by Darwin's metaphorical "struggle" into Spencer's more sensationalized, literal version: the "struggle for existence" a *bellum omnium contra omnes*, in which purposeful cruelty was transformed into nature's method for biological progress. (1994, p. 26)

To understand the subtleties of the Social Darwinists' take on Darwin is to see clearly the launching pad of the eugenics movement: Social Darwinists were steadfastly against all governmental programs to aid the poor. It was precisely a reaction to this mentality that led to the rise of the Progressive movement and the subsequent translation by eugenicists of previously held beliefs regarding race inferiority into more palatable "Progressive" language.

"White Man's Burden"

The late nineteenth century was a period of unheralded imperialism by European nations (Link, 1955; Curti, 1959; Zwick, 1995). Link (1955) explained that in 1898 the United States entered the fray by going to war with Spain to "righteously" (p. 16) save the Cubans from Spanish brutality and tyranny. We might imagine that these events satisfied the Puritan desire to fulfill the *errand*, but they also constituted a significant change in the American epistemology by redirecting the previously isolationist mindset (and reality) to an increasingly international frontier. Justification for outward expansion was cast as a moral obligation that overshadowed economic reality. Montague (1974) observed that "by the middle of the nineteenth century 'racism' had become an important ideological weapon of nationalistic and imperialistic politics" (p. 32).

Imperialism offers unique insight into the peculiarly American combination of race, morality, and public opinion. Anticipating the seemingly incongruous combination of Progressive and eugenic ideology that embodied the social landscape of the 1920s and 1930s, the debate over imperialism at the turn of the nineteenth century combined the newly emerging "science" of race with a vocal and vociferous anti-war movement that spawned anti-imperialist organizations throughout America. Some of the very same people (David Starr Jordan and William Graham Sumner) who would later become leaders of the eugenics movement were, in 1898–1899, instrumental in leading the anti-imperialist movement in the United States (Starr, 1925; Forrest, 1974; Curtis, 1981; Delbanco, 2001). Indeed, anti-Imperialist organizations flourished around the turn of the century, largely in response to the Philippine-American War that began in 1899. Although their stated motivation was the liberation of the oppressed, anti-imperialists were nevertheless deeply concerned with the maintenance of the status quo (Link, 1955; Zwick, 1995). Without challenging the racial aspects of imperialism, the anti-imperialist movement objected to the acquisition of colonies abroad, believing that such a move was both antithetical to the American principle and dangerous to the future existence and happiness of the nation (Lanzar-Carpio, 1930).

Montague (1974) contended that prior to the civil war, the status of the African American was considered to be a product of caste rather than biology and, as such, slavery and servitude transcended biological inheritance. Over the course of the following decades, class as a basis for oppression was usurped by a biological argument that held physical difference to be an outward manifestation of biological and, by extension, social inferiority. In turn, imperialism extended this "drive to find differences in the 'races' of mankind" (p. 127) to all people worldwide. In what was to become a symbol of the debate over imperialism, Rudyard Kipling (1899) penned a poem entitled *The White Man's Burden* wherein he called for an expansion of empire and outlined the costs involved. The poem sparked a flurry of reaction from the chambers of the U.S. Senate to newspaper and magazine editorials on both sides of the Atlantic (Zwick, 1995). At issue was the underlying motivation of imperialist intent and whether it had to do with material yield, in the form of new possessions and new trade opportunities, or whether it was the extension of moral righteousness and protection of helpless brethren.

Anti-imperialists were specific in their objection to colonization but were troubled by the fact that the Philippines were already in American hands and could not in good conscience be given back to Spain. Therefore, anti-imperialists advocated instead that the Philippines be made a protectorate of the United States (Lanzar-Carpio, 1930). Hofstadter (1968) reminded us that the Spanish-American War started as a surge of popular idealism over the freedom of Cuba and that initially, the imperialist implications were unforeseen. An 1899 editorial in *The San Francisco Call* demands a re-evaluation of the burden thusly: "Rightly considered the White man's burden is to set and keep his own house in order. It is not required of him to upset the brown man's house under pretense of reform" (p. 3). At the same time, in a speech delivered on the floor of the U.S. Senate, vice-president of the Anti-Imperialist League Benjamin Tillman (1899) explained anti-imperialist efforts in this way:

> It is not because we are Democrats, but because we understand and realize what it is to have two races side by side that can not mix or mingle without deterioration and injury to both and the ultimate destruction of the civilization of the higher. We of the South have borne this White man's burden of a colored race in our midst since their emancipation and before . . . Those peoples are not suited to our institutions. They are not ready for liberty as we understand it. They do not want it. Why are we bent on forcing upon them a civilization not suited to them and which only means in their view degradation and a loss of self-respect, which is worse than the loss of life itself? (Tillman, 1899, p. 5)

Neither side of the debate had, as its root motivation, any form of racial equality or emancipation. Nevertheless, there was deep public sentiment that regarded American intervention in Cuba and the Philippines as a generous and ideological effort, so much so that war enthusiasm surrounding the Spanish-American War could be considered "the greatest stimulus to the moral awakening of Progressivism"

(Hofstadter, 1968, p. 171). The development of the construct of race as a pivotal issue in the betterment of society was not finished and a rearticulation of older race theory led to the new science of eugenics.

Eugenics and Science

Towards the turn of the century, a shift occurred within the academic community regarding the nature of heredity and the role of the environment. This shift was spurred largely by newly emerging concerns about the morality of a strictly "survival of the fittest" approach to social concerns. Much of the dogma governing competition and social and industrial effort began to be questioned on the grounds that "survival of the fittest" was inherently unfair and that "privileged conditions which admit of monopoly should not be granted in control to any person or set of person, but should belong to and be used for the community" (White, 1989, p. 224). This new direction was not, however, indicative of a new concern for racial and class equality. Instead, some, like Loeb (1900), advocated for a *municipal socialism* which focused on a break with the past rather than possibilities for the future. Concerns about utilities, transportation, telephone, and telegraph service drove proponents of municipal ownership and helped to recast Social Darwinism in terms of acquisition and economy rather than questioning the underlying racist and classist tenets.

The core argument of Social Darwinism, that natural selection provided the only law of moral and physical progress, became, by the turn of the century, "a dying faith" (White, 1989, p. 224). In the late 1800s populists argued that society was doomed to extinction if it chose to await the advent of universal betterment through the unfolding of natural economic laws. Arguments emerged that called for an ideological transition from traditional "optimistic fatalism" to a "vigorous professionalism" (p. 224). Natural order began to give way to a new form of "social sanitation" (White, 1989). Two men, Francis Galton and Karl Pearson were instrumental in translating the ideas of their time through provision of language and scientific validity for hierarchical and racial assumptions contained in Social Darwinism (Chesterson, 1922/2000; Blacker, 1952; Kevles, 1985; Hasian, 1996; Numbers, 1999).

Francis Galton

Francis Galton (1822–1911), explorer and anthropologist, well represents men of his class during the latter half of the nineteenth century. Galton and his cousin, Charles Darwin, descended from Erasmus Darwin (1731–1802) who first described his theory of evolution in 1801 (Darwin, 1801). Thanks to a sizable inheritance, Galton spent decades travelling among "primitive" cultures and writing about them for the educated public at home (Blacker, 1952). One of Galton's primary beliefs was that family pre-eminence in certain fields was hereditary and it was this that led him to coin the word *eugenics* in 1883 (Galton, 1889). It is interesting to note that in addition to the Darwin legacy on his mother's side, Galton's father descended from a long line of wealthy bankers and gunsmiths and was the youngest of seven children (Forrest, 1974). This family structure may be regarded as a virtual blueprint for what was later termed "positive eugenics" and opens the door to questions about the relationship between eugenic ideology and the maintenance of the status quo. A further discussion of Galton's contribution to eugenic ideology will appear in Chapter Five, for now it is important to note his influence on Karl Pearson (1857–1936) who was instrumental during the transition of Social Darwinistic thought into eugenic thought.

Karl Pearson

Karl Pearson, known primarily as an eminent statistician, was influenced by the publication of Galton's (1889) *Natural Inheritance* to change the course of his career and subsequently wrote 18 papers between 1893 and 1912 entitled *Mathematical Contribution to the Theory of Evolution* (Pearson, 1938). Pearson later became the Galton Professor of Eugenics at University College in London from 1911 to 1933 (Numbers, 1999). Pearson (1901) articulated a form of Social Darwinism that appealed to the public's sense of progress by declaring that racial struggle provided the very means of improving civilization. For Pearson, "this dependence of progress on the survival of the fitter race . . . gives the struggle for existence its redeeming features; it is the fiery crucible out of which comes the finer metal" (p. 21). Clear about the role of science, Pearson called his view "the scientific view of a nation" and argued that society could only be "kept to a high pitch of internal efficiency by insuring that its numbers are substantially recruited from the better stocks" (p. 27).

In order to achieve this level of efficiency Pearson employed elaborate statistical analysis to Galton's law of ancestral heredity. In what was to become one of the most powerful provocations for those interested in societal betterment (and one of the most contested tenets of eugenics), Pearson predicted that a population could, within a few generations of selective breeding, "breed true" for a selected characteristic (Pearson, 1894). Anticipating the development of the first intelligence test by Binet in 1905,

Pearson enthusiastically took on Galton's (1889) contention that mental ability was determined by heredity and began to apply his newly developed statistical tools to the problem of inherited mental ability. This work sparked a great deal of further research, especially in the newly developing field of psychology, and became a primary tool in efforts to limit immigration and create more efficient schools.

Progressive Movement

The Progressive era has been described as the period of time between 1900 and 1914 that was marked by a great deal of political and social reform (Hofstadter, 1963). One of the distinguishing characteristics of Progressivism is the extraordinary level of activism around a variety of issues such as prohibition, immigration restriction, racial segregation, super-patriotism, religious fundamentalism, the application of business-model efficiency to government and education, fear of communism and socialism, labor-union busting, and birth control (Hofstadter, 1963). Driving this activism was the certainty that social ills would not fix themselves and that social progress required government intervention.

This may seem antithetical to the Darwinian notion of natural selection and evolution which was used to justify the hierarchical access to wealth and power—whites and men had access because they were biologically superior and thus destined to occupy the pinnacle. It is, however, the same logic that drove the activist. Because of the perceived increase in the number of defectives in society (due to immigration and subsequent 'prolific' breeding), the process of evolution was thought to be simply too slow to adequately handle the needs of civilized society. Government must help nature along and defend civilization from the biologically inadequate (Spencer, 1857).

It is overly simplistic to present eugenics specifically, or Progressive thought in general, as simply an extension of nineteenth-century Social Darwinism, or even that eugenics was the concern of the conservative branch of the Progressive movement. In her book *The Politics of Heredity*, Diane Paul (1998) explains that there were important segments of the Left (as well as the women's movement) that were also supportive of eugenic ideas. "Indeed," Paul tells us, "in Britain and the United States there once existed a movement known as 'Bolshevik Eugenics' " (1998, p. 14). It is here we begin to see some of the overlap between eugenic and Progressive thought. H. J. Haller, the scientist most prominently associated with socialist eugenics argued that, since the bourgeoisie would never willingly relinquish access to power, revolution was needed because only in a society which offered equal opportunities to its citizens would it be possible to overcome the blurring effects of heredity and environment.

An examination of historical literature (Link, 1955, 1963; Conti, 1959; Hofstadter, 1963; Pickens, 1968; Zinn, 1980; Selden, 1999) regarding the Progressive movement reveals a clear consensus regarding the level of complexity among the ideologies, actions, and motivations of the times. In addition, one finds a consistent portrait of the period dividing the era into constituent movements including social justice, agriculture, immigration, education, birth control, efficiency, the nature nurture debate, and continuing debate over what to do about the "Negro problem" (DPI document, 1928). In general, the historical literature tends to regard and analyze these separate constituent movements in terms of how they differed (despite their common claim to progress) yet neglects to address common assumptions.

Contributing to the difficulty in identifying a clear role for the Progressive movement is the fact that there was no single united campaign called Progressive (Hofstadter, 1963). Link (1955) describes Progressivism as a revolt of the middle class stemming from their dissatisfaction with a power structure that maintained the privileged class ownership of wealth. Even in cases where differing groups called for the same reforms, they did so for different reasons. Hofstadter, on the other hand, sees the Progressive movement as "an attempt to develop the moral will, the intellectual insight, and the political and administrative agencies to remedy the accumulated evils and negligences of a period of industrial growth" (1963, p. 3).

Traditional portrayals of Progressivism describe a period of unrivaled optimism whose leaders were proud and excited to be part of a time that rejected and corrected the preceding era of materialism and corruption (Hofstadter, 1963). From the end of the civil war to the close of the nineteenth century, Americans were reeling from remarkable material development, but, according to Hofstadter, they were also suffering from a bankrupt moral fund from which to draw.

The lesson here is that understanding the role of Progressivism in developing and perpetuating the ideology of eugenics is not simply a matter of *sides* as is the case with so many political and ideological arguments. We might even speculate that eugenics has been protected by a shield of invisibility precisely because there is no easy way to identify who believed what and why. In any case, it hardly matters from the present vantage point whether eugenicists were liberals or conservatives, Democrats or Republicans. What does matter is that we begin the process of exposing the long-dry riverbeds that once flooded our collective memory and social institutions with a racist ideology that has (again, from the present vantage point) little to do with biological fact.

Many conduits served to develop and enervate those racial and class assumptions that led up to the eugenics movement in America. The suppositions that have produced and nurtured the cultural heritage that is "race" in America go back a long way, but they have never wanted for encouragement. Intellectual iterations of racial degeneracy are ubiquitous; their investigation holds hope for the future of education, for racial and class equity, and for humanity. From the Puritan legacy of the "myth of errand and progress" to the refining power that positivism offered to achieve the myth within a new era, ours has been a cultural adaptation. As I said in the introduction to this chapter, the challenge of identifying and rectifying our racial memory is an act, not of re-framing, but of de-framing. That the Puritan conceptions of mission and morality have, in America, synergistically interacted with a capitalistic infrastructure and a positivistic verve for solving social maladies requires of us that we question all of our motivations, not just the ones that seem obviously misguided. All along this path of intellectual history we see intentions that are blind to their own motivations. The following chapter focuses exclusively on eugenic ideology, its fundamental beliefs, imperatives, and modes of dissemination.

5

Eugenics: Content and Context

It might be said of many things that what makes them distinctive and understandable is that they arose from a specific set of historical and social circumstances. Indeed, in our human grappling with everything from teen phone chatter to institutional analysis, there is rarely a lack of reference to historical and social circumstances. Nevertheless, such circumstances can be, and often are, inaccurate or worse, downright misleading. This chapter explores the contextual circumstances, fundamental beliefs, and imperatives of the eugenics movement. In order to understand education in the present I argue that it is imperative to acknowledge the historical and social circumstances in which it was conceived and developed. They are inextricably connected, each impacting and utilizing the other in ways heretofore unacknowledged.

It is painful to look at, this sordid past of ours, but more painful is the possibility that because of our reluctance to see, we may be perpetuating racial divisiveness in ways we have yet to understand. Worse, a continued lack of acknowledgment on the part of educators and citizens alike suggests that we may continue to deliver eugenic ideology unto the most vulnerable segment of society, children. After all, as Black (2003) put it,

> in America, this battle to wipe out whole ethnic groups was fought not by armies with guns nor by hate sects at the margins. Rather, this pernicious White-gloved war was prosecuted by esteemed professors, elite universities, wealthy industrialists and government officials colluding in a racist, pseudo-scientific movement called eugenics. The purpose: create a superior Nordic race. (xv)

Human beings, thousands of them, were victims of the eugenics movement in the United States (Haller, 1963; Pickens, 1968; Kevels, 1985; Tucker, 1994; Gould, 1996;

Hasian, 1996; Paul, 1998; Selden, 1999; Allen, 2000; Black, 2001, 2003). Black (2001, 2003) argues the programs and policies of the eugenics movement spread to every continent on earth and were ultimately responsible for the Holocaust. The victims fell into roughly three areas: poor, minority, and socially deviant. Poor whites, both urban and rural, were often deemed mentally "unfit" and labeled with the dubious term "feebleminded." They ranged from unwed mothers and young boys who masturbated, to anyone whose poverty, isolation, language, or habits rendered them unacceptable by "polite" society. Eugenicists ran a formidable anti-immigration campaign seeking to deny entry to anyone deemed "unfit" by standards based largely on speciously employed intelligence tests (Gould, 1996; Lemann, 1999). This is the backdrop for the development of modern education and it is high time that we began to explore the ramifications of the fact that many so-called Fathers of Curriculum were active believers in the eugenic desire to purify the white race.

Eugenic Beliefs and Imperatives

Eugenic ideology emerged from the numerous strands of racial thinking that preceded it, and when combined with imperatives of the Enlightenment and Puritan ideologies, eugenics made for a highly popular form of social betterment in the minds of many Americans. Although Francis Galton coined the word *eugenics* in 1889, he published his ideas much earlier in an 1865 two-part article for *Macmillan's Magazine* (Kevles, 1985). Between 1865 and his death in 1911, Galton provided America with the essential form and content of the eugenics movement through a series of speeches and publications (Galton, 1889, 1909/1996). Like most Victorian scientists Galton wrote books and gave lectures for the general public and took great pains to use language that was accessible to the widest possible audience. Given that Galton approached his subject from the perspective of a statistician he was particularly successful in establishing a conceptual link between science and progress (Kevles, 1985). This link, confirmed for the public by the evidence of human mastery over inanimate nature provided by the technology of the Industrial Revolution, proved to be both an integral and ultimately highly questionable part of the eugenics movement.

Heredity

Heredity was the primary concept behind all eugenic thought. Galton (1889) described eugenics as "the science of improvement of the human germ plasm through better breeding" (p. 3). Another definition held that eugenics was "the application of human intelligence to human evolution" (Wiggam, 1924, p. iii). The role of heredity in creating a wide range of human traits and characteristics was spurred largely by the turn of the century rediscovery of Gregor Mendel's experiments on smooth and fuzzy peas (Paul, 1998). Early eugenic writings were filled with charts, graphs, and family trees showing the traversing of dominant and recessive genes through generations and, in the case of Galton, provided an exacting statistical analysis (Galton, 1901; Wiggam, 1924). With the evidence of science behind them, eugenicists expertly infused the concept of heredity into a wide range of popular culture forums from Fitter Families Contests which graded families on their fitness as human beings, to lecture series, pamphlets, displays, books, magazines, and cartoons (Haller, 1963; Kevles, 1985; Selden, 1999). The subject of heredity, however, did not go unchallenged in America and by the late 1910s the strict reliance on hereditary determinism that characterized early eugenic writings began to take on a softer tone.

Admitting that human behavior, appearance, and health were influenced by a variety of factors and that "we can not directly apply Mendelism to human beings" (p. 59), Wiggam (1924) nevertheless explained that Mendelian genetics had "greatly clarified our conception of heredity, and will aid us in developing the science of eugenics" (p. 59). For Wiggam (1924), the complication was irrelevant. He wrote,

> We see better than ever how it comes about that some men have but one talent, some two and some five. And, for practical race improvement that is all we need to know. Intelligent, wholesome, sane, energetic, moral people have more factors in their germ-cells for these virtues than have the unintelligent, the immoral, neurotic, and stupid. The high injunction of Mendelism to eugenics is then that these good factors can be concentrated in families, and by wise marriages preserved there and handed down to bless the race. (p. 60)

Though controversy abounded regarding the inheritance of acquired traits and the role of the environment, the debate did little to alter the basic form of eugenic ideology. Galton (1889, 1901) worked from the premise that eminence and reputation in society provided a reliable indicator of inborn ability. Conversely, Galton believed an absence of eminence indicated an absence of ability and further, that social circumstance did not affect outcome in either case. As other measures of ability were developed, Galton's defense of reputation as an index of inborn ability proved to be somewhat less than enduring because of its exclusive focus on positive eugenics, defined as increasing the birth rate of superior stock. Nevertheless, the notion of heredity as a central component of eugenic thought remained unchallenged even as it was disproved by advances in genetic research (Paul, 1998).

Important to the eugenics movement was the notion that heredity was responsible not only for physical characteristics, but also for the determination of temperament and behavior. One of the most widely read books on the hereditary nature of social pathology was Richard Dugdale's (1877) study of the Jukes family wherein he traced seven generations of criminals, prostitutes, and social misfits to a single set of ancestors. Pickens (1968) argued that Dugdale's work represented a new from of "practical anthropology" (p. 168) largely evident in the expanding field of social work. Interestingly, Dugdale's work actually attributed a significant portion of the Juke's misfortune to environmental degradation and stressed the role of cultural isolation in the creation of pauperism. Despite this, and evidencing the profound inclination at the time for deterministic ideology, naturalistic reformers and social scientists used the book to defend hereditary determinism and to attack environmental advocates (Pickens, 1968; Kevles, 1985).

Another study which contributed to the public's understanding of heredity was Goddard's (1912) *The Kallikak Family: A Study in the Heredity of Feeblemindedness*. Goddard was most well known as the director of the Vineland Training School for the Feebleminded in New Jersey and for his work with the Binet Intelligence Quotient (IQ) test (Pickens, 1968; Gould, 1996; Selden, 1999). According to Gould (1996), Goddard's work with the Kallikak family was the result of mere "guesswork" in its reliance on visual cues in the identification of feeblemindedness. Nevertheless, Goddard's Kalliaks "functioned as a primal myth of the eugenics movement for several decades" (p. 198). Goddard (1912) traced the lineage of Martin Kallikak, a pseudonym derived from the Greek words for beauty (*kallos*) and bad (*kakos*). The trouble began when Martin, on his way to fight in the Revolutionary War, dallied with a feebleminded barmaid. The union resulted in 480 descendents, of which, according to Goddard's report "only forty-six have been found normal" (p. 18). In contrast, Goddard "discovered" that the progeny of Martin Kallikak's later marriage, to a Quaker woman of impeccable virtue, were all found to be upstanding members of the community (Goddard, 1912).

Beyond the questionable research methodology employed in the study, a more sinister misrepresentation occurred in the case of photographs used by Goddard to document his argument (Gould, 1996; Selden, 1999). Gould (1996) demonstrated that the majority of the multiple photographs of Kallikak descendents were altered to create a more menacing look among those members of the family identified as possessing the Mendelian inheritance of feeblemindedness. "Genetically afflicted" (p. 202) hairlines were drawn in, eyebrows darkened and slanted, and eyes and mouths were darkened so as to "produce an appearance of evil or stupidity" (p. 202). One photograph that remained untouched depicts Deborah Kallikak, who

Goddard judged to be a high-grade moron and the greatest threat to society due to her attractive outer appearance and ability to introduce imbeciles and morons into the population (Goddard, 1912).

References to the Kallikak family appear in numerous writings and illustrations throughout the next two decades. Writing in 1924, Wiggam called Goddard "one of our highest authorities on feeble-mindedness" (p. 7). Arguing that "blood will tell," Wiggam wrote that

> blood has been telling its stories of tragedy and splendor ever since the days of Eden; but seldom has it painted in such clear contrasting colors as upon this little chart of the blood of the Kallikaks. Every parent and every young man and woman, every educator and statesman, should study this simple, but dramatic canvas. (1924, p. 8)

Although his praise of Goddard's work was lofty, Wiggam's view represented a slight shift in emphasis from earlier representations of the Kallikak tale. Wiggam (1924) cautioned his readers that heredity was not the definitive cause of the differences between the two lines of Kallikak descendents "since the factors of heredity and environment are not separated" (p. 10). Wiggam allowed for the possibility of environmental factors but he nevertheless felt sure that "heredity and not environment was the chief cause" (p. 10). Eugenicists understood that an overly deterministic stance would be deleterious to the acceptance of their message by the general public. An increasingly Progressive public sentiment, they surmised, needed evidence that civic effort to improve society and themselves was not wasted.

Fifteen years later, the same softening of the deterministic thrust of Goddard's work appeared in the popular trade book *You and Heredity* (1939) written for the general public "from the viewpoint of the layman peering into the laboratories of the scientists" (Scheinfeld, 1939, p. vii). Referring to the Jukes and the Kallikaks as "our pet horrible examples" of the tendency of insanity and feeblemindedness to run in families, Scheinfeld is careful to explain that "the factor of environment in governing mentality was completely overlooked" (p. 152). Despite a careful explanation of the uncertainty of hereditary considerations, Scheinfeld's (1936) rendition of the Kallikaks is the same as Wiggams, especially as evidenced by an illustration that shows the two lines of descendents in cartoon fashion (p. 362). On one side of the tree the heading is labeled "While in service he dallied with a feeble-minded tavern girl" and pictured are a series of male and female faces with pointed ears, tongues sticking out, facial hair, and looks which appear to depict either evil or stupidity. On the other side of the diagram the heading "—after the war he married a worthy young Quakeress" and the depictions of these offspring show a series of demure, smiling faces with closed eyes, long eyelashes, and neat hair. The captions included with the drawings further explained that the barmaid "bore a son whom she called Martin Kallikak, Jr.—later known as "Old Horror" . . . From "Old Horror" came 10 children who spawned hundreds of the lowest humans, with the worst heredity. On the Quakeress side of the tree we are told that "she bore him seven fine, healthy, upright children . . . From these came hundreds of the most worthy type of humans, with the best heredity" (p. 362). This illustrative depiction of heredity is seemingly incongruous with Scheinfeld's earlier insistence that environment ought to be given equal consideration and demonstrates that by the late 1930s little had changed in terms of public depiction of the dangers of wanton breeding.

Used as it was in popular and academic venues alike, the Kallikak family provides an apt illustration of the way eugenicists popularized eugenic ideology for the public. Also illustrated is the porous nature of the boundary between popular culture, education, and academia. In his quantitative analysis of biology textbooks used between 1914 and 1948, Selden (1999) showed that during this period the story of Martin Kallikak was cited in over 60% of the high school biology texts and in educational psychology classrooms for decades.

Another example of the use of heredity by the eugenics movement was the research of Charles Davenport, arguably the most influential eugenicist in America (Kevles, 1985). An accomplished biologist, Davenport studied engineering in preparatory school, was well versed in mathematics, and was deeply influenced by Karl Pearson's (1894) papers on the mathematical theory of evolution. Davenport, a successful leader and promoter of eugenics, enthusiastically channeled his career into a well-documented quest for a quantitative approach to evolution (Chesterson, 1922/2000; Hofstadter, 1944; Haller, 1963; Pickens, 1968; Ludmerer, 1972; Chase, 1975; Kevles, 1985; Hasian, 1996; Selden, 1999; Allen, 2000; Black, 2003). Using what Kevles (1985) called his "protoplasmic social purposefulness" (p. 54), Davenport lobbied the newly endowed Carnegie Institute of Washington for the establishment of a research station where he could conduct experimental evolutionary research (Black, 2003).

In 1904, 30 miles from New York on Long Island's North Shore, Davenport set up the Cold Spring Harbor research station dedicated to the study of eugenics in conjunction with the previously existing biological laboratory of the Brooklyn Institute of Arts and Sciences, of which Davenport was already director. The small initial staff was recruited from the successful graduates of the biological laboratory and by all accounts, both Davenport and his staff provided a valuable contribution to the study of inheritance in animals (Kevles, 1985). The study of human inheritance began with eye, hair, and skin color and eventually led to the exploration of a broad range of human traits (Haller, 1963). Unable to experiment on human beings directly, Davenport set about collecting inheritance data by developing a "Family Records" form and distributed hundreds of copies to medical, mental, and educational institutions, as well as to individuals, college alumni lists, and scientists (Kevles, 1985).

By 1910, Davenport streamlined his techniques and he sought the financial backing of Mrs. E. H. Harriman who had recently assumed management of her late husband's immense railroad fortune (Chesterson, 1922/2000; Hofstadter, 1944; Haller, 1963; Pickens, 1968; Ludmerer, 1972; Chase, 1975; Kevles, 1985; Hasian, 1996; Selden, 1999; Allen, 2000; Black, 2003). According to Kevles (1985), Mrs. Harriman's daughter Mary was a social activist with a liberal bent who worked in Davenport's laboratory while an undergraduate at Barnard. Mary brought her mother together with Davenport and the result was that Mrs. Harriman bought 75 acres up the hill from the Cold Spring Harbor station and funded the establishment of the Eugenics Record Office (ERO). So pleased was she with the work that she supplied the ERO with 20,000 dollars per year until 1918, at which time she turned the institution over to the Carnegie Institution (Kevles, 1985).

The work of Charles Davenport and the ERO provided the eugenics movement with a focal point that acted as a "center for research in human genetics and for propaganda in eugenics" (Haller, 1963, p. 64). Between 1920 and 1938 the Eugenics Record Office published the "avidly racist and restrictionist" (p. 149) tract *Eugenical News*. In 1938, the name was changed to *Eugenics Quarterly* under the auspices of the American Eugenics Society, and finally, in 1968, the *Journal of Social Biology* (Selden, 1999).

The family records forms distributed by Davenport eventually formed a large repository of data which provided the basis of Davenport's (1911) book *Heredity in Relation to Eugenics*. Cited by more than one-third of high school biology texts between the wars (Selden, 1999), the book is considered by many to be the era's most important treatise on eugenics (Ludmerer, 1972). Davenport (1911) devoted over half the pages of his book to a discussion of the inheritance of dozens of human characteristics including mental deficiency, pauperism, feeblemindedness, sexual deviance, and laziness. Additionally, ERO data served as "the source of bulletins, memoirs, and books, on such topics as sterilization, the exclusion from the United States of inferior germ plasm, and the inheritance of pellagra, multiple sclerosis, tuberculosis, goiter, nomadism, athletic ability, and temperament" (Kevles, 1985, p. 56).

Many (Kevles, 1985; Gould, 1996; Selden, 1999; Black, 2003) have questioned the ability and motives of the field-workers collecting Davenport's data, but regardless of their ability, the impact of their work cannot be denied. In her investigation into eugenic "field-workers" employed by Davenport between 1910 and 1924, Bix (1997) reported that the 258 students (85% of them women) often struggled with the goal of their task. Bix discovered that, as they collected information about families, individuals, and communities, many recognized that their results did not support eugenic assumptions but were bound by "gendered expectations and other obstacles" (p. 627) to compromise their commitment to scientific ideals. That the field-workers collecting some of the eugenic movement's most fruitful body of data questioned the assumptions their work was meant to support provides another example of the resilience of the movement to attacks on its integrity.

By 1914, universities were offering courses devoted in whole or part to eugenics. Between 1914 and 1928 the number of colleges offering courses in eugenics increased from 44 to 376 (Selden, 1999). These included Harvard, Columbia, Cornell, Brown, University of Wisconsin, Northwestern, and Clark (Haller, 1963). In 1918, Popenoe and Johnson published the first of many editions of their college textbook *Applied Eugenics*, relying heavily on data provided by Davenport and the ERO. While *Applied Eugenics* had much to say about the role of education, it is their explication of race that is most relevant for this section. The emphasis of the text, the authors tell us in the preface, is "laid on the practical means by which society may encourage the reproduction of superior persons and discourage that of inferiors" (p. v) or, in other words, to enact both negative (sterilization) and positive eugenics (Popenoe, 1918). More specifically, Popenoe and Johnson offered a clear definition of the societal scope and aim of eugenic policy:

> The problem of eugenics is to make such legal, social and economic adjustments that (1) a larger proportion of superior persons will have children than at present, (2) that the average number of offspring of each superior person will be greater than at present, (3) that the most inferior persons will have no children, and finally, that (4) other inferior persons will have fewer children than now. (1918, p. v)

In addition to the outline of the problem and solution of eugenics, the authors also provided a definition of "superior" germ plasm as manifest in humans. They wrote,

> A eugenically superior or desirable person [is possessed of] the following characteristics: to live past maturity, to reproduce adequately, to live happily and to make contributions to the productivity, happiness, and progress of society. (p. v)

One might wonder about the influence of environment, culture, class, and gender considerations in defining the meaning of the above conditions but, in an example of the movement's talent for appealing to the broadest audience, the authors assured us that while eugenics had biology as its foundation, the "superstructure" (p. vi) was sociology. By broadening the scope of eugenic aims to sociology, eugenicists allowed for definitions of "happiness," "productivity," "contribution," and "progress" that would be most closely aligned with the dominant cultural worldview of upper class Nordic or "old stock" Americans. Relying on a biologically deterministic approach to human variability, eugenicists successfully set parameters and provided social institutions with a framework on which to construct programs and policies attendant to their assumptions about race.

Race and Difference

During the early years of the eugenics movement, the field of anthropology was instrumental in providing the language and rationale for the differentiation of human beings into hierarchical categories. Anthropologists believed that modern racial differentiation was the result of a split in the family tree and that the darker races represented on that tree were not as evolved as the lighter ones (Bean, 1932; Hooten, 1937). During the latter half of the nineteenth century anthropologists increasingly brought to Western and European public attention cultures and societies that were unfamiliar and previously unknown. In the south, a continued desire to justify slavery prompted a proliferation of "pseudoscientific" writers who attempted to prove African inferiority and incapability of advancement (Osofsky, 1967, p. 104). In 1853 in his book *Negroes and Negro Slavery: The First, an Inferior Race—The Latter, Its Normal Condition* Dr. J. H. Van Evrie represented the pseudo-scientific school of writers who charted the foundation of eugenic ideologies and belief about race:

> The Negro is a man, but an inferior *species* of man, who could no more originate from the same parentage with us than could the owl from the eagle, or the shad from the salmon, or the cat from the tiger, and can no more be *forced* by human power, to manifest the qualities or fulfill the duties imposed by the Almighty on the Caucasian man than can either of these forms of life be forced to manifest qualities other than those eternally impressed upon them by the hand of God. (Van Evrie, 1853, quoted in Osofsky, 1967, p. 105)

Although the writing about racial difference took on a slightly more sophisticated tone by the 1900s, the essential belief in the biologically determined, hierarchically arranged difference between Caucasian and other races remained unchanged. The primary difference in the thrust of these writings was spurred by the rediscovery at the turn of the century of Gregor Mendel's laws of inheritance.

Between 1900 and 1915 the science of genetics was polarized into two camps, the "Mendelians" and the "biometricians," who by 1915 had lost credibility (Ludmerer, 1972, p. 45). In his historical appraisal of genetics in America Ludmerer explained that the Mendelians were primarily concentrated in America and focused most of their attention "upon so-called 'quantitative' or 'metrical' characteristics . . . such as height and intelligence in man" (p. 45). Ludmerer claimed that the field of genetics in America was in decline by the 1930s and "rested on shaky intellectual foundations" (p. 48) primarily because of its intricate association (in all countries but particularly in America) with the eugenics movement and its focus on human genetics. In America, the two most important centers for research in human heredity were the Committee of Eugenics of the American Breeders' Association and the ERO at Cold Spring Harbor, both headed by Charles Davenport (Ludmerer, 1972; Kevles, 1985; Keller, 1994).

Prior to World War I, eugenicists had gained a great deal of public support by disseminating the myth of "a rising tide of feeblemindedness" spawned by books like the *Jukes* and the *Kallikaks*. The myth held that feeblemindedness was (a) hereditary, (b) determined by a single gene, and (c) dramatically rising in incidence in America (Ludmerer, 1972). During the war years many geneticists began to appreciate the complexity of inheritance and questioned the feasibility of eugenic programs. According to Ludmerer, as the support for eugenic claims eroded in the scientific community, the eugenics movement "came to be led by men making rash and pretentious claims about the power of heredity" (p. 83). One popularizer writing for *Eugenical News* claimed "there is no trouble breeding any kind of man you like" (Stokes quoted in Ludmerer, 1972, p. 83). The problem, according to Ludmerer, was that although geneticists had come to realize the impossibility of eugenic claims, the majority of eugenicists, as well as the general public, did not. By the close of World War I, "the eugenics movement was preparing for a decade of intensive legislative campaigning" (1972, p. 87). The liturgy of racial purification rose in pitch and intensity:

> Obviously, it is this prodigious spawning of inferiors which must at all costs be prevented if society is to be saved from disruption and dissolution. Race cleansing is apparently the only thing that can stop it. Therefore, race cleansing must be our first concern. (Stoddard, 1922, quoted in Chesterson, 1922/2000)

In the above quote, Lothrop Stoddard (1920, 1922) voiced the perceived threat that America was being overrun by non-white races. Stoddard, a founding member of both the Galton Society and the American Eugenics Society, authored two widely read books *The Revolt Against Civilization: The Menace of the Underman* and *The Rising Tide of Color: Against White World Supremacy*. Both articulated his "worship of the Nordic" (p. 49) and his abiding fear for the "mongrelization and destruction of civilization" (Stoddard quoted in Haller, 1963, p. 49). Among eugenicists there was wide acceptance of the idea that national and racial identities were equated and that behavioral characteristics were determined by race. Like heredity, the construct of race difference was so ubiquitous in eugenic thought that it is difficult to discuss eugenic beliefs about race separately from other of their programmatic imperatives. Furthermore, eugenicists believed in a hierarchical construct of *worth* that superceded race to include class, habit, and behavior. Nevertheless, a brief exploration of the diametric tensions imposed by racial assumptions is in order.

Eugenic belief about race was often at odds with democracy and, as Chesterton (1922/2000) argued in the heat of the debate,[1] such beliefs were more closely aligned with a capitalist paradigm and the desire to accumulate wealth than a democratic one. In the hugely popular college text *Applied Eugenics*, Popenoe and Johnson (1918) suggested that when Jefferson wrote "all men are equal" in the Declaration of Independence, "he may have been thinking of legal rights merely" and that furthermore he was "expressing an opinion common among philosophers of his time" (p. 75). According to Kevles, some eugenicists possessed an "unabashed distrust, even contempt" for democracy and quotes Henry Fairfield Osborn, president of the American Museum of Natural History:

> The true spirit of American democracy that all men are born with equal rights and duties has been confused with the political sophistry that all men are born with equal character and ability to govern themselves and others, and with the educational sophistry that education and environment will offset the handicap of heredity. (Fairfield, 1923, quoted in Kevles, 1985, p. 76)

The imperative of hierarchy would not allow for the possibility that the "unfit" might participate in the governance of the "fit." The case was made clearer for the public through dissemination of books, tracts, and lectures by leading anthropologists and eugenic popularizers.

An editorial in *The Saturday Evening Post* of May 7, 1921, called "The Great American Myth" paid tribute to Gregor Mendel and the new breed of scientific writers who had brought the dangers of wanton breeding to the attention of the public. The editor George Horace Lorimer specifically names Madison Grant's bestseller *The Passing of the Great Race* (1916) and Lothrop Stoddard's *The Rising Tide of Color* (1920) [with an introduction by Madison Grant]. The former, Lorimer (1921) explained, "recounts in glowing words the waxing and waning of the unsurpassed Nordic race" while the latter "shows in the most impressive manner how White supremacy throughout the world is threatened by the yellow, brown and other colored races" (quoted in Chase, 1975, p. 174). Finally, the editorial went on to explain that both writers had based their theses on recent advances in the study of heredity and other sciences. Grant and Stoddard were quoted frequently in eugenic writings and were instrumental in defining for the American public the reasons they should be afraid and distrustful of anyone who did not belong to the white genteel classes.

Madison Grant, a prolific non-scientist, was a much sought after popularizer of the eugenics movement (Haller, 1963; Chase, 1975; Selden, 1999). Grant kept busy until his death in 1937 as co-founder and active officer of the American Eugenics Society, the Galton Society (co-founded with Charles Davenport), the Eugenics Research Association, and as treasurer of the Second (1921) and Third (1932) International Congresses of Eugenics. Grant also ran the Bronx Zoo, the Save the Redwoods League, the American Zoological Society, as well as a host of other legislative and lobbying crusades for the termination of Jewish and other non-Nordic immigration. Needless to say, Grant garnered significant social and political influence. According to Chase (1975), Grant's position in the movement was regarded with some coolness by his colleagues particularly because of his devotion to the cause of total annihilation of the Jews. In addition to a very public debate with Franz Boas, America's best-known anthropologist of the time and one of the leading voices against eugenics, Grant lashed out publicly to senators as well. Boas infuriated Grant when he publicly dismantled the cephalic index myth of scientific racism. Chase (1975) reported that in an April 12, 1912, letter to Senator F. M. Simmons, Grant wrote,

> Dr. Boas, himself a Jew, in this matter represents a large body of Jewish immigrants, who resent the suggestion that they do not belong to the White race, and his whole effort has been to show that certain physical structures [head forms], which we scientists know are profoundly indicative of race, are purely superficial. (quoted in Chase, 1975, p. 163).

Grant involved himself for years in efforts to have Boas dismissed from his position as chairman of the Columbia University Department of Anthropology. In response to the growing professionalization of the field of anthropology, and the subsequent reduction of influence by philanthropists and non-scientific opiners, Grant, Davenport, and Professor Henry Fairchild Osborn teamed up to create a rival anthropological entity they named the Galton Society. The plan for the society mirrored organizations and offshoots around the country in its desire for exclusion and control of discourse. In a March 9, 1918, memo Grant described the society as

> a central governing body, self elected and self perpetuating, and very limited in members, and also *confined to native Americans*, who are anthropologically, socially, and politically sound, no Bolsheviki need apply. (quoted in Chase, 1975, p. 165 emphasis in original)

What this explicates is the remarkable resilience of eugenicists to organize around their profoundly racist views despite increasingly tepid support from the scientific community. Early on, eugenicists and leading scientists were one and the same persons, but by the mid-1920s the movement had shifted its attention from an adherence with science to a social and public policy stance. Science had served its purpose by providing early legitimacy and introducing eugenic ideology into the public mindset. By the time scientists began to cool in their support for eugenic assumptions, public acceptance had embraced the movement.

The identification of the "other" took many forms. For example, the Eugenics Society of Northern California, located in the Capital Bank Building in Sacramento, published pamphlets[2] for free distribution "for classroom use in any university or college upon request from any professor" (CIT, n.d., p. 1). Pamphlet number 16 includes vignettes such as *A Feebleminded Tries Train Wrecking; What Are Our Eugenic Assets*; and *How Can We Eugenically Conserve?* One vignette entitled *Rat-like Marijuana Vendors* warned readers:

> One section of the narcotic trade is largely in the hands of Mexicans who came north in the great trek of the twenties. Lowpowered intellectually, they were the first to become jobless in the Depression: Ratlike brains among them, familiar with the power of marijuana in Mexico, turned to that trade here. (CIT, p. 6)

The story continued to describe a family that was arrested for selling as many as 1,000 marijuana cigarettes a day to school children. The sheer volume of literature devoted to the identification of people as menacing, dangerous, and defective is indicative of the public appetite for such material. The eugenics movement may have been organized and perpetuated by a relatively small but powerful and articulate group of scientists and pseudo-scientists, but the ideology was quickly and readily absorbed into the mainstream and taken up by social workers, educators, and professionals of all stripes.

Ability and Degeneracy

During the 1910s and 1920s eugenicists concentrated their efforts on defining, in numerous ways, those people they deemed "unfit" and of degenerate stock. The eugenic imperative was defined as a two-part program:

1) Reducing the racial contribution of the least desirable part of the population.
2) Increasing the racial contribution of the superior part of the population (Popenoe, 1918, p. 156).

In order to achieve the reduction of the "least desirable" segment of the population eugenicists focused on immigration restriction, sterilization, birth control, and marriage restriction. Meanwhile, increasing the birthrate of "superior" stocks was encouraged through contests like "Fitter Families," baby contests, lectures, and literature. In order to successfully present their program to the public eugenicists needed to identify what constituted "normal" and what constituted "defective." Eugenicists' use of terms like "desirable" and "undesirable" created a national conversation that equated morality with social salvation. The range of persons identified as "undesirable" and therefore unfit to reproduce was broad and included the "blind, insane, feebleminded, epileptics, paupers, alcoholics, tramps, prostitutes, beggars, unmarried mothers, morons, idiots, imbeciles, sexual deviants, children who masturbated, and criminals" (Popenoe, 1918, p. 42). Legislation passed during the first three decades of the twentieth century targeted these individuals and state institutions began to forcibly sterilize, often as a condition of release, any person who fell within these defined parameters.

In North Carolina, as in many other states, philanthropists played a significant role in the establishment and promotion of eugenic research and organizations. Philanthropist and physician Clarence J. Gamble contributed to the establishment of a genetics research center at Wake Forest University and to the Human Betterment League of North Carolina (Schoen, 1995). Following his own interest in the applications of eugenic programs in conjunction with his love of poetry prompted Gamble, heir of the soap fortune of Proctor and Gamble, to write a poem. In the first of twelve stanzas Gamble begins:

> Once there was a MORON, that means
>
> a person who wasn't very bright.
>
> He couldn't add figures

or make change

or do many things

an ordinary man does.

So he couldn't find a job

and the RELIEF OFFICE

had to help him out

for YEARS and YEARS. (Southern Historical Collection, n.d.)

Reflecting the common belief that mentally defective persons were draining state and federal coffers, Gamble made the argument in his poem that the situation was a preventable social crisis. Eugenicists frequently made reference to federal and state expenditure, including education expenditure, when making their arguments for policy and legislation to prevent the spread of "defective strains" (Haller, 1963; Pickens, 1968).

In order to prevent crime, drunkenness, and other "undesirable" conditions eugenicists focused on identifying and eradicating the common denominator of feeblemindedness. Instrumental to the identification of feebleminded individuals was the development of the first intelligence tests by Alfred Binet, director of the psychology laboratory at the Sorbonne in Paris. In 1912, a further refinement by German psychologist W. Stern added the construct *quotient* which he derived by dividing the mental age of those tested by their chronological age (Gould, 1996). Although Binet himself did not believe that his tests measured innate intelligence, eugenicists enthusiastically embraced the new IQ tests as an infallible measure by which educators, social workers, and health and welfare workers could easily identify and definitively diagnose feeblemindedness.

The categorization of mental deficiency in America was a serious undertaking for many educators and scientists in the early twentieth century. Still common in the popular vernacular, the ubiquity of the words "idiot" and "imbecile" belies their technical origin: "idiots could not develop full speech and had mental ages below three; imbeciles could not master written language and ranged from three to seven in mental age" (Gould, 1996, p. 188). Imbeciles and idiots were easily identified as "not like us" by the public and professionals alike and were not the primary concern of eugenicists. More dangerous and insidious for unsuspecting "normal" people was the "high-grade defective" who could be trained to function in society, but whose progeny contributed to what many eugenicists referred to as "the rising tide of feeblemindedness."

The feebleminded "are merely mental children" (p. 355) wrote Wiggam (1924). Wiggam stated that if institutionalized, the feebleminded should be allowed to marry. If allowed to be at large, on the other hand, the feebleminded should be persuaded (or coerced) to be sterilized. He continued:

> This especially applies to the higher grades of feeble-mindedness, the morons. Many morons are most effective factory workers and enjoy the monotony of tending simple machines or carrying out simple industrial processes. (Wiggam, 1924, p. 355)

Feeblemindedness thus defined was a motivating force behind the development of technical and agricultural as well as gifted and talented education programs.

Popenoe and Johnson (1918) offered another example in the case of a young woman inmate of H. H. Goddard's Training School at Vineland, New Jersey. A "high-grade imbecile" belonging to a "thoroughly normal, respectable family" was explained to have been so afflicted because of her mother's experience, while pregnant, of caring for a sister-in-law who was "quite out of her mind" (p. 72). This mother, they explained, had "fretted" and "rebelled" due to this experience and "it is obvious that mothers who fret and rebel are quite likely themselves to be neurotic in constitution, and the child naturally gets its heredity from them" (p. 72). This twist in interpretation represents a common theme in eugenic writing. By engaging their readers in common mythology and claiming to recast it in light of current science, eugenicists were quite successful in maintaining common definitions of the working of heredity in humans.

The Social Crisis: Immigration

That a tremendous influx of immigrants occurred around the turn of the century has been well documented by historians (Hofstadter, 1944, 1963; Cremin, 1961; Zinn, 1980; Kliebard, 1995), but this was not the first time America had been flooded by immigrants. Between 1790 and 1840, America saw an equally prodigious, but substantially different wave of immigrants who, while not "White" compared to their "old stock" neighbors, hailed primarily from Ireland and Northern Europe and who, by the turn of the century, were included in the public perception of white.

The decade of the 1880s saw the arrival of 5,246,613 immigrants, but it wasn't until the turn of the century that alarm begin to spread. Between 1900 and 1914 immigrants were pouring in at a faster rate than before, averaging about 80,000 per year, but instead of being primarily of Irish and German ancestry, they were Northern Italians, Russians, Jews, and Greeks (Hofstadter, 1944; Zinn, 1980).

Eastern European immigrants represented a new threat in the eyes of eugenicists. In addition to the cultural unfamiliarity of Eastern Europeans, these immigrants brought with them new ideologies such as Marxism and Anarchism that were particularly alien to the old American stock. Labor unrest, largely a reaction to horrible working conditions, intensified during the 1910s and 1920s and added to the growing public perception of danger.

The realization that the world had grown smaller and that "men are everywhere in close touch" (Stoddard, 1920, p. 303) permeated both popular and academic writings. There was great fear that the white race was destined for destruction if immigration was not stemmed. "If White civilization goes down," wrote Stoddard (1920), "the White race is irretrievably ruined" (p. 304). At the center of this threat was the element of *blood*:

> It is clean, virile, genius-bearing blood, streaming down the ages through the unerring action of heredity, which, in anything like a favorable environment, will multiply itself, solve our problems, and sweep us on to higher and nobler destinies". (Stoddard, 1920, p. 305)

The alarmist nature of these warnings was instrumental in the spread of fear and distrust among the public. The aristocracy of old stock America was being threatened and through their influence and power they were able to translate that into a threat to the country as a whole.

At the same time, there was an incredible centralization of wealth and power in which a few families controlled the majority of industrial and economic capital. A vast separation between the rich and poor existed, where the rich were not subject to disease or the "depression from dismal and squalid surroundings" but were able instead to concern themselves with art, literature, education, and science (Zinn, 1980, p. 215). Disrupting attempts at political and economic stability, and driving the search for reasoned answers to societal problems were sporadic yet potent reactions from the poor and labor movements wherein they protested the

> new industrialism, the crowded cities, the long hours in the factories, the sudden economic crises leading to high prices and lost jobs, the lack of food and water, the freezing winters, the hot tenements in the summer, the epidemics of disease, [and the] deaths of children. (Zinn, 1980, p. 215)

These uprisings were occasionally directed towards the rich, but just as often their anger was translated into "racial hatred for blacks, religious warfare against Catholics, [and] nativist fury against immigrants" (Zinn, 1980, p. 216). Along both ends of the economic spectrum, racist hostility became an easy substitute for class frustration. Finally, with these events and attitudes as a foundation, the late nineteenth century saw enormous economic growth and a level of corporatization that has continued into the present. Standard Oil, U.S. Steel Corporation, J. P. Morgan, Chase Manhattan Bank, and American Telephone and Telegraph all had profits in the millions by 1890. The significance of this for education is the increased belief in, and dedication to, business practices in general and the idea of efficiency in particular and the possible application of these ideas to social policies of all kinds.

Poverty

Meanwhile, working class families existed in grinding poverty, squeezed into tenements without the benefit of toilets, garbage removal, sewers, fresh air, or water, all of which contributed to continual epidemics of typhoid, typhus, and cholera (Link, 1955; Hofstadter, 1963; Zinn, 1980). The government's response was to criminalize poverty, making it equivalent to immorality. Eugenic proscriptions frequently contained warnings about the importance of hygiene, equating it with purity and breeding, through advertising in children's books and teacher's manuals (Shannon, 1904/1915; Sanger, 1922; Scheinfeld, 1939). The 1930s witnessed profound change, most obviously due to the depression, but also in a new questioning of the status quo. In 1931, Henry Ford stated (just prior to laying off 75,000 workers) that the problem was "the average man won't really do a day's work unless he is caught and cannot get out of it. There is plenty of work to do if people would just do it" (quoted in Zinn, 1980, p. 378). News clippings of the era provide a glimpse into the continued atmosphere of crisis and fear surrounding the poor and immigrant segments of the population:

> *Chicago, April 1, 1932.* Five hundred schoolchildren, most with haggard faces and in tattered clothes, paraded through Chicago's downtown section to the Board of Education offices to demand that the school system provide them with food.
>
> *Boston, June 3, 1932.* Twenty-five hungry children raided a buffet lunch set up for Spanish War veterans during a Boston parade. Two automobile-loads of police were called to drive them away. (Zinn, 1980, pp. 380–381)

Government attempts at an ameliorative response to the Depression did little to affect Black Harlem where 350,000 people lived, 233 persons per acre as compared with 133 for the rest of Manhattan. In 25 years, its population had multiplied six times. Ten thousand families lived in rat-infested cellars and basements; tensions ran very high, race riots ensued. Despite how difficult the Depression was for millions of middle-to upper-class whites, the extent of the denial by white Americans for the plight of those not of their race or social class became readily apparent.

Crime and Dependency

Racial difference was often identified as the causal factor in crime and dependency. A display chart[3] (HHL) circa 1921 entitled *Relative Social Inadequacy of the Several Nativity Groups and Immigrant Groups of the U.S.: Crime, Dependency* lists, from top to bottom by country, Scandinavian and Northern European countries down to Eastern European countries with the rate of crime being highest for Eastern European and South American countries. The chart was presented in graph form with countries listed for both the crime and dependency categories.

In contrast to this fairly technical rendition containing a great deal of tiny writings, another display image[4] is more graphic. Entitled *Burglary and Larceny, Rankings of Native Whites of Foreign Parentage* (APS) this chart is drawn in cartoon style, a tall brick building with a vertical row of windows. The windows are labeled "Polish-Austrian, Spanish, French, Near Eastern, Irish, Scandinavian, Italian, British, and Teutonic and numbered from one to nine respectively and show sinister looking men in burglar attire (bands around the eyes, striped shirts, and unkempt whiskers) are climbing out of the windows with their bags of loot. Although not clearly delineated, the presumption is that "1" represents those "Native Whites of Foreign Parentage" who are most likely to commit burglary and larceny and "9" represent the least likely to engage in criminal activity. What is clear is that "old stock" Americans, while granting the designation of white to these fellow citizens, nevertheless considered them to be of degenerate stock and therefore prone to criminality.

Eugenicists promoted the idea that the inheritance of criminality extended beyond mere trends in families to mental digression on the part of the mother. This is evidenced by a story in Shannon's tome *Eugenics* published for decades (1904/1915) with gilded edges and a black leather cover looking very like a bible. The story tells of the mother of a young man recently hanged who declares that she had tried to get rid of him before he was born and wished that she succeeded. "Does it not seem probable," wrote Shannon, "that the murderous intent, even though of a short duration, was communicated to the mind of the child, and resulted in the crime for which he was hanged?" (p. 228). Not all eugenicists were as brazen in their claims but maintained nevertheless their adherence to deterministic hereditary explanations.

In *Applied Eugenics*, Popenoe and Johnson (1918) took great care to distinguish between what they saw as a pure eugenics from increasing charges of "pseudo-science" by naming and discrediting certain prevalent and popular "myths" (p. 70). These myths are instructive of the degree of public dialogue regarding inheritance, race, and ability and its reliance on the less-than-definitive science of the day. In their chapter on *Modification of the Germ Plasm* the authors devote much discussion to what are "popularly known as 'racial poisons' " (p. 44). Most of the section discussed alcohol as the most pernicious of racial poisons but they also discuss in detail the aforementioned myths. Claiming that "older readers will remember" the case of murderer Jesse Pomeroy whose father worked in a meat market and whose mother's eyes regularly "fell upon the bloody carcasses hung about the walls" (p. 66) we are then assured that these cases are in no way based in fact and that any manifestation of defective germ plasm was present independent of any actions by the mother.

It is important to note that in their conception of race and difference eugenicists were careful to declare that not all Caucasians were of equal heredity. Often their descriptions contained references to culture and stereotypes offered within the context of discussions about heredity. In the section on heredity and "the races of man" (p. 226) Shannon (1904/1915) wrote that while "as children we learned that the human family is divided into five general races" (p. 226) that each race is again divided and subdivided.

> Within the Caucasian or White race one may readily distinguish the different nationalities having their peculiar form and features, traits and characteristics. By these they are distinguished from all other tribes and families. The Irishman is as unlike the German as the Jew is unlike the Swede. The brawny, cautious Scot is the opposite of the vivacious Frenchman, and the sturdy, slow-going Englishman can not sympathize with the irascible Spaniard. (p. 226)

Another example of how eugenicists presented race and heredity to the public is a "flashing light sign" used in displays to promote Fitter Families Contests (APS). In large white lettering in the middle of a large black board are the words "Some people are born to be a burden on the rest" with smaller signs above and below this message. The smaller sign above says

> This light flashes every 15 seconds: Every 15 seconds $100 of your money goes to the care of persons with bad heredity such as the insane, feebleminded, criminals, and other defectives.

Two smaller signs are below: one on the left and one on the right. The sign on the left reads "This light flashes every 16 seconds: Every sixteen seconds a person is born in the United States." On the right, the message is this:

Thio light flashes every $7^1/_2$ minutes: Every $7^1/_2$ minutes a high grade person is born in the United States who will have the ability to do creative work and be fit for leadership. About 4% of all Americans come within this class (APS).

Between these two lower signs is an image of Uncle Sam with a cloaked, presumably eugenically "fit" person standing in his hand and an advertisement promoting the Fitter Families Contests. Eugenicists were able to redefine the Progressive inclination towards charity by encouraging people to re-evaluate their own potential to burden or contribute to society. That a crisis is at hand is clearly communicated by the flashing lights, two of which flash at 15- and 16-second intervals and one, the "preferred" of the three, flashing only every $7^1/_2$ minutes.

Eugenicists used the constructs of heredity and race to define normalcy in society in virtually every aspect of public life. A great deal of scholarship (Chesterton, 1922/2000; Hofstadter, 1944; Blacker, 1952; Link, 1955; Haller, 1963; Ludmerer, 1972; Chase, 1975; Kevles, 1985; Degler, 1991; Gould, 1996; Paul, 1998; Lemann, 1999; Selden, 1999; Stoskopf, 1999; Allen, 2000; Black, 2003) exists tracking the infiltration of eugenic ideology into organizations like Boy Scouts of America, the Young Men's Christian Association, a wide array of "Human Betterment" associations as well as a proliferation of state and federal policies and legislation.

The Moral Solution

And one day he met
another MORON
who wasn't any cleverer than he was.
But SHE was nicer to him
than anyone had ever been
And so he MARRIED HER.

And soon there was a BABY
and then ANOTHER,
and ANOTHER
and ANOTHER.
And the welfare department
had to pay the family
MORE of the TAXPAYER'S
MONEY
and MORE
and MORE
and MORE. (HBL-SHC)

Eugenicists developed a three-pronged response to the perceived societal threat of wanton breeding by dysgenic classes, infiltration by millions of immigrants, and "the Negro problem" by pursuing public and legislative campaigns to achieve mandatory sterilization laws, increasingly restrictive immigration laws, and laws governing the granting of marriage licenses to mixed race couples. North Carolina philanthropist Clarence Gamble's poem[1] (HBL-SHC) captured the tone of the proliferation of editorials and articles extolling the virtues of sterilization and the couching of the appeals in economic justification. In 1907, responding to the increasing public concern about habitual criminals and degenerate classes, Indiana was the first state to pass a compulsory sterilization law. Washington, California, and Connecticut followed in 1909 (Carlson, 2001). By 1912, Iowa, Nevada, New York, and New Jersey had joined the list and eugenicists took great pains to provide measurements and standards by which to define feeblemindedness and degeneracy. These laws were not without critics and constitutional challenges tried to prevent the spread of these laws over the next two decades. Nevertheless, by the mid-1930s the majority of Americans were subject to sterilization legislation as laws were strengthened and passed in over 30 states. Of all the legislative mandates spurred by eugenicists, sterilization was the most blatantly egregious in the infringement of individual rights and continues to act as the window by which most people in the present are aware of eugenics.

In order to insulate state sterilization legislation from constitutional challenge Harry Laughlin (who succeeded Davenport as the director of the ERO) developed a Model Eugenical Sterilization Law which realized the establishment of definitive definitions to bolster eugenic arguments. "A socially inadequate person," Laughlin wrote, "fails chronically in comparison with normal persons, to maintain himself or herself as a useful member of the organized social life of the state" (1922, p. 447). The definition of "socially inadequate classes" provided by Laughlin included

> 1) Feebleminded; 2) Insane (including the psychopathic); 3) Criminalistic (including the delinquent and wayward); 4) Epileptic; 5) Inebriate (including drug habitués); 6) Diseased (including the tuberculous, the syphilitic, the leprous, and others with chronic, infections and legally segregable diseases); 7) Blind (including those with seriously impaired vision); 8) Deaf (including those with seriously impaired hearing); 9) Deformed (including the crippled); and 10) Dependent (including orphans, ne'er-do-wells, the homeless, tramps, and paupers). (p. 447)

The model law defined heredity as the transmission of physical, physiological, and psychological qualities from parents to offspring and included the transmission "post-conceptionally and ante-natally of physiological weakness, poisons or infections from parent or parents to offspring" (p. 447). By 1930, Laughlin's model law was used to reinstate previously challenged sterilization laws in 30 states.

Estimates of the number of compulsory sterilizations performed in this country vary but eugenicists reveled in the reporting of their successes and numerous charts, lists, and tallies exist throughout the data (American Philosophical Society;

California Institute of Technology Archives; Harry H. Laughlin Collection; Southern Historical Collection). One estimate (Black, 2003) puts the total at 60,000. In their December 2002 exposure of sterilizations in North Carolina the *Winston-Salem Journal* reported that North Carolina ranked third in the nation with 8,000 sterilizations, with Virginia second and California leading the nation with over 20,000 sterilizations (State Archives of North Carolina). Although many state sterilization laws were repealed during the World War II era, it should be noted that in North Carolina more than 80% of sterilizations occurred between 1945 and 1974, long after most other states had repealed their laws (*Winston-Salem Journal*, 2002).

One of the first tests of the law's resilience occurred in Virginia's 1924 implementation. Selected to receive the first sterilization under the new law was a young woman named Carrie Buck, an inmate of Virginia's State Colony for Epileptics and Feebleminded (Tucker, 1994; Gould, 1996). The law, challenged and upheld from local circuit court to the Virginia Supreme Court, culminated in the famous *Buck v. Bell* case heard in front of the 1927 session of the Supreme Court of the United States. Laughlin testified in the lower court proceedings that Carrie Buck, her mother (also an inmate), and her daughter all suffered from "mental defectiveness," Carrie and her mother having scored poorly on an intelligence test, and the infant daughter being possessed by a look that was "not quite normal" (quoted in Tucker, 1994, p. 101). "These people," Laughlin continued, "belong to the shiftless, ignorant and worthless class of anti-social Whites of the South" (p. 101). The case prompted U.S. Supreme Court Justice Oliver Wendell Holmes, Jr., to deliver what Gould (1996) called "one of the most famous and chilling statements of our century" (p. 365):

> We have seen more than once that the public welfare may call upon the best citizens for their lives. It would be strange if it could not call upon those who already sap the strength of the state for these lesser sacrifices, often not felt to be such by those concerned in order to prevent our being swamped with incompetence . . . Three generations of imbeciles are enough. (*Buck v. Bell*, 1927, p. 207)

Never revealed during the disposition of the case (and not until a half a century later) was the fact that Carrie Buck had been raped by a relative of her foster parents and subsequently committed to the institution to hide her condition and protect the perpetrator (Gould, 1984). Examples of the abuse and oppression of women, men, and children at the hands of these lawmakers abound. Young women especially were often institutionalized and sterilized to protect family members from charges of incest.[2] The law upheld by Holmes was implemented in Virginia from

1924 to 1972 resulting in 4,000 sterilizations at Virginia's State Colony for Epileptics and Feebleminded and nearly 8,000 statewide. The common conception is that support for eugenics waned as scientific errors contained in eugenic assumptions began to come to light in the late 1920s but as Paul (1998) showed, the movement actually strengthened during the depression. Throughout the 1930s the number of sterilizations climbed and the procedure was legalized in Germany (1933), British Columbia, Canada (1933), Norway (1934), Sweden (1934), Finland (1935), Estonia (1936), and Iceland (1938) (Paul, 1998).

Marriage and Immigration

In addition to their work on sterilization eugenicists worked to restrict immigration and marriage in the name of creating a more eugenic future. Chase (1975) offered the following June 26, 1921, Boston *Sunday Herald* headline as an example that summarized decades of editorializing about immigration and race:

DANGER THAT WORLD SCUM WILL DEMORALIZE AMERICA

If We Don't Do Something About Immigration
We Shall Have a Mongrelized America. (p. 173)

In 1919, George Horace Lorimer, editor of *The Saturday Evening Post*, assigned a former Army intelligence captain to do a series of articles (the above headline represents one installment) which were eventually republished as a best-selling book entitled *Why Europe Leaves Home* (Roberts, 1922).

Marriage was presented to young people as a procreational responsibility and marriage for love or convenience was disparaged as selfish and anti-social. A great proliferation of eugenic writings focused on sexual relations, the form and function of the family, the raising of children, and health and hygiene (Shannon, 1904/1915; Robinson, 1916; Stopes, 1918/1931; Jefferis, 1925; Bell, 1933; Frank, 1937). In the preface to the seventh edition of *Married Love* Stopes (1918/1931) told her readers that her book was addressed to those who are "nearly normal" (p. x) and are either married or about to married and need to know how to "make their marriages beautiful and happy" (p. x).

In *Some Aspects of Adultery* Bell (1933) explained that adultery is inevitable given the state of society and "society has no right to punish unfits for its collective fault" (p. 54). Instead, he argued, it is the duty of society to make adultery unnecessary [by] divesting marriage of the supernatural, by freeing it from the bondage of superstition, by making it a purely secular institution. (p. 55)

Eugenicists were convinced that marriage restriction represented society's best opportunity to enact positive eugenic progress. By appealing to patriarchal mores regarding the proper role of women and the function of family in civic participation, eugenicists ensured that their message would be spread from pulpits throughout the land.

In a handwritten note[3] dated May 25, 1928, Manley Allbright told the unknown recipient that the "enclosed is the manuscript of a sermon preached by me at the regular morning service of our church on Sunday, May 20, 1928" (APS-AS, p. 1). Allbright was the minister of Allston Congregational Church in Allston, Massachusetts. The sermon entitled *Eugenics* proclaimed that "it is the scientist that has shown us a more excellent way of breeding a race of men and of perpetuating the civilization which our high-grade forefathers brought to these shores" (p. 3). "We have learned," Allbright continued,

that charity doled out by the rich for the care of defectives, is far less Christian, however good the motive may be, than to prevent the propagation of defectives. The science of Eugenics has come to our rescue, and we are moving toward a more natural and biologic way of living. (APS-AS, p. 4)

Anticipating an underlying national trend, Allbright goes on to sermonize that science may be replacing religion in the hearts and minds of the public. Given the historic division between religious factions who favored creation theory and scientists who favored evolution over creation theory, the fact that eugenic rhetoric made its way into the sermons and programs of churches was remarkable indeed. The melding of civic and social duty with biological moral imperative was apparently an irresistible combination for a Progressive-minded public.

Disseminate the Message

Although examples of eugenicists' use of dissemination techniques have already appeared throughout this text, a discussion outlining the plan and intent of the movement is warranted. As is probably already apparent, from the very outset of the movement eugenicists were experts at disseminating their beliefs in a variety of ways. In fact, dissemination was part of the original imperative because eugenicists realized that without public acceptance and support their ideas would fall victim to the temptations of carnal desire and/or a desire for scientific proof that did not exist. Driven by the fear that the American population was declining in quality, eugenicists turned their attention to the institution of education.

According to a 1938 booklet[4] on *Practical Eugenics* produced by the American Eugenics Society (NCSA), eugenics education should be thought of as having two main objectives. First, eugenicists should strive to develop in the public an understanding of the principles of heredity to be followed by more specific studies of the theoretical and practical aspects of the eugenic program. Second, eugenics education should focus on the intellectual, emotional, and physical development of individuals "for the fulfillment of their roles as participants in family life, and especially as parents" (NCSA, 1938, p. 4). The proscription is very specific as it continued: "to attain these objectives would require a reorientation of the whole educational process with reference to eugenic values" (p. 4) starting with the introduction in elementary schools to "the simpler aspects of biology and genetics" (p. 5) through nature programs.

The development of public opinion, the American Eugenics Society booklet continued, required planned and orchestrated activity because "the education of leaders of public opinion is the first step toward the practical realization of eugenic aims" (NCSA, 1938, p. 5). The importance of interaction with such leaders was essential not only for the realization of aims, but also "contact with such leaders will give eugenicists new insight into the practical application of a eugenic philosophy . . . and learn from them how eugenics can best be reconciled with other social needs" (NCSA, p. 6). The movement's leaders clearly had their finger on the pulse of the Progressive heart of the nation and understood the need to translate their beliefs into a language and methodology that would endear it to the widest possible audience. The American Eugenics Society pamphlet concluded:

> This part of the Society's program calls for a continuing series of conferences in many fields and with many groups. It calls for discovery and publication of new facts bearing upon the science and practice of eugenics through periodicals and newspapers. It should aim to develop eugenic applications, and at the same time to create a public opinion sufficiently discriminating to approve of large families of good quality and discourage large families of low quality, in whatever class of society either may be found. (NCSA, 1938, p. 6)

The fact that the degree and direction of the dissemination campaign was planned to this extent helps to explain the quick and thorough penetration of eugenic ideology into so many corporate, scientific, educational, religious, civic, and social organization within such a short period of time.

Applied Eugenics took a different approach to the subject of dissemination. For Popenoe and Johnson (1918), the success of eugenics depended on its ability to proceed towards its goal upon multiple roads at the same time. The authors claimed that eugenics proposed no definite goal, set no one standard to which the human race should conform. Instead, they claimed, by "taking man as it finds him, it [eugenics] proposes to multiply all the types that have been found by past experience or present reason to be of most value to society" (p. 165). By offering the promise of societal ascension to virtually anyone, eugenicists successfully appealed to segments of the population who were not members of the aristocracy by birth. Everyone had at least some reason to feel good about themselves; at least they were better than *someone*. At the same time, eugenicists retained their distinctly unscientific claim on methods of evaluation "found by past experience or present reason" (p. 165) that actually defined the value to society of each particular individual. So, although they used the promise of meritocracy, eugenicists nevertheless retained control over the entrance requirements.

A three-page typewritten document with a penned signature "field worker" offers tips to "student workers" who approach potential members of the American Eugenics Society (APS-AS, n.d., p. 1). The document encouraged the student worker to memorize a few phrases about eugenics so as to be able to "counter any resistance" (p. 1) with enthusiasm and confidence. After explaining that the worker should announce to the prospect that he has been nominated as a member of the Society, the document went on to present possible questions that might be asked and to suggest answers.

Prospect: Oh, yes, I have heard of the American Eugenics Society. What is it? Tell me more about it? What does it do?

You: The American Eugenics Society is an organization of thoughtful people of the United States bonded together for the benefit of humanity to do what it can to raise the hereditary endowment of the human race to the end that the human race may become happier. (APS-AS, p. 2)

The questions continued to probe the relative costs and benefits of membership. In the middle of a discussion about the *Eugenics Magazine* (one of the benefits of membership) a parentheses appears containing the following: "Right here it might be advisable to tell the people what eugenics really is so that they will not have a mistaken notion about it" (p. 2). What this document reveals is that the leaders of the movement understood there to be a distinction between the bland answer to the "what is eugenics" question that focused on the happiness of the human race and the "real" eugenics which was aimed at specific reform and exclusion.

What is striking about many of the eugenic mandates to disseminate their message widely is the expert use of grassroots campaigning to achieve their goals. Those who work for non-profit environmental and consumer organizations do a daily grind of "canvassing" neighborhoods in order to sign up new members. Such grassroot appeals require a great deal of skill and stamina, while the level of training involved is substantial. Eugenicists were clearly focused and deliberate in their efforts to increase public support for eugenic campaigns. Given the number of doctors, lawyers, pubic office holders, and prominent scientists who publicly supported eugenic ideology, it is not much of a stretch to imagine that eugenic leaders hand-picked their targets for support. By targeting the most prominent members of society early on, eugenicists were able to create a broad spectrum of public support the importance of which superceded the support of geneticists which proved to be less than consistent.

It is impossible to overstate the impact of books like Madison Grant's (1916) *The Passing of the Great Race* and Stoddard's (1920) *The Rising Tide of Color: Against White World Supremacy* on the translation of public perception of racial difference into one of impending threat. This translation was orchestrated in part by the nation's leading editors and publishers (in an era before radio and television), many of whom were enthusiastic supporters of eugenics.

Grant was representative of many non-scientists who preceded and succeeded him in that he "suffered the delusion that if a person *writes* about science—however well or badly—this literary fact automatically qualifies him as a working scientist" (Chase, 1975, p. 163). But Grant was careful to elicit feedback from men of prominence in eugenics as evidenced by a letter to Madison Grant from Harry Laughlin, director of the American Eugenics Society, dated November 19, 1932, regarding the manuscript of a new book Grant had written (Harry H. Laughlin Collection). After expressing his enjoyment of perusing the manuscript with Grant, Laughlin told Grant that the new book would "perform a very valuable service in the re-establishment of American Racial ideals, and in the determination of the American people to direct their own racial evolution" (1932, p. 1). Laughlin agreed to offer, as requested, "frank criticism" and although he believed the book to be "remarkably free" from statements not supported by the evidence, he identified three places with a "tinge of 'explosion' " which if not corrected would "injure the value" of the book (p. 1). Laughlin's first warning to Grant:

> (1) Reference to the Hindus. I believe the statement about Gandhi is irrelevant, and that while vigorous opposition to the Hindus as desirable or assimilable as American immigrants should be made, general contempt should not be shown for Hindus in India . . . the Hindu, although a colored man, being more intelligent

than the Negro, and claiming "Aryan descent," would be more insistent in demanding race equality, and in trying to destroy the barriers to mixture between the White and the colored races, than would any other non-White race which has come to our shores. (Harry H. Laughlin Collection, 1932, p. 2)

Laughlin, in this moment of candor, showed his awareness that contempt was often the common basis of eugenic rhetoric. In his claim that Grant's book was "remarkably free" (p. 1) of unsupported statements Laughlin also showed his awareness that much eugenic writing of the period was not so free of inaccuracy. Also of note from this passage is Laughlin's discrimination between types of immigrants and people of color. Laughlin characterizes people from India as being more intelligent than other people of color, a stereotype that persists into the present, and as such they are more dangerous to the maintenance of "barriers to mixture" (p. 2).

Laughlin's second objection to Grant's manuscript concerned the treatment of democracy. Clearly, Laughlin was cognizant of the national debate concerning democracy and the vulnerability of eugenic ideology where democratic notions of freedom and equality were concerned. Laughlin, in yet another example of his expert recasting of core American principles to coincide with his own agenda, offered a solution to the problem:

(2) Statement about Democracy. This was made in such a manner as to constitute a shot at Democracy, rather than to reinforce the historic argument of capacities differential between the Nordic and the colored races. The statement to the effect that "in experiments in self-government the Nordic races, due to their finer inborn sense of square dealing and their self-control, have been infinitely more successful in self-government than the non-Nordics" would cover the ground. (Harry H. Laughlin Collection, 1932, p. 1)

In this statement Laughlin employed a logic that set democratic ideals on the same ground as "the historic argument of capacities differential" (p. 1) which completely eradicates those problematic definitions of equality, liberty, and freedom. By substituting self-government for democracy, and establishing the prerequisite for success at self-government as a white cultural norm, Laughlin exposed the mechanism by which eugenicists had so successfully attached their racist ideals to preexisting political constructs.

The final objection voiced by Laughlin regarded Jews in America and his comments reflect the deep and abiding way in which Jewish people represented a key threat to Nordic superiority. Far more than the "Hindus," Jews had the capacity to "pass" as White and Laughlin's comments about this threat have a ring of the fear surrounding the high-grade morons who, by virtue of their outward normal appearance, could, with ease, incorporate themselves into society. As usual, Laughlin had a plan:

> (3) Criticism of the statement that "if the remainder of the Jews could be prevented from coming to the United States." This has a tinge of "Damn Jew" about it. It would . . . constitute a more forceful statement if it were pointed out that the United States has already one out of five of the World's Jews, and that further concentration and unassimilated Jews . . . would tend to develop anti-Semitism here. (Harry H. Laughlin Collection, 1932, p. 2)

Laughlin went on to argue that the "Jewish problem" (p. 2) was not that bad yet but that further immigration by Jews was highly undesirable. Acknowledging that the marriage barrier between Jews and Gentiles was rapidly breaking down, Laughlin believed that if the flow of immigrants was stopped then the country would survive because

> [t]hree-percent Jews in the United States evenly distributed and assimilated over a period of say two hundred years would not leave a serious imprint of their qualities on the American stock. (Harry H. Laughlin Collection, 1932, p. 3)

Again, Laughlin relied on stereotype for his analysis when he said that the mate selection between Jew and non-Jew was compensated by "wealth and cultural status" (p. 3). Eugenicists had a clear and definitive view of the future that calculated risks and assessed relative damages. Laughlin closed his (1932) letter to Grant with a request that the preface contain a statement that no American ever be found to apologize for standing up for the "finest qualities of American racial and family stocks" (p. 3). He argued that since all races, including the white race, had been scrutinized that "no member of any race can object [to the] sharp and from the shoulder" (p. 3) truth.

This letter provides a number of insights into the premises upon which eugenicists rested their arguments. Laughlin complained about unassimilated alien groups who "loudly demand the right to promote their own racial interests" (1932, p. 3) and was indignant that they "at the same time cry 'persecution' when persons of Old American stock attempt to re-establish the basic racial interests of foundation Americans in America" (p. 3). Laughlin closed his letter by saying that any person of alien stock who promotes their own racial interests and in so doing decries the efforts of Old American stocks "should be deported as an undesirable resident" (Harry H. Laughlin Collection, 1932, p. 3).

One of the primary methods of dissemination used by the eugenics movement was an active lecture circuit. Lectures were well publicized and the posters are filled with quotes from prominent men and women extolling the virtues of both the speakers and the subject of their speeches. Kevles (1985) reported that demand for lectures on eugenics was high and requests came from ethical, debating, health, and philosophical societies, as well as school and university campuses, women's clubs and a variety of civic and social betterment organizations. Dr. Alfred E. Wiggam, author of *The Next Age of Man, The Fruit of the Family Tree*, and the 1923 bestseller *The New Decalogue of Science* was a journalist and lecturer who "stood out for the way he melded eugenic science with statesmanship, morality and religion" (Kevles, 1985, p. 59). Posters (TCS-LOC)[5] picture Wiggam as an imposing bespectacled man, describe him as "The Apostle of Efficiency" (TCS-LOC, n.d.) and characterize his lectures as offering "A hopeful, helpful, inspiring, philosophy of life for these times" (TCS-LOC, n.d.). The list of subjects upon which Wiggam would lecture included "Who Shall Inherit the World—the Strong or the Weak. The Intelligent or the Stupid?" (TCS-LOC, n.d.). The poster lists Wiggam's credentials which include his position on the writers staff of *Reader's Digest* "the most widely read magazine in the world," and his position on the editorial staff of National Newspaper Services. Wiggam wrote a regular newspaper column *Let's Explore Your Mind* which, according to the poster "reaches 5,000,000 readers daily" (TCS-LOC, n.d.). Wiggam was also a regular contributor to *Good Housekeeping, Ladies Home Journal, American, Cosmopolitan* "and many other magazines" (TCS-LOC, n.d.). Regardless of the accuracy of one poster's claim that "over a million people have paid to hear Wiggam lecture" (TCS-LOC, n.d.), it is clear that Wiggam was practically ubiquitous in American culture.

Lectures rested on a number of possible angles to draw people in. One poster headline proclaims "The American Woman Is Rapidly Becoming Ugly" (TCS-LOC, n.d.) and shows a photograph of a white marble statue of a mother and daughter, presumably not "ugly." The smaller text gives the details:

> Prof. Ross has proved it. When the low immigrant is giving us three babes while the Daughter of the Revolution is giving us one it means that the Gibson and Harrison Fisher girl is vanishing. Her place is being taken by the low-browed, broad-faced, flat-chested woman of lower Europe. If this continues it means a Progressive loss of racial excellence, intelligence, and power. (TCS-LOC, n.d.)

In addition to a wide and diverse lecture circuit, dissemination of eugenic ideology took on other cultural forms as well such as the drama performed by Katherine Oliver-McCoy. Described as "A Wonderful Drama Dealing with the Foremost

Problem of the Day—Eugenics" (TCS-LOC, n.d.) the play called *Tomorrow* was written by Percy MacKaye. A reviewer representing the medical profession wrote that

> the high culture, exquisite art, and intense moral earnestness of the speaker added doubly to the force of the message—which is . . . engaging the attention of parents and educators. (TCS-LOC, n.d.)

As eugenic ideology entered the American lexicon in ever more creative ways, the public responded by finding their own ways to engage in active dissemination of the eugenic cause.

We have seen that dissemination occurred on many fronts, but not all were sponsored by eugenics organizations. So enthusiastic were some members of the public that spontaneous bursts of organizing and proselytizing took place throughout the country. One example of this was revealed in a letter to Harry Laughlin from E. S. Gosney, president of the Human Betterment Foundation headquartered in Pasadena, California (SHC-HBL, 1938). Dated August 17, 1938, the letter requests advice regarding Mrs. Marion Norton, a woman from Princeton, New Jersey, who had submitted several unsolicited papers she had written, developed four pamphlets, and in general expressed her interest in the cause of the sterilization of the unfit. Gosney explained that having never met the woman he and his colleagues were interested to know what Laughlin thought of her and whether she was possessed of "personality, tact, common-sense, [and] judgment about such things as to know when to talk and when not to talk." Laughlin responded, in a letter dated September 1, 1938, that it was his belief that Mrs. Norton was "doing good work." "I agree," Laughlin continued, "that she is rather enthusiastic and forward at times, but she seems to know what eugenics is about" (SHC-HBL, 1938). Laughlin expressed his belief that since the New Jersey sterilization law had been attacked and defeated, and the state now had a legislator who could "write a good, conservative, constitutional eugenical sterilization law," Mrs. Norton may be "of very substantial service" in the passing of a new law (SHC-HBL, 1938). Like any good grassroots movement, eugenics took advantage of enthusiastic believers to work towards the cause. This example also shows the degree to which the boundary between promotion of eugenic ideology and the performance of civic duty overlapped. Mrs. Norton represented white Americans who felt the fear that saturated popular culture and press and responded by becoming active in the movement.

From Galton's belief in the inheritance of societal eminence, to the beliefs of eugenicists on a wide array of value-laden moral imperatives, Chapters Five and Six have investigated the essential elements of eugenic ideology. Although initially concerned with heredity as it concerned the "superior germ plasm," this early focus on eminence grew to include a widely cast net. Heredity covered not only physical characteristics but also temperament and behavior including alcoholism, truancy, laziness, imbecility, and feeblemindedness. Eugenicists helped to foster an already deep and abiding fear of the "other," who they identified as the millions of immigrants from Eastern Europe, poor whites, and African Americans. Using heredity in combination with older hierarchical versions of race theory eugenicists successfully convinced the public that race, ability, and essential human worth were correlated.

The contextual elements of immigration, industrialization, poverty, and crime were incorporated into the eugenic analysis and ultimately related to race and heredity. Due in part to their successful campaigning, eugenic legislation spread throughout the county over the course of the 1920s and 1930s. These laws applied mainly to the sterilization of the unfit and marriage restriction, but subtle variations sought to control and define degeneracy in as many ways as possible. Finally, eugenicists were expert grassroots campaigners. Their plans and programs of dissemination were built in to the earliest mandates and nothing was left to chance. Eugenic leaders displayed a sophisticated awareness of the power of public opinion very early in the century and were therefore able to insulate eugenic ideology from scientific advances.

It was the idea of the heritability of feeblemindedness and intelligence that would have the most profound impact on education. With the development of mental testing, eugenicists had found a diagnostic tool that enabled them to identify, classify, and sort institutional populations of all kinds, including school children. The following chapter traces the integration of eugenic ideology into educational mandate.

7

Education—A New Frontier

Education in its modern form was largely conceived as an academic discipline during the early decades of the twentieth century when eugenics was promulgated. Many argue (Tyack, 1974; Eisner, 1992; Kliebard, 1995; Pinar, 1995; Apple, 1997, 2001; Eisner, 1997; Kliebard, 1997; Selden, 1999; Stoskopf, 1999) that despite valiant efforts, not enough has changed since then in terms of the practice and public conception of education. This is not to say that mention has never been made, or that inklings have not been had, but for the most part the extent to which there may be a link between eugenic ideology and education has remained under the public radar. The reasons behind the profound lack of public awareness regarding the impact of the eugenics movement are complex and integrally related to the cooptation of education. I would hazard that these connections are missed precisely *because* we are talking about education. Education as a social institution was conceived and developed during the height of the eugenics movement and in many ways is the product of eugenic ideological thinking that must, in order to survive in the present, exclude introspection.

The first three decades of the twentieth century saw enormous growth and change in education. Public education was widespread in America by 1870 but there was considerable variation with respect to race, ethnicity, class, gender, and region (Cremin, 1988, p. 644). Over the next century those variations were erased and the character of education became virtually universal. This was due in part to the establishment of compulsory education laws which by 1918 had been passed in every state. According to Cremin (1988), although most states began to actually enforce compulsory education laws during the 1920s and 1930s, large segments of the population, primarily immigrants, remained "outside the influence of truant officers and outside the concern of education authorities" (p. 644). Despite these exceptions, by 1920 over 90% of American children between the ages of 7 and 13 were reported as enrolled in school and by 1950 the number had risen to 96% (Cremin, 1988, p. 645). In terms of potential influence on the mindset of the American public, schools provided a rapt audience for the inculcation of ideas.

A New Frontier

By the close of the nineteenth century, mental discipline had been largely replaced as education's fundamental mechanism of operation (Pinar, 1995). New fields of inquiry, and new careers, were being forged in education and the fledgling field of psychology. As we have seen, society was gripped, but hardly paralyzed, by a profound fear of the "Other" due to massive immigration, burgeoning urban populations, and the effects of industrialization. Social activists were consumed by a defensive strategy that called for the eradication of the socially inferior and the preservation of "old stock" American values and genetic material. Education, as we will see, was not immune to these social forces.

Out of the perception of extreme calamity on the part of White America came a renewed enthusiasm for the possibility of education to provide a solution to the crisis at hand. Over the course of the 1910s and 1920s much of the vociferousness of eugenic rhetoric that called for the elimination of defective germ plasm[1] was muted by an increasing realization (provided in part by advances in genetic theory) that America was, in effect, stuck with a diverse population. Reflecting this concession, Wiggam (1924) wrote that eugenics was

> a program in which the most ardent believers in heredity and the most ardent believers in environment can unite with the utmost good will. It will give ample scope to the desires and passions of both. Such a union of both the environmental and hereditary forces all along the line is, indeed, the only hope for race improvement. If the workers for good environment and those who advocate good heredity can thus join their forces, as they are rapidly doing through the new education of the younger generation, it will mean but one thing for the future—a constantly improving race of people dwelling in a constantly improving world. (p. 60)

Without letting up on their efforts to effect both positive and negative eugenic reforms in the areas of sterilization and immigration, eugenicists broadened their "environmental" scope to include those social institutions that offered the most promise for affecting eugenic progress, especially education.

Eugenically motivated reforms in schools came in many forms. In a November 1916, article for *The North Carolina Educational News*, a publication of the State

Department of Public Instruction[2] (NCSA-NBL, 1916), the State Board of Health advocated the establishment of "School Health Clubs," designed to establish health laws and sanitary teaching to the student body and by association to "the other members of his family" (NCSA-NBL, 1916). The clubs were to be under the guidance of teachers, but officers were to be selected from "the most efficient boys and girls" who would oversee the teaching of hygiene, health, and sanitation. Furthermore, the program enlisted students in the process through the selection of "sanitary scouts." These scouts were a key component to the program since they would "report the health conditions in general and . . . any nuisances or unsanitary conditions that exist about the school" and report them immediately to the teacher and superintendent (NCSA-NBL).

School programs like these, a hidden curriculum, speak to the inherent approach to "undesirable" populations, the categorization, the civic duty imbued upon students, "school scouts" whose role it is to identify, judge, and report on their fellow students. We might be tempted to pass this off as an interpretation of the "cleanliness as godliness" maxim that was popular at the time, or even a new awareness of the importance of preventing disease. Such arguments would not be inaccurate, but they would be shortsighted given the extent to which elements of popular culture were infused with eugenic ideological principle. In other words, even though the work of birth-control advocate Margaret Sanger, for example, contributed an enormous element of freedom to millions of women doesn't repudiate the fact that eugenic principles were the motivator. The benefit to women is not denied, the deeply embedded assumptions ought to be.

In language that mirrors that of eugenicists, another article in the same 1916 volume titled *Work of Schools during the War* refers to the need of education to provide "skilled mechanics and high-grade helpers" for the war effort (NCSA-NBL). "The Bureau of Education," the article continued, "warns particularly against the relaxation of standards, pointing out that half-baked mechanics will in the end impair the efficiency of any branch of service." Elsewhere, *The North Carolina Educational News* (NCSA-NBL, 1916) reported on a community schools program that travelled around the state offering teachings by federal and state representatives on matters of home economics. At the meeting of state and federal leaders including "the United States Bureau of Education, State Department of Agriculture, A. & E. College, State Board of Health, State Highway Commission, State Bureau of Markets, the State Normal and Industrial School, Farm-life schools, and the state Department of Education" the program included topics ranging from the "schoolhouse as the hub" of the community wheel and how it "might better be used for service" in the "treatment of defective school children" (NCSA-NBL, 1916).

A series of letters[3] to the State Superintendent of Schools in 1921 regarding the recent adoption of D. S. Mussey's (1920) high school history textbook show that strong racial feeling and a sense of persecution ran strong in North Carolina (NCSA-DPI). These letters were the product of a well-organized campaign on the part of the Daughters of the Confederacy, but also came from lawyers, doctors, teachers, and other concerned professionals. One writer complained that the "author calls slavery 'the terrible system of gondage' [*sic*]" and opined, in a claim that has become the stuff of legend where southern justification of slavery is concerned, that "the negro in the south was the happiest and best cared for peasantry the world ever saw" (NCSA-DPI, n.d.). This writer also took offense at the textbook author's characterization of *Uncle Tom's Cabin* as "an exaggerated but powerful portrayal of the moral degradation to which slave-holding reduces a man." "Horrid tommyrot": the letter writer continued, "Only the ignorant or vicious can believe that slave-holding, as it prevailed in the south was 'morally degrading' " (NCSA-DPI, n.d.). A final example from this author's three-page, single-spaced objection refers to the history text's claim that the southern position in the civil war represented an unworthy cause. The author called this characterization "Yankee calumny" and declared that "the teaching of this kind of history" to the children of North Carolina was "scandalous" (NCSA-DPI, n.d.). One woman, representing the Charlotte chapter of the United Daughters of the Confederacy requested action by the State Superintendent in more dulcet tones, requesting that "in the name of truth and justice, you lend your influence in abolishing" the text "and any other book that is unfair" from the school curriculum.

In what appears to be an early incarnation of the current debate over accountability in education, Popenoe and Johnson (1918) delicately broached the subject of teacher discretion over what is taught in classrooms. The authors were concerned that

> the individual teacher may accept or decide, either consciously or unconsciously, what seem to him to be the important ideals which shall dominate the instruction which he gives to his students. (p. 44)

They are quite clear that the emphasis of ideals should not be left up to chance. The solution to such wanton disregard for the conscious direction of ideals in public schools is to encourage faculty to "decide for itself what will be the dominant ideals of the institution, after taking into account the individuality of the students" (p. 44). An interesting juxtaposition occurs here in the clear definition and establishment of dominant ideals and the individuality of the student. Clearly, the authors had no intention of taking student individuality into account when it came to the direction and content of the curriculum. While the above may merely hint at reflected eugenic thinking, we will see shortly that the depth and extent of racial feeling present in the 1920s extended very much to school curriculum.

Early Conceptions of Curriculum

> The history of American Eugenics has more often than not been a history of the categorization of individuals and groups for the purpose of legitimizing a set of existing social, institutional, and political relations. (Selden, 1999, p. 85)

So too, is the history of American *education* implicated in the categorization of individuals and groups. Cremin (1990) argued that overall, there have been three "abiding characteristics" (p. vii) of American education; the *popularization* of American education, its *multitudinous* nature, and the degree of inevitable *politicization* that it engendered. While these were, Cremin argued, not uniquely American characteristics, their combination was. It is important to go beyond mere identification of "abiding characteristics," or even of the manifestation of them by instead pursuing a deeper analysis of the motivations behind their development in the first place.

The first characterization, popularization, Cremin (1990) defined as the tendency to make education widely available in increasingly diverse forms that would reach the largest number of people. This characteristic of education in America is inherently tied to the eugenic goal of conjoining what Wiggam (1924) referred to as the "hereditary and environmental forces" (p. 60). Eugenicists desired to exert as much control as possible over the indigent and defective populations and considered schools to be an ideal mechanism by which to do so.

In large part, compulsory education was used to accomplish this goal. In *Applied Eugenics* Popenoe and Johnson (1918) reflected the eugenicist stance on the promise of education with their contention that

> [c]ompulsory education, as such, is not only of service to eugenics through the selection it makes possible, but may serve in a more unsuspected way by cutting down the birth rate of inferior families. (p. 371)

Education "of service to eugenics" allowed for the "very desirable" (p. 371) condition that "no child escape inspection" (p. 371), a goal that in 1918 had yet to be realized by the public educational system. In addition to the selection made possible by compulsory education, eugenicists also advocated for vocational education.

Vocational and agricultural education programs flourished during the 1920s and 1930s (Cremin, 1988) and were instrumental in realizing the eugenic objective to achieve "as perfect a correlation as possible between income and eugenic worth" (Popenoe, 1918, p. 371). The belief was that this correlation would occur when individuals were trained for jobs that are most suited to them. Moreover, compulsory and vocational education would provide the "distinct advantage" (p. 372) of allowing "superior young people" (p. 372) to get established earlier, and avoid the vice and temptations of eugenically unsound societal influences. Especially, earlier establishment of young people into the societal roles for which they were best suited, "the boys being fitted for gainful occupations and the girls for wifehood and motherhood" (p. 372) would especially further the likelihood of eugenically sound propagation and thus the furthering of racial purity.

Eugenicists also helped define the parameters of educational aims by attaching the notion of ability to heredity. By defining the ability to learn as a function of heredity, eugenicists successfully ensured that only those segments of society who approached their clearly defined "superior" standards would receive the kind of education that allowed for independent thought. It must be remembered that just as vocational education was promoted and encouraged by eugenicists, so too did the gifted education movement originate in eugenic ideology. Selden (1999) reported that Leta Hollingworth, a professor at Teachers College, Columbia University, known for her research and advocacy of "the top two percent" was unconcerned with the feebleminded and instead focused her efforts on "the biologically meritorious" (p. 100).

Cremin's (1990) second "abiding characteristic" (p. viii) of education was its *multitudinous* nature, referring to the proliferation and multiplication of institutions to provide America with an educational system that was widely available and increasingly accessible. A survey of the wide variety of institutions that appear throughout both the educational and eugenic literature indicate that indeed there was a great deal of variation in the educational institutions common during the first decades of the twentieth century.

An illustration of the dialogue in North Carolina concerning the disposition of "the feeble-minded and defective in the state" can be found in a letter[4] dated January 12, 1912 (NCSA-DPI). Written on the official letterhead of the North Carolina School for the Feebleminded in Washington, NC, by the secretary of the school, Dr. Ira M. Hardy the letter is addressed to the Superintendent of Public Instruction Dr. J. J. Joyner (NCSA-DPI, 1912). Hardy requested that Joyner provide his views on Hardy's idea, to establish institutional training and care for the feebleminded and defective. Hardy stated his belief that the Governor would give his approval for the plan. Hardy argued that the establishment of more institutions to relieve the state's current inability to properly care for this population would

> relieve the homes and the social body of the unguarded presence of these persons, and help the taxpayers to spend their money more wisely than they would do eventually if this same wandering mass became criminals, insane and the like, to be supported in the most expensive way to the taxpayers. (NCSA-DPI, 1912)

Hardy went on to describe the function of the "the committee (to be hereafter named)," (NCSA-DPI, 1912) and its possible course of action in organizing support for the creation of more institutions. Sensitive to public opinion, Hardy further stated his belief that "public sentiment would respond more quickly in supporting a committee than it would any institutions that would seemingly have 'an axe to grind' " (NCSA-DPI, 1912). Hardy was willing to participate in "a great deal of persistent work" to obtain a "correct" list of the feebleminded confined in jails, alms houses, and public institutions "as directed by the Board of Trustees last June." The ultimate aim of this effort was to identify the feebleminded and defectives "in the homes and public schools" so as to interest people in the counties to secure legislation that would bring them relief (NCSA-DPI, 1912).

Politicization, defined as the effort to solve certain social problems indirectly through education rather than directly through politics, is the third and final of Cremin's (1990) characterizations of education. We have already seen that eugenicists sought to expand the frontier of their activities and focused their gaze on education. We have also seen evidence of the politicization of education in the sampling of archival data from the North Carolina Department of Public Instruction. Education leaders in the state were on the cutting edge of eugenically influenced education reform and participated in the implementation of clearly eugenic imperatives.

Cremin (1990) argued that America's long-standing tendency to "solve social problems through education" has placed an enormous burden on schools, but more fundamentally, this tendency "involves education in the most fundamental aspirations of the society" (p. xi). Taking into account the highly charged, racially motivated social atmosphere that inevitably was reflected in the schools provides some explanation. What is inexcusable, however, is continued ignorance of the knowledge that educational theory, philosophy, and practice were developed both within and as a mandate of this atmosphere. To attempt educational reform in the present without this knowledge amounts to mere folly and perpetuation.

Humanists and Mental Discipline

According to Kliebard (1986/1995) turn of the century education was characterized by four competing groups: *humanists, developmentalists, social efficiency educators,* and *social meliorists.* Admitting that the end result was a "not very tidy compromise" (p. 25) for American education, Kliebard described the impact of these four competing groups on early conceptions of curriculum. *Humanists* tapped in to the positivist perspective's encapsulation of the spirit of the enlightenment and were concerned with traditional notions of reason most closely associated with what we call "the scientific method" today. This group represented the early positivists' desire to find a reliable measure of reality with which to make sense of a societal context characterized by perpetual flux. For the humanists, a reasoned approach to the world involved accurate observation, the keeping of thorough and accurate records of those observations, engagement in an analysis which classified and categorized the observed data and finally making correct and accurate inferences.

Humanists, at least this early, positivist iteration of the camp (as opposed to the Erikson, Rollo May, etc., camp) were also associated with the doctrine of mental discipline which had been the status quo of American curriculum throughout much of nineteenth century (Kliebard, 1986/1995). Mental disciplinarians believed that the mind was like a muscle and that certain subjects, if taught with monotonous drill, harsh discipline, and verbatim recitation, could strengthen the facilities of memory, reasoning, will, and imagination. The doctrine of mental discipline defined proscriptions about what to teach, as well as what rules to apply to the practice of teaching. It also had broader implications, like balance and integration in the curriculum, which make the legacy it imparted to education difficult to erase. Kliebard (1986/1995) explained that by the 1890s, the theory of mental discipline began to unravel largely as a function of new theories of social transformation. Despite being rather removed from the professional debate, humanists nevertheless continued to exercise a strong measure of control over the American curriculum in to the twentieth century (Kliebard, 1986/1995). Although educational theorists such as Bobbitt and Thorndike were associated with eugenics (Selden, 1999) and the move away from the humanist perspective, mental discipline provided a rich precedent in later conceptions of curriculum that sought to categorize and sort students by ability.

Developmentalists and Child Study

Another group garnering significant influence on education at the turn of the century were the *developmentalists* who proceeded from "the assumption that the natural order of development in the child was the most significant and scientifically defensible basis for determining what should be taught" (Kliebard, 1986/1995, p. 11). A pivotal figure in the developmentalist school of thought was leading American educator Granville Stanley Hall. Hall is most well known for his development of Child Study, a major strand of twentieth-century curriculum. The implications of our current conception of Child Study and individual approaches to education are challenged when we acknowledge that eugenicists were of the opinion that

> [i]t is very desirable that no child escape inspection, because of the importance of discovering every individual of exceptional ability or inability . . . the public educational system has not yet risen to the need of this systematic mental diagnosis. (Popenoe, 1918, p. 371)

In other words, individual approaches to education act as a euphemism for "systematic mental diagnosis" (1918, p. 371). Developments in mental testing and curriculum reform over the next 75 years would remedy the problem that, as Popenoe put it, education has not yet "risen to the need." Between 1866 and 1924 Hall's 14 books and over 350 published papers reflect a "fairly consistent social philosophy" (Curti, 1935/1959, p. 396) built upon a foundation of naturalism. Hall argued that the "probable destination [of the] great army of incapables" should dictate the manner and extent of education for American students (quoted in Kliebard, 1986/1995, p. 12). Selden (1999) reported that "believing in the heritability of the 'criminal mind,' it was Hall's contention that negative and positive eugenics were necessary components of social policy" (p. 43). In their search for ever more accurate scientific data on which to base their curricular efforts, developmentalists shared their penchant for positivism with the humanists. However, instead of a blanket prescription of mental exercise, developmentalists pursued the subject of curriculum from a biologically deterministic perspective that defined the differing stages of child and adolescent development, as well as the nature of learning.

Social Efficiency and Sorting

Kliebard (1999) identifies the third group of educational reformers in the late nineteenth century as the *social efficiency* educators. Reflecting the general societal trend, social efficiency educators were "imbued with the power of science" (p. 24) and believed that the application of business and industrial standards would eliminate waste in education. It should be noted that in the literature (Curti, 1935/1959; Kliebard, 1975/1997, 1986/1995; Cremin, 1988; Pinar, 1995) it is with social efficiency educators that eugenic imperatives are most often associated, although eugenics itself is not named. While Kliebard (1999) did not specifically acknowledge the power of popular culture to influence curricular ideology, he described the influence of a series of nine articles by Joseph Rice, a self-appointed educational reformer, on the development of the social efficiency movement. Rice, who was German educated, published these articles between October 1892 and June 1893 and caused an "immediate sensation" (Kliebard, 1999, p. 18). These articles, later published as *The Public School System of the United States* (1893), were, in fact, critical to the development of what Kliebard (1999) called a "veritable orgy of efficiency that was to dominate American thinking generally in the decades ahead" and which in fact "became the overwhelming criterion of success in curriculum matters" (p. 24).

Anticipating themes from later eugenic emphases in education, social efficiency was concerned with the extent to which curriculum could provide more functional training and thus conform to the eventual adult roles that America's future citizens would occupy. Functionality or, as it was soon to be known, vocational education was a major trend in education whose roots are directly planted in the eugenics movement. In *Applied Eugenics*, Popenoe and Johnson (1918) state that one of the "greatest services" educators can provide eugenics

> will probably be to put a lot of boys into skilled trades, for which they are adapted and where they will succeed, and thus prevent them from yielding to the desire for a more genteel clerical occupation, in which they will not do more than earn a bare living. This will bring about the high correlation between merit and income which is so much to be desired. (p. 374)

Eugenicists believed ability was innate and that it was the job of education to successfully sort students and match them to the vocations for which they were best suited. By matching inborn ability with the appropriate path society would achieve a system of meritocracy where income and ability were directly correlated.

Social Meliorists and Justice

Finally, to conclude Kliebard's (1999) sketch of the competing forces in American education at the turn of the century the *social meliorists* "saw the schools as a major, perhaps the principal, force for social change and social justice" (p. 25) and directly challenged the Social Darwinist assumption that the key to human betterment was genetically based. Social meliorists believed that the power to change society was a function of the ameliorative possibilities that education offered. By directly addressing race, gender, and class inequality in the curriculum, this group believed that a new generation of students would be equipped to eradicate social problems.

The extent to which each of these four groups continued to influence education in the twentieth century fluctuated with social forces, "economic trends, periodic and fragile alliances between groups, the national mood, and local conditions and personalities" (Kliebard, 1999, p. 25). That they all exerted influence to varying degrees is evidenced by the wide range of reforms that were attempted in education during the following decades. What is less clear is the residual role of collective memory and popular culture to influence, create, and sustain the ideologies of any one of the groups. As we continue to explore the relationship between eugenic ideology and early conceptions of curriculum, we will see that the development of the field of education was predicated in part on popular cultural conceptions of racial hierarchy and ability. Taken in sum, the historical context in terms of masses of immigration, education's new found infatuation with the salvation offered by science, and the competing influences operating within the field of curriculum offers a foundation from which we can begin to understand the penetration of eugenic ideology into educational thought.

Confluence of Philosophies

The conjoining in the 1910s of newly emerged conception of the legitimacy offered by science and the newly developing field of education has had profound implications for generations of American students. The manifestation of this conjoining was what many theorists (Tyack, 1974, 1982; Stone, 1985; Kliebard, 1986/1995; Pinar, 1995) referred to as *scientific curriculum*. Scientific curriculum is most identified with the rise of the field of educational psychology and particularly with the work of Edward L. Thorndike (Pinar, 1995). Stone (1985) described the scientific curriculum movement in terms of three generations of curricularists, culminating with Ralph W. Tyler and his now infamous "rationale" embodied in his book *Basic Principles of Curriculum and Instruction* (1949). Stone's description is useful because it allows us to see directly the flow of intellectual influence as it occurred from the late nineteenth century through the middle of the twentieth century.

The first generation of curricularists, Stone (1985) explained, was comprised of William James and Wilhelm Wundt. James, a consummate American philosopher and psychologist, is most famous for his influential *Principles of Psychology* (1890) and is credited with bringing psychology to America (Cremin, 1988; Pinar, 1995). James sought to "apply the doctrines of evolution to the phenomena of the mind," and counted among his students both Edward Thorndike and John Dewey (Cremin, 1961, p. 106). Wundt, on the other hand, was described by Cremin (1961) as part of "the paternity of American psychology" and one of the "three titans of German science" (p. 101). According to Stone (1985), Wundt mentored Charles Judd who, along with W. W. Charters, Franklin Bobbitt, and George Counts mentored Ralph Tyler. In her genealogy, Stone places Thorndike and Dewey between the first and second generations of curricularists who applied the scientific approach to curriculum (Stone, 1985, p. 203).

In 1928, C. C. Little wrote that "education has long felt the need for an adequate body of scientific data to provide for it the foundation necessary to any properly established profession" (quoted in Selden, 1999, p. 45). Education and eugenic leadership in America felt the imperative to fill this need. The conduits comprising the interface between eugenic ideology and education was formed through a combination of historical, political, socially Progressive, and demographic influences in play during the first decades of the twentieth century. This combination resulted in decades of policy formation directed by a prolific group of ideologues. We must examine the philosophies of those activists who created scientific curriculum and, I will argue, opened the gate for eugenic ideology in American education.

Thorndike

The bulk of E. L. Thorndike's *Principles of Teaching* (1906) and subsequent work dealt with the design and choice of teaching materials, instructional organization, adjusting to individual differences in the classroom, and assessment. So influential was Thorndike during the genesis of the field that Cremin (1961) was inspired to comment that virtually "no aspect of public school teaching during the first quarter of the twentieth century remained unaffected" (p. 114). By means of chickens in boxes with levers Thorndike developed a new theory of learning and new "laws" wherein "learning involves the wedding of a specific response to a specific stimulus" (Cremin,, 1961, p. 111). Thorndike's theory consists of three primary laws: the law of *effect*, the law of *readiness*, and the law of *exercise*. Each of these have been deeply embedded in our thinking about the way children learn and, consequently, have been enacted through curriculum and policy mandates.

Thorndike's (1913) law of effect holds that those responses to a situation which are followed by reward are strengthened and become habitual. The law of readiness builds on the first by theorizing that responses can be chained together in a series in order to satisfy a desired goal. Finally, Thorndike believed that stimulus–response connections become strengthened with practice and weakened without it; this he called the law of exercise. In the larger context, Thorndike's theory exacted a revolution of sorts on conceptions of learning and imbued educational psychology with previously unrealized influence. As Cremin describes it,

> in one fell swoop it [Thorndike's theory] discards the Biblical view that man's nature is essentially sinful and hence untrustworthy; the Rousseauan view that man's nature is essentially good and hence always right; and the Lockean view that man's nature is ultimately plastic and hence completely modifiable. Human nature, Thorndike maintained, is simply a mass of "original tendencies" that can be exploited for good or bad depending on what learning takes place . . . Thorndike's goal was a comprehensive science of pedagogy on which all education could be based. (Cremin, 1961, pp. 112/114)

Thorndike is quoted "ad nauseum to the effect that everything that exists exists in quantity and can be measured" (Cremin, 1961, p. 114). Thorndike did not limit his vision for the impact of science on education to methods but ultimately believed that the aims of education could be scientifically determined as well (Cremin, 1961). This brings us to Bobbitt and how scientific curriculum fit into the intellectual scheme in the 1920s and 1930s.

Bobbitt

John Franklin Bobbitt was a founder of the curriculum field and author of the classic curriculum policy text *The Curriculum* (1918). Writing at a time when mental discipline as a theoretical basis for the curriculum was well on its way out, and Social Darwinism was being replaced by eugenic ideology around the country, Bobbitt articulated his early ideas on the subjects of race, class, and ability in an article entitled "Practical Eugenics" (1909). Bobbitt shared the view common among eugenicists and Social Darwinists before them that social policy should seek to remove the protective characteristics of civilized society and allow the force of nature to take its course in sorting human worth. Bobbitt believed that "our schools and charities supply crutches to the weak in mind and morals," and, reflecting a common eugenic theme, he furthermore asserted that schools and charities "corrupt the streams of heredity which all admit are sufficiently turbid" (Bobbitt, 1909, p. 387). As we read in the previous chapter, social turbidity was the topic of the day in 1909 and the confluence of science and racist ideology was well established in the minds of many as the key to racial purity and subsequent societal betterment.

Bobbitt's article, which appeared in the journal *Pedagogical Seminary*, edited by colleague and eminent psychologist G. Stanley Hall, confirms his clear alignment with eugenic ideology. It is hardly surprising, but nevertheless somewhat shocking, that one of the premier constructors of education in America adhered to such blatantly racist ideas. Bobbitt was confident that the problem of child training would be solved by limiting the right to procreate to individuals of "sound sane parentage" since there was little to be done for the children of "worm-eaten stock" (p. 385). In order to purge society of the unfit, Bobbitt proposed the abolishment of the public school system, all charities, and any other public agency that went out of its way to "preserve the weak and incapable" (p. 393). We will see that Bobbitt later learned to tone down his rhetoric even though the essential elements of this early philosophy remained intact.

Over the course of the following decade, Bobbitt, echoing social reformers of all stripes, conceded that eradication and elimination of society's unfit was an unrealistic goal and set about developing a theory of education that would be able to function within these newly realized parameters. Bobbitt's philosophy led him to devise a curriculum based on social efficiency that allowed schools to function as a societal hub for organizing and sorting children according to their relative worth to society. It was Kliebard's (1975/1997) contention that the most crucial element of Bobbitt's theory was his emphasis on curriculum as preparation for later life because of its implication that "the end products of curriculum [could] be stated with great particularity" (p. 32).

Philosophically, Bobbitt was most closely aligned with the social efficiency quadrant of the reformist movement. The "scientific method in curriculum making," as Bobbitt (1918, p. 41) called it, appealed to both the public and professional educators because both segments of society were familiar with science applied to business in the form of scientific management and there was "no reason why scientific principles applied to education would not meet with the same success" (Kliebard, 1975/1997, p. 31). For Bobbitt though, it was not enough to simply apply management techniques to education. Rather, Bobbitt enabled the establishment of a new hegemony of professional educators by providing the concepts, metaphors, and language "needed to create an aura of technical expertise" (Kliebard, 1975/1997, p. 32).

Regarded as perhaps one of the most influential curriculum texts in American educational history, Bobbitt's *The Curriculum* (1918) defined curriculum in two ways:

1. It is the entire range of experiences, both undirected and directed, concerned in unfolding the abilities of the individual; or
2. It is the series of consciously directed training experiences that the schools use for completing and perfecting the unfoldment. (p. 43)

In what may be regarded as a direct reference to his eugenic theoretical stance, Bobbitt (1918) further stated that "education must be concerned with both [directed and undirected training experience], *even though it does not direct both*" (p. 43; emphasis mine). In other words, "undirected" experiences are those that are imbued by heredity, be they functional ability or economic status. To discover the "appropriate" education for "any special class," Bobbitt believed, required a close inspection of the "total range of habits, skills, abilities, forms of thought, valuations, ambitions, etc., that its members need for the effective performance of their vocational labors" (1918, p. 43).

Bobbitt's philosophy is indicative of the common conception of differences between groups, not only in terms of ability, but also in terms of their habits and proclivities. By using habits and proclivities as a tool to discover appropriate education for members of various groups, Bobbitt effectively brings together curriculum form and function with dominant racial and class definitions of difference. For Bobbitt, the central theory was simple. Given that human life, regardless of its origin, consisted in the performance of specific activities, along with the fact that those activities could be discovered, ensured that conceptions of ability embedded in the curriculum were defined by racial and class-determined differences.

The possibility that appropriate education could be discovered through measurable individual markers rested on the presupposition that education was "established on the presumption that human activities exist upon different levels of quality or efficiency" (Bobbitt, 1918, p. 48). The result of this approach to the assessment and development of education for the widest variety of ability allowed educators to rest assured that "performance of low level is not good; that it can be eliminated through training; and that only the best, or at least the best attainable is good enough" (p. 48). Education had always functioned as a form of societal promise and progress, only now education did so within the boundaries of an ideology that described learning and ability in terms of race and class limitations. It was Bobbitt's contention within the confines of this definition, that "education should aim at the best" and "scientific investigations as to objectives should seek to discover the characteristics of only the best" (p. 50). Bobbitt was to get his wish in the form of testing.

We have seen that, for eugenicists, the great compromise (having re-prioritized the ultimate goal of racial cleansing) when it came to the institution of education was that it direct students, according to their inherited lot, into the workplace. These end products, what have come to be known as curricular objectives, have proved to be one of the most enduring legacies of scientific curriculum as it was originally conceived.

Another enduring element of Bobbitt's curriculum theory was his ability to combine specificity and ambiguity into a coherent whole. Perhaps reflecting the cultural perspective from which eugenic ideology was derived, Bobbitt's theory was simultaneously specific and ambiguous. It is interesting to note that Bobbitt's proscription for curriculum provided specificity for practical and clearly desirable skills, but his theory was vague and ambiguous where value issues were concerned (Kliebard, 1975/1997). Although Kliebard never mentions eugenics specifically, he nevertheless felt suspicious enough to refer to Bobbitt's combination of specificity and ambiguity as reflective of a "submerged ideology" (p. 34).

The influence of Bobbitt's curriculum theorizing on education has been acknowledged by education historians and scholars (Curti, 1935/1959; Callahan, 1962; Kliebard, 1975/1997, 1986/1995; Eisner, 1992; Pinar, 1995; Selden, 1999) but the degree to which Bobbitt rested his philosophy on proscriptions and assumptions that were closely aligned with what the eugenics movement was advocating at the time has yet to be acknowledged to the same extent. In *The Curriculum* Bobbitt (1918) showed an alignment with a number of eugenic themes regarding the role of vocational education, good citizenship, moral and religious education, physical training, and scientific efficiency.

If, as Kliebard (1968/1995) argued, the central element to curriculum theory is embodied in a dialectic, then it is clear on which side of the fence Bobbitt's curriculum theory sits. On one side of the argument is the belief that curriculum is proscriptive and therefore engaged in the provision of a "blueprint" by which to live. On the other side is the belief that curriculum consists of an attempt to understand the present in terms of the interrelationship between complex historical and cultural factors, amounting to a version of nature/nurture. Any theory of curriculum that relies on preconceived ideas which correlate ability with race, class, and gender clearly takes a stance on the side of "blueprint." Curriculum is, in this conception, a means for treating deviations from the norm; at the same time as it accounts for the whole curve. Selden (1999) wrote that "the history of American Eugenics has more often than not been a history of the categorization of individuals and groups for the purpose of legitimizing a set of existing social, institutional, and political relations" (p. 85). Education shares that history, in part, because of the work of Bobbitt and other early education theorists.

Hall

G. Stanley Hall first came to prominence at the age of 37 with the publication in 1883 of his *The Content's of Children's Minds*. This, along with his subsequent appointment as full professor of pedagogy at Johns Hopkins and his "soaring reputation as a scientist" (Kliebard, 1990/1997, p. 37) led, in 1909, to his presidency of Clark University (where Bobbitt received his degree). Cremin (1961) claimed that the "link between Hall's general psychology and its application to pedagogy" lies in his belief that "ontogeny, the development of the individual organism, recapitulates phylogeny, the evolution of the race" (pp. 101–102). Redolent of nineteenth-century's "Great Chain of Being" theory, Hall's position on education "paved the way for some fundamental changes in American pedagogical opinion" (Cremin, 1988, p. 103). First, Hall's work shifted the definition of teaching to "meeting the needs" of the students, needs that were defined by then current conceptions of race, ability, and heredity. Next, Hall provided a new emphasis on the "scientific study of feelings, dispositions, and attitudes" (p. 104) which dovetailed nicely with Bobbitt's (1918) theory by supplying the information needed to assess the "habits, skills, abilities, forms of thought, valuations, ambitions" (p. 43) needed to construct an appropriate curriculum. "Most importantly," Cremin (1988) suggested, was the consequent shift in meaning of the notion of equal opportunity in education to an idea that established "the right of all who attended school to receive something of meaning and value" (p. 104). The merging of society's Progressive inclinations, where education was concerned, with definitions and forms of curriculum based on hierarchical ideology ensured the support of both the public and educational leaders.

Throughout the latter half of the nineteenth century, psychology became a popular subject pursued by men of means in top European universities. In particular, German psychologist Wilhelm Wundt trained a number of young Americans in experimental methodology, including Hall and James Cattell, who together created the field known as educational psychology. Educational psychology was distinguished from child study and pedagogy by its focus on mental testing. Wundt's reliance on biological assumptions caused him to emphasize physiology and the experimental method in his research and teachings. This emphasis deeply influenced American social science by providing psychological thought with a foundation of Darwinian premises, evidenced particularly in the work of a generation of early social theorists including Hall, Cattell, William James, Franz Boas, and John Dewey (Pickens, 1968). By 1914, American psychology was a well-defined discipline with clear cut fields. The philosophy of William James and the prolific work of G. Stanley Hall were instrumental in the popularity of instinct psychology.

Along with Thorndike, Hall was a leader in American educational psychology. Despite what Curti calls his "impressionistic" and "often self-contradictory" writings, Hall's 14 books and over 350 published papers put forth a clear and consistent social philosophy (Curti, 1959). Little wonder that three of the four best known of Hall's students, Cattell, Goddard, and Terman, spent their careers as strong advocates of eugenics (Selden, 1999). Dewey was the lone dissenter. For Hall, the primary role of education was to be a mediating influence between the individual and the institution. Hall adhered strongly to evolutionary theory which kept him from regarding education as anything more than ameliorative. Writing about the "faults, lies and crimes" of youth, Hall (1906) identified the source of degeneracy. Attesting to the power of collective memory to transport base assumptions from one group of people to another over time Hall wrote that "the vagrant, itinerate, vagabond, gadabout, hobo, and tramp, is an arrested, degenerate, or perverted being who abhors work [and] feels that the world owes him a living" (p. 125). Continual references to the drain on society incurred by non-superior peoples has appeared throughout the past century.

In addition to its mediating influence, Hall believed education should take seriously its role in preventing the repression of feelings, moods, and impulses that represent the stage of development of the race being recapitulated by the child. Were education to repress the natural instincts of the child, Hall contended, they would likely surface in adulthood in anti-social and illegal behavior. Hall believed that "almost the only duty of small children is habitual and prompt obedience" (p. 207). For Hall, the real goal of the self-knowledge afforded by not repressing feelings, moods, and impulses was

> [t]o bring the richest streams of thought to bear in interpreting the ethical instincts, so that the youth shall cease to live in moral interregnum. (p. 208)

Child-centeredness, as it has come to be known, actually originated as a way to access the inherited, highly variable, natural inclinations displayed by children in order to insert the "richest streams of thought" possessed by professional educators, psychologists, and social theorists. The 1912 textbook *Introductory Educational Psychology: A Book for Teachers in Training* averred that "the work of the educator is to utilize the materials at his disposal in such a way that the mental and spiritual changes in the developing child will all tend to the production of the highest type of socialized individual" (Sinclair, 1912, p. 9). Again, it is the production of socially acceptable individuals that education is concerned with; an "uplifting" of sorts from the "moral interregnum" of base instinct.

Goddard

During the 1920s, educational psychologists claimed that through testing they could understand the structure of personality, learning, motivation, emotion, individual heredity, and environment. At the same time, the promise of scientific vindication from aristocratic monopolization of resource and power, a common theme during the Progressive era, was applied to education. Henry Herbert Goddard, a student of G. Stanley Hall, was the first American psychologist to recognize the potential of intelligence testing for furthering eugenic ideals. Goddard first entered the public eye with the publication of his book *The Kallikaks* in 1912 wherein he traced the progeny, as discussed previously, of a union between a misguided revolutionary soldier and a feebleminded barmaid. Goddard's book was immensely popular and used in educational psychology classrooms for decades after its publication (Selden, 1999). In order to test his hunch regarding the usefulness of mental testing for the eugenic cause, in 1912 Goddard visited Ellis Island to administer his newly revised Binet intelligence tests to immigrants hoping for entry into the United States. The tests, according to Goddard's interpretation, proved the inferiority of Jews, Italians, Hungarians, Poles, Russians, and others with blood "known" to be inferior. The tests were used as a tangible measure for declaring certain immigrants ineligible to enter the United States (Chase, 1975).

Goddard is also famous for his revision of the Binet test and in particular for his system of classification which gave a mental-age value to imbeciles, morons, and idiots. Goddard's ideas appealed to the public because for the first time there seemed to be evidence that connected hereditary determinism with mental ability. The possibility that mental capacity could be preserved "as long as any given strain is kept pure" (p. 89) did much to bolster public acceptance of mandatory sterilization laws and fear of cross-breeding among races (Pickens, 1968). Popular on the lecture circuit, Goddard continually warned the public about the "rising tide of feeblemindedness," a warning that was commonly repeated throughout the press. Differences in children required different educational responses, Goddard (1924) wrote, and

the school must not lose sight of the fact that the making of good citizens is accomplished more successfully by teaching children to control their natural tendency to steal and to lie than by teaching them to read and write. (p. 174)

The greatest threat to society, according to Goddard and repeated in the press, was the "high grade", or "moron" type of feeblemind because although they were unfit to reproduce, they nevertheless were able to function in society and thus were a threat to the gene pool.

> Here we have a group who, when children in school, cannot learn the things that are given them to learn, because through their mental defect, they are incapable of mastering abstractions. They never learn to read sufficiently well to make reading pleasurable or of practical use to them. Under our present compulsory school system and our present course of study, we compel these children . . . and thus they worry along through a few grades until they are fourteen and then leave school, not having learned anything of value or that can help them to make even a meager living in the world. (Goddard, 1912, p. 16)

Thus was the central dogma of eugenics, that "poverty and its pathologies, like affluence and its comforts, were in the blood—and not in the environment in which human beings were conceived, born, and developed" (Chase, 1975, p. 149). What eugenicists really needed, in order to continue to guide the human race towards purity and high levels of intelligence, was a scientific way to establish difference, the provision of divergent paths for students that have different abilities, and the support of the public in doing so.

It has been accepted dogma in the United States since the 1920s that intelligence is congenital and unchanging (Gould, 1996). By connecting intelligence with heredity, the Binet testing scale ensured that education policy would be based on a philosophy of biological determinism. In 1897, and again in 1917, psychologists using intelligence testing found that African Americans lacked higher powers of intelligence and concluded that providing them with industrial rather than literary education was the fair and just thing to do because it met the innate qualities of the individual. This policy enabled the public to feel positive about advocating the themes of Progressive education, an approach ostensibly designed to meet the innate needs and interests of the child, while at the same time providing the legacy of nineteenth-century racism with scientific and public support. In other words, nineteenth-century racism was validated by twentieth-century science.

Charters

We have seen that, during the first three decades of the twentieth century, popular eugenics was supported by a cadre of well-known members of American society. Under the leadership of men like Charles Davenport and Harry Laughlin, the eugenics movement held enormous sway over a well-integrated set of national orga-nizations. Selden (1999) revealed that leading American educator W. W. Charters, and colleagues Leta Hollingworth and E. L. Thorndike, actively participated in the race betterment conferences and eugenic congresses and lent their names and prestige to the furthering of eugenic causes in general. Little surprise then that, like the curriculum theorists we have already discussed, Charters too carried the ideology into his conception of curriculum.

By 1924, the work of Bobbitt, Hall, and Thorndike had established curriculum as a legitimate field of inquiry (Curti, 1935/1959; Tyack, 1974, 1982; Kliebard, 1975/ 1997, 1986/1995; Pinar, 1995; Selden, 1999). Curriculum theorists successfully rede-fined the purpose of education from the acquisition of comprehensive knowledge towards a concern with societal and individual usefulness. Pinar (1995) characterized the work of these early curricularists as part of the *developmentalist* phase of theoriz-ing, a phase which extended until roughly 1980 when it was supplanted by the *recon-ceptualists*. "There was little sense," Pinar (1995) wrote of the developmentalists, "of developing a field devoted to accumulation of knowledge [or] to the enhancement of understanding" (p. 15). Instead, these theorists directed their writing specifically to elementary and secondary teachers emphasizing the improvement of skills, actions, and results over understanding and inquiry. Charters, a student of Dewey and rep-resentative of "a major statement of the social efficiency educators" (p. 100), was instrumental in completing the transformation of the curriculum being enacted by Bobbitt, Thorndike, and Hall. Charter's work in particular functioned to focus the curriculum away from content and towards the means to determine that content. This was, according to Pinar, "an important shift in curriculum theory that persists to this day" (1995, p. 101). An essential element to Charters' (1923) theory was his treat-ment of the aims of education.

The problem, according to Charters, was that while writers on the curriculum, including Plato, had successfully begun with a statement of the aim of education, they had failed to derive a curriculum logically from their stated aim. Charters (1923) quoted Plato's contention that "the man whose natural gifts promise to make him the perfect guardian of the state will be philosophical, high-spirited, swift-footed, and strong" (p. 7). Charters then proceeded to deride Plato for his "mental leap" (p. 7) that music and gymnastics would provide the training for the "ideal guardian" (Charters, 1923, p. 7). The fault lay in the fact that "their ideals [are] isolated from their aims" and, because "one fact is as virtuous as another, sub-ject matter cannot be derived from virtue as the aim of education" (p. 9). Instead, a *useful* curriculum was determined when the aims of education were stated "in terms both of ideals and of activities" (p. 11).

Arguing that the public schools had failed to progress along with science and the then current knowledge regarding the importance of individual activity and action, Charters claimed that in addition to the problem of aims, *ideals* themselves must be examined. Referring to the failure of education to accurately reflect current thinking, Charters (1923) wrote that as a result of this failure,

> the curriculum has been under the domination of the idea that the youth should be given a birds-eye view of the knowledge of the world rather than a compendium of useful information. (p. 4)

Given the common assessment of the American student body at the time, a reflection of the broader society in terms of race and ability, it is hardly surprising that Charters should take umbrage with the idea that the "richest streams of thought" (Hall, 1906, p. 208) would be handed over willy-nilly to a generation of morons and imbeciles. After all, Charters (1923) argued, "the inheritance handed down through the schools to the young is so massive that it can never be assimilated" (p. 5).

"The standards of our day," Charters (1923) concluded, demanded that "we should frankly accept usefulness as our aim rather than comprehensive knowledge" (p. 4). Charters developed a basic methodology for the construction of curriculum which he proceeded to apply to a wide variety of fields such as secretarial science, pharmacy, library science, veterinary medicine, and teacher training (Pinar, 1995). Further evidence of the extent of Charters' influence is the fact that he presided over a "number of lucrative consultancies" (p. 102) that provided states and school districts with curricular assessment and the means to "devise procedures by which curriculum could be developed scientifically" (p. 102). In 1860, Spencer asked the quintessential curriculum question "what knowledge is of most worth?" By the mid-1920s, that question had been transformed into a quest for the means to determine what should be taught and relied on popular conceptions of ability and race to determine those means.

8

Ability and Degeneracy in the Schools

"Rid your room of mental deficients" urged the opening sentence of an undated memorandum[1] from the North Carolina Teachers' Association (NCSA-DPI, n.d.). The memo, addressed to "Every Grade Teacher in North Carolina" continued:

> You owe it to the enormous majority of normal pupils. You owe it to the deficients who are entitled to special education. You owe it to the tax payers on whom these deficients, when adults, unless specially educated, will be a burden. Finally, you owe it to yourself. You can no more do your grade work properly with a deficient child in your room than you could do it were a blind or a deaf and dumb child put into it. For the protection of your own professional character, take the action which we urge. (NCSA-DPI, n.d., p. 1)

Like the eugenic rhetoric saturating the media in the surrounding society, this imperative by the North Carolina Teachers' Association casts the identification of deficients in light of civic, charitable, and personal duty. Confident that the request to identify deficiency in their classrooms would be greeted with relief, the memorandum stated "we need not add that there is even a distinct personal reward in the removal of a wholly unwarrantable wear and tear upon your nerves" (NCSA-DPI, n.d., p. 1) In the final paragraph, the executive committee explained that "the Superintendent of Public Instruction has appointed the undersigned sub-committee to get you to report with a view to helping you" (NCSA-DPI, n.d., p. 1). Signing off with a request that the teacher be "accurate and prompt" the memo attached the forms and information teachers would need to "rid their rooms of mental deficients."

The second page of the Teachers' Association memo tells teachers that what follows is meant to provide them with the means to decide whether "a case is unfit for education in the public schools" (NCSA-DPI, n.d., p. 2). Titled *Diagnosis for Mental Deficiency* the document provides credit as to the source followed by a 11-point list of the symptoms of deficiency. A supplement supplied to North Carolina Teachers for this purpose of identifying the "unfit" is credited to eugenic operator H. H. Goddard, the superintendent of the Vineland, New Jersey training school. The superintendent's expertise is established by the claim that he has "360 deficient children of both sexes under his care" (NCSA-DPI, n.d., p. 2), in the school where Carrie Buck, the 17-year-old rape victim, along with her mother and sister were forcibly sterilized (Gould, 1984).

The memo (NCSA-DPI, n.d., p. 2) requested that teachers "bear in mind that no one symptom is significant, unless excessively marked, while several strangly [*sic*] marked or many clearly marked are important, if taken in conjunction." The list is as follows:

1. Blinking, twitching of the mouth, squinting, nervous movements of the hands and feet.
2. Inco-ordination, especially irregularities of gait.
3. Spasms, fits, hysterical crying and laughing.
4. Cold and clammy hands and excessive pallor or blushing.
5. Drooling, especially if accompanied with sore mouth, ears, eyes.
6. Slight malformations of the cranium, eyes, ears, teeth, palate, and limbs.
7. Carelessness, indolence, inattention, unreliable memory, obstinacy and either passion or stolidness.
8. Incapacity for simple acts, e.g. to tie knots, button clothes, go up and down stairs properly, catch ball, etc.
9. Imperfections of speech, sight, hearing, etc.
10. Excessive exaggerations, falsehood, pilfering, and poor moral sense.
11. In ability to keep up studies, as shown by persistent excess of the child's age over the average age of his class. (NCSA-DPI, n.d., p. 2)

A telling list indeed, it is tempting to go through it point by point to examine the ways each can be explained by qualities other than mental deficiency, but I believe the list speaks for itself. This tool must have provided a fairly fine sieve through which to filter and sort students, but as we will see, by the 1950s, having found a new tool for the purpose, North Carolina was beyond such crude measurements for the identification of deficiency.

The final document in the three-page memo delivered to North Carolina teachers statewide is a double-sided form to be filled out and sent to the State Superintendent of Public Instruction (NCSA-DPI, n.d., p. 3/4). The form requests the numbers of boys and girls that fall into 14 categories. Item six asks for the number of students with defective speech. Item seven asks teachers to identify "number who are putting out their tongue [or] put it slightly to either side." Ever sensitive to the distastefulness of the task, in brackets, the memo allows that "if objectionable to teacher this question may be omitted." Teachers were asked to indicate the number of students who drooled, who could not follow a coin readily as it was moved from side to side or up and down, and who had a slovenly gait and twitching muscles (NCSA-DPI, n.d., p. 3).

This memorandum, sanctioned by the State Superintendent of Public Instruction and delivered to North Carolina's teachers via the State Teachers' Association provides clear evidence that eugenic ideology and imperative had entered the educational arena. Teachers and students were enlisted in the movement to eliminate the unfit, unhygienic, and deficient from schools. Reference is made in *Educational News* to resources provided by the federal and state boards of health including pamphlets and posters. The boards also recommend that students engage in debates and write essays on health and hygiene. By engaging students and teachers in activities devoted exclusively to the identification of difference must certainly have impacted collective memory. In a review of Selden's (1999) *Inheriting Shame*, geneticist and longtime documenter of the eugenics movement Elof Carlson (2001) commented on Selden's discussion of eugenics propaganda used in classrooms saying "I well remember those illustrations and cautionary tales from my own childhood, reading my assigned texts in New York City classrooms" (p. 407). So ubiquitous had eugenic rhetoric become that no citizen in America was immune from some exposure.

During the summer of 1933, a flurry of correspondence occurred[2] regarding the role of education and the responsibility of taxpayers therein (NCSA-DPI, 1934). These letter writers included the State Superintendent of Public Instruction, the Honorable A. T. Allen, and various community leaders. After the end of the civil war, a movement in North Carolina to "segregate Negro taxes for Negro schools was pressed for two generations" (Paul, 1954, p. 18). In 1869 a public school law that provided for a uniform school system for "both" races was passed, but the debate continued. In a letter dated July 12, 1933, addressed to Superintendent Allen, H. G. Connor of Wilson, North Carolina, speculated about the state of public education and queried, "Why the public schools anyway?" (NCSA-DPI, 1934). The schools were "under severe fire from all sides" and, Connor explained, "the leaders of Education and I do not classify teachers as exclusively the leaders" of the uprising. The problem, according to Connor, was that everyone had lost sight of the fact that schools were there to serve children, who had the right to expect the best.

On July 25, 1933, Superintendent Allen responded to Connor with his own vision of the purpose of public schools. Allen wrote:

> I have never been one who conceived of the public school as a great mill grinding out people exactly alike in every particular [and while] this doctrine does not leave any room for stratification on the basis of birth and wealth . . . it does make provision for much stratification as may occur on the basis of merit, worth or industry. (NCSA-DPI, 1934)

Allen then brought up the subject of vocational education and urged an expansion of the scope of education. "We hear on every side," Allen wrote, "that there is too much education offered; that the educational opportunity offered now is far and away beyond the needs of our great population" (NCSA-DPI, 1934). Mirroring the recommendations of Bobbitt and other educational leaders of the time Allen wonders, "is that so, or is the trouble with the kind of education?" (NCSA-DPI, 1934).

Allen sent copies of his correspondence to Durham business leader J. O. Carr requesting his ideas on the subject (NCSA-DPI, 1934). Carr responded on July 29, 1933, saying that he had discussed the matter with the governor and both were in agreement that "no man [Allen] in public life today . . . has rendered a greater public service and who now occupies as trying position as you in connection with the school system" (NCSA-DPI, 1934). In an unusual display of personal angst Carr continued:

> The truth about it is the matter is so distressing that we are all endeavoring to go along without mentioning the depressing side of it. Still, there is something wrong, and radically wrong, but probably not more so with the schools system than with our changed method of living. (NCSA-DPI, 1934)

Apparently, some in North Carolina were still smarting from emancipation and later proclamations of equality issued by the federal government. Carr continued by explaining that, based on his practice before an election of "going to sundry barber shops," "sentiment in favor of public schools is in danger of collapse, especially among those who have to support them" (NCSA-DPI, 1934). The public was "bitterly opposed," to a proposed fifteen cent supplemental education tax and believed that "giving education beyond the elementary grades [was] a mistake" (NCSA-DPI, 1934). Carr concludes that the real antagonism to the schools was rooted in the tax burden, and thus it arose not so much from business interests "as from the small and more numerous taxpayer" (NCSA-DPI, 1934). We can see that public concern regarding education was high and also that there was a great deal of public discourse on the subject.

Other writers concurred with Carr's assessment such as Duke Professor A. M. Proctor who said in his August 29, 1933, letter to Superintendent Allen:

> We do not need to re-sell the principle of universal education [but] of course there are individuals, as there have always been, who are aristocrats at heart and who believe that the working class must be kept in their place and there are other individuals among the working class who believe in a sort of predestination and who look forward to only a hand to mouth existence who do not care for educational advantages for their children. (NCSA-DPI, 1934)

These are the people, he concluded, who are responsible for defeating the special tax elections. The reference to a belief in "predestination" on the part of members of the working class is interesting for its suggestion of a public acceptance of a eugenic analysis of worth and ability. That the controversy extended across traditional class lines goes to the heart of my argument that the integration of eugenic ideology was as successful as it was because of the unique spin eugenicists were able to create that allowed adherence to eugenic imperatives to coincide with notions of civic duty.

It must be noted that Superintendent Allen was a deeply thoughtful and earnest contributor to the dialogue with these members of the public. Although his ideas and recommendations were at times in line with prevailing eugenic recommendations such as an emphasis on vocational education, he was hesitant about it, writing that

> I should like to see vocational education delayed as long as possible so that the child will get acquainted with the world in which he lives before he is called upon to make a selection of his life's work. (NCSA-DPI, 1934)

He believed in self determination and a move away from "blind conformity to existing conditions" (NCSA-DPI, 1934). In another letter responding to school teacher Mrs. W. C. Taylor, Allen stated his reservations in even stronger tones. "If I understand the philosophy of your letter," he wrote,

> You would go back to training people for different vocations, fix them in a groove from which they could not escape, and compel them, on account of birth or on account of limited training provided in youth, to go down that groove from the cradle to the grave without hope of better conditions or better training. It seems to me that in this new civilization of ours that we need more initiative and more power of determination than we now have rather than less of it. (NCSA-DPI, 1934)

Two years later, "race relations" had become part of the vernacular in education, vocation was still a popular topic and under the rubric of improving relations among the races plans were being made.

In the mid-morning of May 20, 1935, on the third floor of the alumni building at the University of North Carolina in Chapel Hill, a meeting convened[3] to assess the state of race relations in education in North Carolina. Members of this committee of the *Conference of the Division of Cooperation in Education and Race Relations* (NCSA-DPI, 1935) included N. C. Newbold, of the North Carolina Department of Public Instruction, numerous Drs, and president Few of Duke University. Presiding over the meeting, Dr. Howard Odum, member of the North Carolina Human Betterment League (SHC-HBL), offered some opening remarks. Odum expressed concern that "inequalities are actually increasing in the present period of economic and social stress." Odum expressed the opinion that

> America is the most nearly perfect laboratory of cultural evolution [given that] there are more Negroes at the present time in this country than there were people in the United States under Jefferson. The Negro population affords a striking example of maladjustment. Mass power of emotion will grow unless ways for closing gaps are discovered. (NCSA-DPI, 1935)

For Odum, the problem was not the "gaps" themselves, which, after all, provided evidence from the laboratory that was America, but the threat of the "mass power of emotion" (NCSA-DPI, 1935). The conference then, would focus on the provision of "practical, tangible, workable, ways for bridging gaps" (NCSA-DPI, 1935).

We might imagine this group of doctors sitting around a large conference table, on the third floor of the alumni building. Each participant would stand while speaking their part, after having acknowledged his predecessor's comments. So it was when Newbold stood, "thanked Dr. Odum for his excellent statement," (NCSA-DPI, 1935) and expressed his confidence that the division would "achieve worthwhile results in light of its purposes" (NCSA-DPI, 1935). Many speakers rose and provided suggestions which included the sharing of textbooks from year to year, and requesting copies of theses and books "by or about the Negro" to be sent to the division (NCSA-DPI, 1935). The subject of "in-state Negro members" of the committee arose and it was suggested that they should form their own separate committee "in order to insure the complete participation of Negroes in the project" (NCSA-DPI, 1935). We cannot know why Newbold "gave assent to this suggestion without hesitation" or even whether this was an attempt at exclusion or motivated by the spirit of inclusion. However, given the previous remarks concerning "Negroes" in America it seems likely that it was the former. Further evidence of this is suggested by Dr. Trigg's list of suggested problems that might be "studied by the Division in their relation to the Negro" (NCSA-DPI, 1935). The first suggestion is to study retardation in the primary grades of the public school. The problem is that "in some situations as much as 64% of the total school enrollment is on the first three grades" which mirrors the estimates provided by eugenic literature (NCSA-DPI, 1935). Second on the list is

> Curriculum adaptations. A study of the extent to which the present curriculum is adapted to the local interests, aptitudes and needs of the Negro population should prove helpful for the total school situation. (NCSA-DPI, 1935)

Bobbitt's, 1918 suggestions had apparently become the general conception of how schools could best provide for racial and social difference. The adaptation of this curriculum meant, as we have seen, that the inclusion of vocational education and the provision of more opportunities that were devised to match the aptitude of the masses of morons and imbeciles. Interestingly, the third suggestion deviates from conventional eugenic thought while preserving its language in its call for "the discovery, nourishment, and preservation of racial genius" (NCSA-DPI, 1935). A study to discover "any racial genius peculiar to the Negro" suggests an acknowledgment of the existence of non-white "genius" but one must wonder at the addition of the word "peculiar" given the overarching tone of the time (NCSA-DPI, 1935).

In any event, a glance through the Division of Instructional Services January 1936 version of the fifth grade *Introduction to American History* curriculum[4] shows that school curriculum continued to reflect a romantic view of African Americans (NCSA-DPI, 1935, v22). When reading Unit VI, titled *North Carolina Blighted by the Civil War*, one must wonder at the impact of those 1921 letter writers opposed to a history text that shed the south in a less than admiring light. Under the question "What were the major problems?" the curriculum lists "Civil Rights Bill, 14th Amendment, and Negro" (NCSA-DPI, 1935, v2). Lest one wonder about possible alternative explanations for listing these items as "problems," under the "Suggested Activities" column the recommendation is to "promote appreciation of deeds of forefathers; faithfulness of Negroes; and heroism of N.C. women" (NCSA-DPI, 1935, v3). Finally, Unit VII, *North Carolina's Return to Prosperity since 1900* urges teachers to show "how the new generation began to manage State governmental affairs, eliminating the Negro from politics." Exactly what this curricular objective refers to is unclear, but the tone is not unclear.

African Americans were subject to a distinctly biased representation in the common language of education in the mid-1930s. A letter dated January 21,

1936, from the Supervisor of Elementary Schools P. L. Byrd and addressed "Dear Co-worker," Byrd announced a new program initiated by the state's "Interracial Commission" (NCSA-DPI, 1935 v3). The program institutes "penny day" at high schools throughout the state with proceeds to go towards "interracial work." The letter requested that local superintendents urge their schools to participate and stated that participating counties would not be published because "we would like to have one hundred percent if possible" (NCSA-DPI, 1935 v3). The letter cited the added benefit that "the children will learn about the work of the Interracial Commission" (NCSA-DPI, 1935 v3). The linking of non-white races with charity was doubtless not lost on the state's high school students given that racial strife was so often expressed by the public and in the media in terms of tax burden.

Seminal educational leader and historian Elwood Cubberley (1934) wrote about the influence of the "foreign born" on education. "These Southern and Eastern Europeans," Cubberley explained,

> [w]ere of a very different type from the North and West Europeans who preceded them. Largely illiterate, docile, often lacking in initiative, and almost wholly without the Anglo-Saxon conceptions of righteousness, liberty, law, order, public decency, and government, their coming has served to dilute our national stock and to weaken and corrupt our political life . . . popular education everywhere has been made more difficult by their presence. (1934, p. 485)

It is clear indication of the entrenchment of racist, eugenicist ideology, I argue, that Cubberley is referenced so extensively (see, e.g., Curti, 1935/1959; Kliebard, 1986/1995; Pinar, 1995) with no mention of his definitive bias. Claiming that "our national life, for the past quarter of a century, has been afflicted with a serious case of racial indigestion" (p. 486), Cubberley explained that World War I had "opened the eyes of our people to the danger of having groups of non-assimilated peoples living among us" and that "the schools have proved to be our greatest agency for unifying diverse elements of our population" (p. 489). Although "Americanization" was a popular theme, it was not the only tack taken by education leaders. Sorting, testing, defining, and categorizing were all important functions of education as well.

Ability

While degeneracy was a major concern of eugenicists and educators alike, so too was the plight of the "gifted," vulnerable to the degenerative influence of their peers on all fronts. Like Hollingworth, Hall too was especially concerned with the gifted child, and felt that current "mass methods" of schooling were especially harmful to them. Hall was a proponent of industrial training in schools and justified the aims of such training by means of his belief that class distinctions corresponded to individual differences in capacity (1909). In order to achieve this definition of individualization Hall argued for the improvement of the economic and professional status of teachers, emphasized the provision of a proper education for the gifted child, de-emphasized special education for the non-gifted, and advocated a popularization of curriculum in order to foster child "interest."

Though she differed from Hall in her express disregard for the feebleminded, Leta S. Hollingworth, considered to be one of America's leading researchers and advocates for gifted education, enthusiastically took up the cause of eugenics in her work (Hollingworth, 1929). Hollingworth strongly believed Galton's original contention that gifted and superior persons reflected a natural meritocracy. The October 1929 issue of the journal *Eugenics* features an article by Hollingworth titled *The Production of Gifted Children from the Parental Point of View* in which she argued that "potential parents of the gifted are probably above average in susceptibility to appeals in favor of the common welfare" (p. 7) and that therefore as much research as possible "tending to establish beyond argument" (p. 7) the need for more gifted children would be instrumental in convincing the superior to procreate. Using the "evidence" of the Stanford-Binet mental tests Hollingworth declared that much had been learned about the "gifted child":

1) the great majority of the gifted originate in families where the fathers are professional men or business executives, including proprietors;

2) very few gifted children originate from fathers in semi-skilled manual trades or in unskilled labor;

3) gifted children existing within the period since mental tests have been available have very few siblings, the average being about one brother or sister each. (Hollingworth, 1929, p. 7)

Like Galton, Hollingworth (1929) expressed deep concern that those persons in society who are most capable of producing superior children "do so with relative infrequency" (p. 3). In what I argue has turned out to be prophetic for education in America, Hollingworth expressed the opinion that it was not "health and economic security" (p. 5) that would "prompt the more learned" (p. 5) to contemplate parenthood, but refers instead to the college student of "recent decades [who is] likely to have assimilated the biological facts about the regression of offspring" (p. 5). That Hollingworth specifically names the "assimilation" by college student of principles of heredity that would lead them to the conclusion that "selfish interests should be sacrificed for the good of the next generation" (p. 6) illuminates the eugenicist contention that eugenic progress could be realized through education.

Hollingworth (1929) connoted that for many women, maternity, especially repeated maternity, was incompatible with "the strong, inherent drive" (p. 6) to satisfy intellectual curiosity experienced by highly intelligent persons. What could be done for these wayward women? After all, " 'Tut! Tut!' spoken sternly, no longer affects them" (p. 6). According to Hollingworth, "They are affected by the teachings of mental hygiene" (p. 6), along with the lesson that sanity is defined by one's conviction to be "fair to one's self as well as to others" (p. 6). This is no small matter for Hollingworth. "Here arises the question," she wrote, "of who is to live *intellectually* and *morally*, as well as physically" (1929, p. 6; emphasis in original). Herein lies the ultimate imperative of eugenic ideology, written in the context of gifted education, by a woman who is recognized to this day as a leader and founder of a very active and vibrant focus of education in the twenty-first century.

Questioning the Rhetoric

Despite the seemingly near universal consensus among social leaders of the period, dissent did exist in both direct and indirect forms. African American historian and cultural theorist (and father of 1960s activist Julian Bond) Horace Mann Bond (1927) saw education as reproductive of the status quo. In a scathing article decrying the abuse and misuse of testing in American education Bond wrote that

> ever since the "measurement of minds" became a popular field in which to pursue investigations, the testing of Negro children has easily ranked as a major indoor sport among psychologists . . . The rules of the game are simple and seem to be standardized throughout the country with but few exceptions. First one must have a *White* examiner; a group of *Negro* children; a test standardized for *White* children tested by *White* examiners; and just a few pre-conceived notions regarding the nature of "intelligence" and the degree to which Negro children are endowed, if at all . . . and the *fact* that the social status of Negro children need not be considered as an extra allowance for scores different from Whites. (p. 257; emphasis in original)

Bond was clear that the intent behind the increasing use of tests to determine ability belied a deeper racist imperative. He ridiculed the claim of fairness so often uttered by proponents of testing by pointing out that the mere "removal" of social implications from consideration in the determination of ability did not by default make the tests fair. "Only one conclusion is to be drawn," Bond wrote,

> if Negro children make lower scores than White, they are inferior, they were born that way and though we had a sneaking suspicion that this was the fact all along,

we are now able to fortify our prejudices with a vast array of statistical tables, bewildering vistas of curves and ranges and distributions and the other cabalistic phrases with which we clothe the sacred profession of Psychology from the view of the profane public. (p. 257)

The sheer volume of tables, graphs, and charts used by eugenicists, and subsequently by educators, to illustrate the validity of their claims played a significant role in the incorporation of eugenic ideology into the popular mindset.

Bond (1927) then focused on the results of his own tests, conducted on 30 "Negro children from laborer-class homes, professional homes, and middle-class homes" and using "the original Binet-Simon, in the revised form produced by Lewis Terman" (p. 258). Contrary to Terman's prediction that only 5% of white children could be expected to equal or exceed an IQ of 122, Bond found that fully 47% of his group exceeded that score. Bond claimed that most white psychologists reported "the average I.Q. of Negro children as falling about 85, placing the race on the border-line between extreme dullness and the moron class." What Bond has articulated is the degree to which social efficiency educators, using mental testing as a device, succeeded in redirecting the implicit definition of schooling. The deeply embedded American notion that schooling represented the promise of social uplift did not change, rather the definition of social uplift was redefined to apply only to the "fittest" members of society. Such was the accidental genius of eugenic ideology that it was able to preserve, and tap in to, previously existing definitions of opportunity and freedom and the commensurate role of education, and use those definitions to support its own, significantly narrowed, definitions.

Bond's scathing dissent notwithstanding, the scales were overwhelmingly tipped in favor of eugenically defined approaches to education. Eugenic ideology had made its way into the curriculum and definitions of the purpose of schooling and was even taught directly in a significant portion of school biology texts, school health policies and practices, and policy mandates. Selden's (1999) quantitative analysis of the appearance of eugenics in high school biology textbooks between 1914 and 1948 showed that 87% of high school and college textbooks offered eugenics as a topic. More than 70% recommended eugenics as a legitimate science. As examples of how inferior blood runs in families, the Kallikak and Juke families were cited in nearly 60% of textbooks as were the theories of Davenport, Galton, Goddard, Wiggam, and Popenoe and Johnson (Selden, 1999). Selden's qualitative analysis of the eugenic content of these texts showed that eugenic ideology was often presented within the context of anticipating a brighter future.

We may surmise that this trend stemmed from arguments of many eugenic leaders (Galton, 1889, 1901, 1914; Thorndike, 1903, 1931; Shannon, 1904/1915; Hall, 1906; Bobbitt, 1909; Pearson, 1909, 1919; Davenport, 1910, 1911; Davenport, Laughlin et al., 1911; Goddard, 1911, 1912, 1916, 1921; Hall, 1911; Grant, 1916; Stopes, 1918/1931; Stoddard, 1920, 1922; Sanger, 1922; Wiggam, 1924; Jefferis, 1925; Sumner, Keller et al., 1927; Davenport and Steggerda, 1929; Hollingworth, 1929; Bell, 1933; Holmes, 1936) regarding the need to convince the younger generation of the import of eugenically sound marriages. According to Selden, students were presented with three possible trajectories for their lives: excellence, competence, or institutionalization. Which direction they went depended on the attention they paid to diligence, hard work, and the betterment of the human condition. The fact that subsequent generations of educational policy makers have so enthusiastically embraced mechanisms of measurement (testing and dependence on IQ), techniques of tracking and sorting (high school tracks, gifted and talented programs), and forms of content presentation (curriculum) that have their conceptual roots in eugenic ideology suggests that the aim of passing the imperative on to the younger generation was successful.

Though their hopes never did materialize, 1932 was, according to Pinar (1995), "the best year Progressive education ever enjoyed" (p. 126). This was the year that George Counts published his famous pamphlet *Dare the Schools Build a New Social Order?* This was, according to Pinar (1995), a "call to arms [and] reactions ranged from 'inspiring!' [and] 'stirring!' [to] 'impractical' [and] 'un-American' " (p. 127). It was a decisive moment for the future of educational policy because "Counts split the Progressive movement beyond reconciliation, and this polarization began the slow erosion and ultimate demise" of progressivism in America (p. 127). John Dewey, who of course had been on the scene since the 1890s, and had provided articulate and memorable opposition to the social efficiency movement and scientific curriculum makers for more than 30 years, responded in 1933 to Counts by recommending the idea that teachers had an "obligation to search for solutions to social problems and that the focus of teacher inquiry should be local" (Pinar, 1995, p. 127). While his language was characteristically calmer than Counts, Dewey agreed with him that schools could and should "function to change society" (p. 128).

Pinar (1995) calls Progressive scholars like Dewey and Counts "authentic social radicals who expressed a deep commitment to social planning and, among other issues, public ownership of the means of production" (p. 129). Kliebard (1995), on the other hand, wants us to know that the "educational theory Dewey so painstakingly developed during his Chicago years was either turned into a pitiful caricature . . . or neglected altogether" (p. 27) and that in fact, despite his well-deserved worldwide recognition, "his actual influence on the schools of the nation has been seriously overestimated or grossly distorted" (p. 27).

Nevertheless, Dewey's ideas hail from within the same context as those of Hall, Goddard, Hollingworth, and Thorndike, and therefore they have the potential to speak a truth that the nation has yet to hear. According to Selden (1999), while there is no direct reference to eugenics in Dewey's work, "this does not suggest his tacit acceptance of its goals or purposes" (p. 113). Having done a search of "the corpus of [Dewey's] work," Selden found that Dewey's philosophy differed significantly from his eugenically inclined colleagues. Dewey did not believe in the use of mental tests for classification. Nor did he distrust democracy or long for "a biologically determined intellectual aristocracy" (p. 113). Finally, Dewey rejected the common belief in the hierarchical worth of the different races and "used his broad understanding of science to buttress that position" (p. 113). Dewey's, 1922 article *Mediocrity and Individuality* showed that his disapproval of the classification of students through the use of mental tests was total. Such classifications would

> postpone the day of a reform of education which will get us away from inferior, mean, and superior mediocrities so as to deal with individualized mind and character. (Dewey, 1922, p. 35)

Dewey did not reject mental testing wholesale, but believed in its use for diagnostic purposes only, and furthermore, he disapproved of the trend towards vocational education as a way to channel students:

> Barring complete imbecility, it is safe to say that the most limited member of the populace has potentialities which do not now reveal themselves and which will not reveal themselves till we convert education by and for mediocrity into an education by and for individuality. (1922, p. 37)

Dewey names the great tragedy of vocational education. It is not the fact of it that rankles, but rather the motivation behind its introduction as a channel of "mediocrity."

Transitioning into the Modern Era

The following section traces the developments in education leading up to, and including, the 1954 Supreme Court decision *Brown v. Board of Education,* and the federal mandate to desegregate the nation's public schools. The reason I have chosen to include this era in my research is that in the case of eugenic ideology, North Carolina was somewhat of a special case. While the majority of states that had passed mandatory sterilization laws had removed them by the end of World War II, due to the actions of Hitler and the horror of the Holocaust (Kevles, 1985), North Carolina was just gearing up. Records show that over 80% of the sterilization in North Carolina occurred after World War II and, in fact, the North Carolina Eugenics Board was in full operation until 1974. Given the level of severe public anger and resentment that occurred during the mid-to-late 1930s, it is hardly surprising that the 1954 Supreme Court decision caused something of an uproar. I do not make any claim to offering a comprehensive history of either education or eugenics in North Carolina. Nor do I do justice to the immensely complex impact of *Brown v. Board of Education*[5] on education both nationally and in North Carolina. Instead, I reach forward into the 1950s in order to provide evidence of the persistence of eugenic ideology within education.

Developments in Education

While America became an active participant in World War II, on December 8, 1941, the actual "course that the American curriculum had been taking over the previous half-century was not so much significantly altered as accelerated" (Kliebard, 1995, p. 205). The role of schools became conjoined with the war effort. In order to contrast the democratic way of life to "that of our totalitarian enemies," Kliebard (1995) wrote that

> youth must participate in scrap metal and paper collection drives, Red Cross work, and receive training in first aid. Schools must also do what they can to counteract the wartime propaganda directed at people of German, Italian, and Japanese descent, and the contributions of different racial and cultural groups should be emphasized. (p. 205)

Though the Eight-Year Study was one of the "most ambitious of the efforts to stimulate education reform at the local level," the results were "something of an anticlimax" and furthermore, because the framers of the study "specifically declined to promote any particular curriculum ideology . . . they wound up at least partially supporting them all" (Kliebard, 1995, p. 182). The purpose of the study was to resolve the criticism that school reform was being hampered by college entrance requirements and so an agreement was reached whereby students from participant schools would be accepted and tracked outside the normal system (Kliebard, 1995). The actual content of the curricular changes that took place in the participating schools "had strong social efficiency overtones" (p. 187) and indeed, according to Kliebard one of the most abiding outcomes of the study, the notion of core curriculum, actually "emerged as a fusion of the social efficiency concern that the schools prepare directly and specifically for the duties of life" (p. 187). In other words, the proponents of social efficiency who argued that "to teach history, algebra, and foreign languages to people who would never use them was an inexcusable waste" were able to gain access to school curriculum "under the aegis of the Eight-Year-Study" (p. 187).

Another reason the Eight-Year Study is relevant to this inquiry is that it is here that Ralph Tyler made his first significant entry onto the educational scene. Although Kliebard reported that Tyler was brought in as the director of research for the study (1995, p. 183), Pinar claimed that this is a common misconception and that he was actually the director of research for the evaluation staff (Pinar, 1995, p. 136). Regardless of his role though, Tyler would become "the single most visible name in American curriculum studies" (Pinar, 1995, p. 136). The impact of the study was somewhat lost due to the onset of World War II, but the stage was set for the re-establishment of scientific curriculum as the prevailing method within school practice.

Scientific Curriculum 1946–1965

As I have suggested, scientific curriculum went into something of a slump during the 1930s and the Progressive movement found an opportunity to exert considerable influence but in actuality, "the chaos that surrounded what was called Progressive education increasingly made it an easy target for criticism" (Kliebard, 1995, p. 195). Pinar (1995) summed up the situation thusly,

> World War II functioned to erase Progressivism's influence, and the post war era began with the partial reappearance of social efficiency, this time in the guise of "life adjustment" education. (p. 151)

Life adjustment education was formed out of the decline of Progressive education and its inability to answer America's new calling for functionality in education due to the war effort. Life adjustment education was primarily focused on secondary education and called for a curriculum that, like Bobbitt's model, provided a preparation for all areas of living that students would need as they entered into adulthood

(Kliebard, 1995). However, "the life-adjustment movement would prove to be short-lived," because shortly thereafter, "the functionality of social efficiency asserted itself simply and forcefully in the Tyler Rationale" (Pinar, 1995, p. 151).

Pinar (1995) characterized the impact of Tyler by saying that he "crystallized a half-century of curriculum development thought in one thin book which sold over 85,000 copies during 36 printings and was translated into seven foreign languages" (p. 149). Elsewhere, he described it as "the single most influential curriculum text ever written" (p. 148). Let us now go into the content of what Tyler contributed in order to fully understand how and why scientific curriculum has persisted into twenty-first-century American curriculum.

Tyler's enormously influential book *Basic Principles of Curriculum and Instruction* (1949) is perhaps most memorable for its brevity and simplicity. The entire book, derived from a course syllabus he used at the University of Chicago, consists of Tyler's answer to four questions which are also the chapter headings in his book:

1. What educational purposes should the school seek to attain? [Objectives]
2. What educational experiences can be provided that are likely to attain these purposes? [Design]
3. How can these educational experiences be effectively organized? [Scope and Sequence]
4. How can we determine whether these purposes are being attained? [Evaluation]. (Tyler, 1949)

In a number of ways, Tyler's work continued and reaffirmed Bobbitt's (1918) conception of the function of curriculum. Both agreed that curriculum specialists should provide guidance for practice, conduct, and research on the content and evaluation of curriculum. Additionally, both sought to conduct empirical investigations that would provide curriculum with scientific basis (Pinar, 1995, p. 34). Apple (1997) described Tyler's book this way:

> Even with its avowed purpose of synthesizing nearly all that had gone on before, it was largely a behaviorally oriented, procedural model. It was of almost no help whatsoever in determining the difficult issues of whose knowledge should be taught and *who* should decide. It focused instead on the methodological steps one should go through in selecting, organizing, and evaluating the curriculum. (p. 345; emphasis in original)

Apple (1997) also noted that "one of the ultimate effects of Tyler's model, though perhaps not intentional, was the elimination of political and cultural conflict from the center of the curriculum debate" (p. 345). Thus, by diverting attention from the political debate inherent in Spencer's classic question "what knowledge is of most worth," and by posing their question in this way, scientific curriculum makers were "determining the kind of answer that could be given," an answer that "is likely to be phrased in terms of functional utility rather than in terms of intellectual virtues. In this sense, the curriculum became the ultimate survival kit for the modern world" (Kliebard, 1975/1997, p. 35).

Cremin (1988) explained that

> It was the Supreme Court, however, that most effectively placed the federal government on the side of desegregation, with the unanimous *Brown* decisions of 1954 and 1955. Not surprisingly, those rulings were greeted by a storm of opposition in the South. Less than two months after *Brown I* was handed down in May 1954, the first White Citizens' Council was organized in Indianola, Mississippi, for the express purpose of preventing the "mongrelization" of the Caucasian race. (p. 259)

Needless to say, North Carolina was not immune to this reaction and, as we will see, while the nation's highest court reflected a more modern interpretation of race and schools, North Carolina most certainly did not.

The Legacy: Race and Education

In order to illustrate the extent of the distress caused in North Carolina by the 1954 Brown decision, this section will draw from two primary sources. The first is titled *A Report to the Governor of North Carolina on the Decision of the Supreme Court of the United States on the 17th of May, 1954* and was written by the director of the Institute of Government at the University of North Carolina Chapel Hill, Albert Coates (Coates, 1954). Part I of the 206-page report to the governor provided a detailed history of education in North Carolina written by Albert Coates, director of the Institute. Part II is comprised of the text of the Supreme Court decision. Part III, which I will concentrate on, provided "An Analysis of the Legal Aspects of the School Segregation Decision and Alternatives Open to North Carolina in the Light of that Decision" and was written by assistant director Paul (Coates, 1954).

The second document,[6] produced by the New Hanover County, North Carolina school district, is dated July 1955 and titled *Non-Segregation Data for Study: Preliminary Report to the State Advisory Committee on Non-Segregation* (NCSA-NBL, 1954). A perusal of the table of contents of this report gives a glimpse into the content:

Part I.   Mentality and Scholastic Standards
Part II.   Social Adjustments and Traditions
Part III.   Physical Conditions and Locations
Part IV.   Economic
Part V.   Health and Social Customs
Part VI.   The Negro Teacher
Part VII.   Subversive and Antagonistic Attacks
Part VIII. The Legality of Decision of Supreme Court & 14th Amendment
Part IX.   Miscellaneous Items. (NCSA-NBL, 1954)

What is particularly compelling about this particular document is that it appears to be a work in progress. Inconsistent formatting, absent pagination, and inserted comments with suggestions for further additions all point to the likelihood that this report was not in its finished form. What is valuable about this is the frankness of the language, which, as we will see, was as inflammatory as any eugenic tome from 30 years earlier.

In what might be regarded as a macabre version of a Saturday Night Live skit called "What They Said: What They Really Meant," I will offer the opinions of both reports on the various issues with which they are concerned. In viewing both versions together, instead of one after the other, we are provided with an insight as to the way language is and has been used to mask underlying assumptions and sell ideas.

Social Impact of Brown

The final chapter in Coates' (1954) comprehensive history of North Carolina Schools, titled *Where Do We Go From Here*, outlines the potential problems of desegregation in the state. Speculating on the "unbridled passions to the public peace" that were likely to occur, Coates stated that "people were not ready for mixed schools in 1866 (referring to the emancipation proclamation) and many raise the question as to what extent, if any, they are ready for it now" (p. 38). So extreme was the reaction, Coates reported, that suggestions ran from a concerted effort at compliance to "resistance to the limit regardless of consequences" (p. 38). "It is not idle to speculate," he warned, "whether this decision will sweep them [schools] forward on a rising tide or pull them under in the undertow" (Coates, 1954, p. 39). After all, Coates reminded the governor, public school doors had closed in 1866 and while the poverty of that era had largely disappeared, "racial feeling has not yet passed in music out of sight" (p. 41). Concluding his chapter, Coates expressed his opinion that "we cannot keep the schools if we do not keep the peace" (p. 44). Towards that end, he wrote:

> Let us pray that it is not too much to hope that the children of a people who found resources in themselves to build the foundations of a new civilization out of the ruins of the Civil War . . . and in 1869 found a way to open the doors of public schools to White and Negro children . . . let us pray that it is not too much to hope that they will bend all of their energies to find a way, if there is a way, within the framework of the 17th of May decision—to save the solid values which three generations have built into those schools. (Coates, 1954, p. 44)

An impassioned statement to be sure, and no doubt sincerely felt, but the staggering lack of recognition anywhere in Coates' comprehensive history of the racially motivated conceptions of ability and degeneracy that saturated public school policy in the state are deafening in their absence. No acknowledgment of the potential ramifications of *Brown* for African Americans in the state was forthcoming. No speculation as to the potential benefits to the population as a whole of drawing on an increasingly rich and diverse populous. Coates' main concern is for the impact on white citizens of the state, who he painted with a broad brush as being uniformly alarmed and angry at the imposition of the Court.

If the contents of the New Hanover County document (NCSA-NBL, 1954) is any indication, perhaps the broad brush of Coates was not that presumptive after all. The language used in the New Hanover County report limns a picture of racial tranquility, an ideal system of separate but equal schools that provided each race with positive self-conception and resource for the future. Along that line the New Hanover County report claimed that "it would be hard to find a place where there is so little racial friction as in New Hanover County. Clashes between schools are unknown" (NCSA-NBL, 1954, p. 13[7]). Part II, the section on Social Adjustment, begins with the following questions:

> Shall we try to preserve the cultural and educational development of each race? Or,
>
> Shall we merge the two? Or,
>
> Shall we integrate only those negroes who show mental ability with the Whites at the White standard of scholarship?

This last must have seemed an attractive compromise given the numbers reflected in the following recommended topics of study to answer the above questions. "Items to be studied are," the report lists:

(a) What has the Negro to gain or lose by integration?

(b) What has the White to gain or lose by integration?

(c) What is to be done with the lowest 2% of the White race and the corresponding 14% of the negroes who rate below the mentality necessary for any formal learning.

(d) How can the next higher 7% of the Whites and the corresponding 29% of the negroes be adjusted socially in school affairs. (Learning ability is very limited).

(e) The next higher 15% of the Whites and the corresponding 30% of the negroes present another problem.

(f) The 76% percent of the Whites and the 27% of the negroes above the moron classification present a further problem. (NCSA-NBL, 1954, p. 10)

Keeping in mind that this was written in 1954, we can see clearly that eugenic assessments of racial ability had clearly made their way into the assessment tools and language of the schools. To integrate "only those negroes who show mental ability with the Whites at the White standard of scholarship" the state would only be responsible for 27% of the African American school population. Using the school population numbers provided by the University of North Carolina report, this would translate roughly into 6,000 students out of a total population of over 63,000 students[8] (Coates, 1954, p. 47). Finally, the "Social Adjustment" section of the New Hanover County report listed the characteristics of "The Negro of New Hanover County" (NCSA-NBL, 1954, p. 12). The list documented the "90-year history" (p. 12) of the 'negro' schools by naming the superior vocation training that had enabled the 'negro' to drive cars, look at television, and eat well, as well as the international fame of the Williston Choral Group. Social organizations within the schools reflected "a demonstration of a social culture, fitted to the race" while extra-curricular activities and the leaders "developed by the above programs . . . rate above the national mental average" (p. 12). The last two items on the list include:

X. *RACIAL PRIDE:* Children by White fathers, once a standard topic of facetious discussion, are reduced to an insignificant number. Contrary to popular legend, these illegitimates were sired mostly by crude, moronic, and beastly Whites—not often by men of brains and culture.

XI. *FRIENDLY RELATIONSHIP WITH WHITE RACE:* In spite of the continuous "hate campaigns" waged by various groups, it would be hard to find a place where there is so little racial friction as in New Hanover County. Clashes between schools are unknown.

Both the White and the negro can point with pride to the adjustment each race has made in working out the most difficult problem of our nation. Each, according to the characteristics and temperament of the race, has produced a racial adjustment unknown in integrated areas, where considerable numbers of negroes live. (NCSA-NBL, 1954, p. 13)

Little did they know that New Hanover County was to host some of the bloodiest and most intense race riots of the twentieth century. As to item X above, we can only assume that the "popular legend" referred to are the stories of white plantation owners impregnating their African American slaves, but that is not certain. What is certain is the continued use of language developed a half-century earlier in tales of the Jukes and Kallikaks. In any event, the presence of "crude, moronic, and beastly" white blood would not constitute an improvement of any kind.

Academic Differences

We have already seen the expectations of school officials in New Hanover County with regard to African Americans, that 70% of African Americans were moronic or imbecile. The University of North Carolina governor's report utilized a decidedly more diplomatic and creative tone. In attempting to find ways to avoid the mandate of the *Brown* decision, the University of North Carolina report (Coates, 1954) suggested that

If local authorities could demonstrate that pupils of one race in a given grade could *not* be expected to participate and keep up with the students of the other race in the same grade level, then it is arguable that immediate integration of the two classes would be unreasonable and delay justifiable. Utilization of such a principle would, it is true, serve to continue the status quo of separate education . . . to forestall contentions that delay for this reason would amount to deliberate noncompliance, there would exist a need for detailed and objective analysis of the facts. (Coates, 1954, p. 158)

This approach seemed to indicate that some form of definitive measurement must be used to create an indisputable demonstration of racial inequality where academic ability was concerned. In other words, the objective of creating proof of inequality existed before the tools to legitimize that objective were brought in to play. By itself, this suggestion proves little, but within the context of the historical legacy of beliefs about race, ability, and degeneracy along with what we know about the development of mental testing as it occurred within the same context, the inevitable conclusion must be that measurement methods developed and used in American schools was born of a less than magnanimous intention.

By 1954, we know that intelligence testing was widely practiced in the schools and not surprisingly, the evidence provided by those tests supported the deeply seated assumptions about race and ability. The New Hanover County report makes no bones about presenting those numbers to support its contention that desegregation would be disastrous. Part I of the report (NCSA-NBL, 1954, p. 2), concerned with "Mentality and Scholastic Standards" begins its presentation as with a table:

1. Intelligence tests show a very pronounced difference in the mental ability of the two races. The following chart shows typical results for 30 year period of testing.
   (a) Over I.Q. 100—(Above average)—White 49%—Negro 8%
   (b) (Low average)—White 26%—Negro 20%
   (c) High grade moron—White 16%—Negro 30%
   (d) Low grade moron—White 7%—Negro 29%
   (e) Below moron—White 2%—Negro 13%

The use, as late as 1954, of the eugenic language and classification of students so widely used by Goddard, Hall, Thorndike, and Hollingworth speaks to the deep embeddedness of the ideology in the institution of education. What this shows is that claims of inherent intellectual inequality were not the exclusive domain of fanatical eugenic thinkers. Such racist assumptions were commonly accepted dogma, and the tests used to prove those assumptions presented as indisputable.

The New Hanover County report provides current test data for the 1954–1955 school year that tells essentially the same story as the "30 year" compilation.

Negro Intelligence Test

I.Q. above 110	0.7%
I.Q. 100-109	5.8%
I.Q. 90-99	22.5%
I.Q. below 90	71.0%. (NCSA-NBL, 1954, pp. 2-5)

Given the glowing characterization of segregated education presented in the report, it might seem surprising that nearly 75% of African American students are classed as imbeciles. However, the quality of education notwithstanding, these numbers make sense when we remember that the expectations preceded the tests, the tests proved the expectations, and therefore school officials could in good conscience claim to have provided the best, most "appropriate" education possible. The report contained numerous other charts and graphs, replete with "I.Q. medians and quartiles" (p. 5) and claims to African American "educational opportunity equal or superior to 90% of the White schools in the state" (p. 5). There is a hint of desperation, and more than a hint of fear contained in the presentation of data on intelligence.

The report put great effort into its contention that dramatic academic inability on the part of African American students occurred despite a long history of state funded education. Lest questions arise about the possibility that racial differences might be attributable to inherent shortcomings in segregated Southern schools, the report contended, under the headline "*Racial Equality?*" that

> For four decades there were more negroes than Whites in the schools. They were taught by White teachers trained in the North. The equipment and supplies were supplied in keeping with that prevalent in the North . . . This Negro community has had educational opportunities equal to, or better than, 90% of the White children in N.C. FOR A PERIOD OF 90 YEARS. They still have equal or superior facilities to more than 90% of the Whites in the South. (NCSA-NBL, 1954, p. 15; emphasis in original)

The basis of these claims is unclear, but there is a clear sense of extreme unfairness and indignation among whites. Should the reader miss the profound implications of what they had presented, the authors made it plain. "If opportunity would bring equality," they conclude, "and lack of it bring inequality, this negro group would rate higher on achievement and intelligence than the White one" (NCSA-NBL, 1954, p. 15). Not surprisingly, the authors claimed that "*The reverse is true*. The White school district always scores much higher in both I.Q. and achievement" (p. 15). Furthermore, there was "not a single one of these White areas, no matter how remote or backward, that will fail to score considerably higher than this negro community with 90 years of school opportunity" (p. 15). In other words, what was the purpose of integrating schools when there was no hope of academic achievement on the part of African American students.

In any event, the report went on, integrated schools do not work. Through the provision of a list of "quotations on racial differences from instructors in integrated schools," (p. 14) that include commentary by the authors of the report, a picture is drawn of the inside of an integrated classroom. The depiction of African American students sounded very like Cubberley's (1924) depiction of immigrants with the New Hanover County authors claiming that non-white students

> lack ambition and initiative, [find it] hard to follow verbal instruction, are quick to take offense, [and] some are a little too aggressive, loud and fussy, with not enough respect for authority and a tendency to take too many privileges (NCSA-NBL, 1954, p. 14)

The quotations from instructors in integrated schools further claimed that African American parents were "losing sympathy with their own children," because, they offer in an aside, "(the inferiority complex is really accentuated in integrated schools)" (p. 14). African American parents are presented as parasitic and indifferent in the following statement

> new glasses were needed—both parents were working—they would not buy them. In such matters the parents seem to be willing to shift responsibility to the school. (p. 14)

This reiteration of non-whites as a tax burden, a lazy shiftless population "lacking in ambition" and swelling the welfare roles was applied to African American teachers as well.

In Part VI, titled *The Negro Teacher*, the New Hanover County report offered the following insight:

> A very large percentage of negro applicants, for teachers, base their main point, in a plea for a position, on the basis that they have a sick mother, father, etc. that is dependent on their support. The welfare idea even extends to this high level position. (NCSA-NBL, 1954, p. 27)

The illustration developed 50 years before had turned out to be resilient. The African American teacher was also presented as "an easy victim of subversive propaganda" (p. 30). The teacher "has adjusted herself to teaching at, or near the level of her pupils," and the "tempo of teaching in negro schools is slower than in White schools" (NCSA-NBL, 1954, p. 28). The horrifying result: "(Some parents in integrated schools, praise this until later—too late—they find their children are hopelessly retarded.)" (p. 28). It is unclear how this result is reconciled with the heritability of ability, but the threat was presented as fact nevertheless.

Another quote echoes the anthropological depictions of Africans from three-quarters of a century prior: "The negroes seem to learn more by mimicry than Whites" (p. 14). Finally, the list of quotes is concluded with this:

> If there is anyone under the illusion (promoted by the communists and pinks) that situations improve as the years go by, just let them study the integrated schools in Upper Manhattan and Brooklyn. So far, . . . no place has been cited (where any considerable number of negroes are found), where integration is working with anything like the satisfaction that segregation works in North Carolina. (NCSA-NBL, 1954, p. 14)

By the 1950s, much of the deep racial and class animosity had been redirected, or rather, expanded to include communists. By attempting to establish that integrated schools were inferior to segregated ones, the authors revert to representations of African American students that are derived almost verbatim from the eugenic rhetoric of the 1920s and 1930s. Their clear enthusiasm for the status quo might reasonably be recast into the adage about "keeping [African Americans] in their place." The communist threats are articulated elsewhere in the New Hanover County report under the headline "Subversive Influence" (NCSA-NBL, 1954, p. 29). After having warned that "the majority [of African Americans] are thoroughly sold on the idea that all colored races should be enemies of the Whites" (p. 29), the report then identified the perpetrator of this threat to tranquility.

> The Russian—NAACP—do-gooder, etc. propaganda machine has been turned on teachers, preachers, "Y" workers and all leaders of youth until it is hard for them to know the difference between the Christian and Communist Religion. (NCSA-NBL, 1954, p. 29)

This provides further evidence of the feeling of persecution felt by white Southerners. The clear divisions established at the turn of the century and before between whites and everyone else remained firmly intact in 1954 North Carolina schools.

Health and Safety

Eugenic ideology was deeply concerned with health and hygiene. A great deal of the public education to promote eugenics was presented within a context that defined the "non-superior" masses as dirty, diseased, and dangerous. By 1954, that view had altered very little and the authors of both reports make use of this perception to further their arguments. The University of North Carolina governor's report (Coates, 1954), Section 6 titled *Taking Account of the Need to Protect the Health of Individual Students*, tackled the problem:

> Some concern has been expressed that mixed attendance in the schools, in some areas, may imperil the health of some of the children in the mixed schools . . . and the question is . . . whether the court would recognize and permit the states to take appropriate action to protect its school children from disease . . . it would seem beyond question that the Court would recognize this interest. (p. 159)

The report went on to weigh the relative merits of the right to a non-segregated public school system versus the right to be free of disease and emotional anguish. That the federal decree abolished segregation on the basis of race alone was presented as an advantage. Were the state to establish other parameters by which to allow segregation to continue, the report contended, and despite the fact that "such a plan might well result in a considerable amount of voluntary segregation," it "does not *ipso facto* violate the law of the Brown case" (Coates, 1954, p. 162). Coates was confident that the state could establish a waiver of some kind that would act as a loophole.

Once again, the language in the New Hanover County report was considerably less guarded. More warnings were forthcoming under the heading "Health and Social Customs" (NCSA-NBL, 1954, p. 26). The report identified "this problem as the most serious of all" (p. 26) and referred for the first time to a need for tact in the presentation of facts in this area. Being that the factors in this field were "of a nature too personal and delicate" (p. 26), the authors cautioned that "to publish without the utmost care and consideration as to how it should be presented" (p. 26) would "arouse latent emotions dangerous to the community" (p. 26). Point 3 of the list of factors to consider in the area of health and social customs brings this worry about "latent emotions" to the fore. It stated:

> There is a very rapid increase in mixed marriages since WW II. One mother in New York City said, "We have learned the hard way, that we must start teaching racial hatred, at birth, to keep down trouble when they grow up. (NCSA-NBL, 1954, p. 26)

The reference to teaching racial hatred, sobering as it is, is indicative of the near pathological fear on behalf of whites where mixing was concerned. "The negro develops sexual awareness at a surprisingly early age" the report explained.

Bus transportation presents the most difficult problem of discipline:

(a) The boy–girl problem.
(b) Feuds between families and localities.
(c) Trouble because of large and small children, etc. Add to this another race— it would be a source of fuel for friction even though none existed to begin with. (p. 26)

The perpetual reference to a previous time of racial harmony is endemic to the infrastructure of racial conception in this argument against school integration. I will close this glimpse of education as it concerned race and ability with a version of the myth provided in the New Hanover County report:

> These consolidated [negro] schools have produced a wholesome and Progressive atmosphere and influenced every phase of life in the community. The young

people show pride in their race and in the success of their own efforts. The result is loyal and productive American citizens. The southern White citizens is [*sic*] proud of the rapid development of his negro neighbor. The North Carolina plan of racial adjustment has proved superior to any yet presented in any part of the world. (NCSA-NBL, 1954, p. 20)

Never mind that 70% of those "negro neighbors" fall below the "low moron" classification. No matter that, in example after example, the authors of this report showed a deep and abiding fear, contempt, and resentment of their neighbors. Finally, the idyllic presentation of racial well-being and harmony gives the following warning:

IT IS THE FIRST DUTY OF SCHOOL OFFICIALS TO INFORM PARENTS, that:

(a) *A mixed racial school is a sub-standard school. Your children will progress more slowly.*
(b) *The educational, social, and health standards will be equally affected.*
(c) Your children can easily be "brainwashed" to accept these standards. It is human nature to follow the easy, lazy road. (NCSA-NBL, 1954, p. 7)

The list had six more points but their inclusion here is unnecessary. The illustration of a fundamentally racist school system is complete.

This chapter has traced the infiltration of eugenic ideology into the conception and form of American education. Admittedly, it has been an emotionally exhausting journey. What the data provide is the exposure of racist ideology which formed a system of education that impacted all Americans. The penetration of eugenic ideology into education began in the nineteenth century, was codified in the early twentieth century, and was evident in the inner workings of schools in North Carolina from the Department of Public Instruction to rural classrooms.

I examined the contextual circumstances which characterized education at the turn of the century and have shown how they combined with societal influences to provide a willing environment within which eugenic ideology flourished. Through the educational philosophies of education leaders such as Bobbitt, Hall, Thorndike, Charters, and Hollingworth, eugenic constructions were developed into a curriculum that provided the framework for the following century. We have seen how eugenic definitions of race, class, ability, and worth were translated into educational parameters. Finally, I have provided the evidence to show that these same eugenic parameters existed within the form and function of schooling in North Carolina through the mid-1950s.

9

Epilogue—Excavating Memory

As in all previous history, whoever emerges as victor still participates in that triumph in which today's rulers march over the prostrate bodies of their victims. As is customary, the spoils are borne aloft in that triumphal parade. These are generally called the cultural heritage. The latter finds a rather distanced observer in the historical materialist. For such cultural riches, as he surveys them, everywhere betray an origin which he cannot but contemplate with horror. They owe their existence, not merely to the toil of the great creators who have produced them, but equally to the anonymous forced labor of the latters contemporaries. There has never been a document of culture which was not at one and the same time a document of barbarism.

—*Walter Benjamin*
Thesis on the Philosophy of History, VII

Of any of the oppressed groups caught under the microscope of eugenic ideologues, entire books could be filled. Not just of their plight and sufferings, but of their resistance and adaptation. What I set out to accomplish in this book was not limited to further documentation of the deeply embedded racialized scientism that has so characterized American society. Rather, I hoped to show that the effects of this legacy impact not only non-Nordic and poor peoples, but everyone. I have heard many of my colleagues who were part of the effort to desegregate schools during the 1960s and 1970s express a profound sadness that the dawning of the twenty-first century has witnessed what Jonathan Kozol has called apartheid education. Why, despite the best efforts of so many, does this state of affairs persist to such an extent?

Since the most recent conservative backlash was ushered in 1983 in the form of a report entitled *A Nation at Risk*, our nation has embraced calls for standards and accountability. Colleges of education across the country are undergoing accreditation nightmares, processes that are contrary to all that has been theorized and advanced in the schools as a result of the reconceptualization. Why, my colleagues ask, are so many of us embracing this new trend? Why do those that oppose it acquiesce despite their opposition? I hope what this book has accomplished is to underscore the fact that we are all complicit, whether we fight, teach, and march in opposition to racism or not. Such is the power of collective memory and the deliverance of institutionalized racism, classism, and gender bias through our nation's schools and churches, families and friends. The civil rights movement failed on one important count—it never addressed the racism as it was embedded in the individuals who were fighting for change. Many people have pointed out this problem—indeed, deficit theory belies the very racist assumptions carried therein.

As we have seen, the eugenics movement was part of the Progressive movement, was carried out by people who sincerely believed they were working to make society and the world a better place. They were not unlike ourselves and it is here that, in my mind at least, the most important point of this book lies. To what extent have we all unwittingly perpetuated that to which we are utterly opposed? How clearly does our silence indicate our contentedness with the way things are? Where does fear lie?

When I was a graduate student, and this work was still an idea, a kind gentleman at an AERA division B mentoring function advised me. Upon hearing that I planned to connect high-stakes testing policy in the present with eugenic ideology (subsequently refocused on the initial connection between education and eugenics)—this gentleman implored me to be sure to end with something positive. He expressed something I have heard many times since—that critical theorists do nothing but complain. Wallowing in the negative, they contemplate the nation's navel and do nothing to encourage people to participate in change. Where there is no hope, this argument goes, there is no incentive to make a difference. I have thought a great deal about this, having always considered myself to be a generally optimistic person. I have since conceded that in light of the present climate, there is little to be optimistic about, but hope—we can always hang on to that. From whence does this desire for a positive spin on tragedy come? I believe it, too, is a part of our collective memory. The maxim issued goes like this: "If you can't say anything nice, don't say anything at all"—so those of us who point out what is wrong are being rude and impolitic. Apparently, we need to feel good about something, on some level, before we can act. Clearly though, simply feeling good is dangerous and fails to interrogate the degree to which that good feeling might in itself be a Trojan horse. It is here, at the very moment when we think we are thinking and acting independently, that ideology operates in its most pernicious state.

Seductive in its ability to objectify moral sentiment and motivate action, ideology defines the structures through which individuals understand the world. Eugenic ideology, replete with imperatives and proscriptions, spawned deep commitment among its followers and defined the national dialogue about race, ability, and degeneracy in ways that are uniquely American. Throughout the twentieth century, the national dialogue regarding eugenics and social engineering has been advanced in the schools and continues to provide the outline of the cultural system that is American education. Operant within this early twentieth century cultural system were two essential elements, science and eugenic ideology, which have endured and continue to represent the current paradigmatic frame in American education. Using the requirements for such a system as described by Clifford Geertz we see that science has provided a diagnostic and critical dimension while eugenic ideology has provided a justificatory, apologetic dimension. The implications for our society of eugenic ideology acting in the capacity described are grave. The data reveal that, indeed, eugenic ideology was successful in establishing and defending patterns of belief and value that defined racial and class inequities in terms of heredity and innate ability.

The ubiquity of the past in our present national conversation about schools and race, test scores and national strength, or immigration and cultural decay underscores a serious need for ideological excavation. Social dialogue in America, co-opted by a Puritan form requiring an aggressive war-like approach to the dismantling of opposing points of view, has entrenched us within our own ideological past. Uncritically examined, the ordering of social and historical time in the national consciousness serves, therefore, not to inform, but to resist change and preserve tradition. No wonder, then, that we have had the same, regrettably uncomplicated, conversions over and over throughout our history. Historical time is not an accurate record of what "happened" but is instead, as Freeden (2003) explains, "a selected and patterned list of events . . . that are woven together to form an ideological narrative" (p. 42). In this sense, ideologies themselves act as signposts through which collective national identity is forged.

A long line of theoretical and ideological predecessors of eugenics played a significant role in both the infiltration and perpetuation of eugenic ideology in American culture. Puritans established an enduring faith in the power of education to aid in the salvation of social ills and inadequacies. Even as attendance at the nation's public schools became compulsory in states across the country between

1871 and 1929, education as a site of transmission for society's most closely held ideals has existed in America since the 1600s. Education is a fundamental component of virtually every institution, organization (both secular and religious), and cultural activity in American life. We do not leave anything up to chance when it comes to the definition of institutional values, goals, mandates, and imperatives. We educate people through issue statements and public declarations, literature and advertising. These things are not open to interpretation in that, in the case of differing interpretations, one simply agrees to disagree. Boundaries remain intact: compromise and consideration are not built in to the system.

One particularly enduring element of Puritan ideology was the provision of a form of social discourse that used competition to create a public sphere that was authoritarian, democratic, hegemonic, and individualistic all at once. The result of this provision was that one did not enter into the public discourse in order to *discover* what one believed; rather, one entered the discourse in order to *convince* and compel others to believe what was presented (Roberts-Miller, 1999). The influence of this early parameter ensured that, from the very beginning, education was a conduit for training and advocacy rather than an environment of discovery and learning. Cultural heritage such as this can be a painful and agonizing reflected image. Presupposing that this heritage is regarded from an intentionally vulnerable stance, the image becomes *story*. This has been the story of the suppositions that have produced and nurtured the cultural heritage that is "race" in America. The intellectual movements that preceded, and provided the infrastructure for, the American eugenics movement revealed numerous examples of ideological replication. Patterns of thought, managed by memory, along with the contextual influence of society, all acted in concert to create the conduits through which intellectual history has flowed.

Another example of early influence comes from Steven Tomlinson's (2005) fascinating account of the influence of phrenology in Europe and America. Tomlinson (2005) provides evidence that the relationship between education and racialized scientism predates the eugenics movement by at least a century. Phrenology, characterized by an interest in the bumps on people's heads as indications of behavior, Tomlinson argues, had a significant impact on education in Europe and America and acted as a foundation for both Social Darwinism and eugenics in America. Unlike the recent interest displayed by Foucault and other social theorists regarding the use of phrenology to "chart the epistemic contours of the nineteenth century mind" (p. xiii), Tomlinson chooses to pursue a more "internal" path by examining the way phrenology operated to unite physiological laws and moral imperatives. He asks how phrenology was tied to the natural theology of secularism and how its basic principles of human classification, inheritance, and development were used to endorse progressive pedagogic and disciplinary practices. Finally, Tomlinson investigates how the early nineteenth-century "Head Masters" wielded the doctrines of phrenology in their many and various efforts to reform schooling and other institutional practices. We see that Horace Mann, a staunch believer in phrenology, based his theories of universal education on the belief that human nature was consistent, and predictable (head bumps) across the globe and that, therefore, sound pedagogical principles superceded national boundaries. In light of this, Mann's view of education, traditional accounts of which portray a vision of school as "the great equalizer," looks a bit different.

Horace Mann died during the same year that Charles Darwin published *Origin of Species*, and, as Tomlinson points out, a mere two months before the birth of John Dewey. Mann, who held unquestioning faith in a divinely ordered and beneficent world, operated within vastly different paradigmatic frame from that of Dewey, who rejected all moral and physical absolutes. Throughout our history, attempts to measure, sort, and classify human beings have been propelled into popular and widely accepted theories of human nature by prominent scientists and intellectuals including leading members of the medical and educational communities. Eventually, at least on the surface, these grand theories fell into disrepute and, like phrenology, come to be regarded, in the words of Mark Twain, as a "'pseudoscientific fad in which hucksters read character traits from the bumps on a person's skull' relegated to fairgrounds and seaside piers" (quoted in Tomlinson, 2005, p. xi). Herein lies the danger, this disregard of ideologies from the past, for it is clearly a matter of historiography, rather than history itself, that the dismissal of what later may be something of an embarrassment requires us to alter what we remember.

The thread of collective memory is witnessed through the tracing of not only ideas themselves but the form of their iterations. Beginning with the Puritans, the development and social application of the theories of naturalism, positivism, and evolution show that no ideology exists in a vacuum. In America, the peculiar combination of nineteenth-century ideological imperatives with the twentieth-century social realities of immigration, industrialization, urbanization, and poverty led to a unique and enduring role for eugenics. There is a distinct common denominator that follows hierarchicalized, racialized thinking from the Great Chain of Being theory, through phrenology, Social Darwinism, and eugenics. Each iteration was focused on sorting human beings based on their declared worth as the result of a socially constructed formula—a formula that makes sense to those wielding it precisely because the basic infrastructure is familiar, a residual part of collective memory.

In 1935, writing in the *Journal of Educational Sociology*, Paul Popenoe argued for a more deliberate social component to school life. Students, being most likely to choose a mate during their high school years, or at least to develop their discerning tendencies, must be steered towards eugenically sound mating practices. Popenoe calls for more "honesty" where family background is concerned and advocates the development of a way to make family histories more public. In addition to the school's role in providing social opportunities for students to put into practice their newfound ability to make wise choices in mating, Popenoe expresses the, by then, commonly accepted relationship between eugenics and education declaring that

> [t]he general facts [of eugenics] can be brought to the attention of students through a wide range of courses in biology, social science, citizenship, history, psychology, home economics, and the like. Then the outlines of sound eugenic policy of population control, in its negative and positive aspects, can be suggested. (p. 457)

Meanwhile, those policies that Americans have generally regarded as emblematic of progress operate, according to Popenoe, in support of eugenic ideology very nicely. "The abolition of child labor," Popenoe explains, "will remove the economic incentive to childbearing in a part of the population that produces children who are, on the whole, below par" (p. 457). Furthermore, "excessive reproduction of the unfit" can be further checked by raising the minimum age for marriage in order to "keep the kind of people who are uneducated or uneducable from getting a long start in parenthood over educated classes" (p. 457). Finally,

> [s]pread of contraceptive information and materials and wider use of voluntary sterilization (with a compulsory provision in the law for use when needed) will prevent the insane and feebleminded, the irresponsible and reckless, the alcoholic and the indifferent, the chronic paupers, and those parents who produce children in order to get their dole increased from multiplying more rapidly than those who are physically healthy, mentally sound, and emotionally stable. (p. 458)

Popenoe is clear that the schools must operate as a mechanism in society that sorts the "fit" from the "unfit" and casts this imperative as one of civic duty. The underlying assumption is that in a democratic society, those citizens who care about the welfare of their democracy will buy in to a need for eugenic reform.

Despite attempts to the contrary, eugenic belief about the connection between race, class, and ability was often at odds with democracy. As Chesterton (1922/2000), one of the more vocal dissenters during the height of the movement, argued in the heat of the debate, eugenic beliefs were more closely aligned with a capitalist paradigm and the desire to accumulate wealth than a democratic one. A common argument, (appearing in both Popenoe and Johnson's (1918) hugely popular college text *Applied Eugenics*, and also in a *Journal of Educational Sociology* article by Goddard (1933) on *The Gifted Child*) suggested that when Jefferson wrote "all men are equal" in the Declaration of Independence, "he may have been thinking of legal rights merely" and that furthermore he was "expressing an opinion common among philosophers of his time" (Popenoe and Johnson, 1918, p. 75). Some eugenicists were possessed of brazen distrust, even contempt, for democracy as evidenced by the words of Henry Fairfield Osborn, president of the American Museum of Natural History:

> The true spirit of American democracy that all men are born with equal rights and duties has been confused with the political sophistry that all men are born with equal character and ability to govern themselves and others, and with the educational sophistry that education and environment will offset the handicap of heredity. (1923, quoted in Goddard, 1933, p. 354)

The imperative of hierarchy would not allow for the possibility that the "unfit" might participate in the governance of the "fit."

Democracy has so far failed to protect all but its most venerated citizens from oppression waged by social institutions and policies of all sorts. Nevertheless, perhaps due to my own participation in an exalted fantasy of equal representation, I wonder if, reconceived, there might be something to salvage from the democratic ideal. As Tomas Englund (2000) sees it, there is hope to be found in the most recent *neo-pragmatic* interpretation of Dewey's (1916) work. Englund understands "the main characteristic of neo-pragmatism to be its concern for communication as a democratic form of life, [one that develops both] communicative and deliberative capabilities for democracy" (p. 306).

Definitions about race, ability, and human worth, provided by race theorists from the nineteenth century, entered into the public vernacular and, subsequently, the collective memory of our nation. That the structure and function of ideology has implications for collective memory was established in Chapter Two by combining the work of Geertz and Halbwachs. Ideology supplies memory with an objectification of moral sentiment, as well as the justificatory and apologetic dimensions of culture (Geertz, 1973). In the United States, that ideology was eugenics. Eugenicists made moral sentiment synonymous with racially based definitions of human and societal betterment. Eugenics provided American culture with the justificatory tools to achieve those ends in the form of testing and classification schemes. Finally, eugenic ideology satisfied the apologetic element of culture by redefining civic duty and virtue such that they reified the inherent assumption regarding human worth. It is exactly at this moment that ideologies like eugenics infiltrate common understanding of the world, and each other: they become part of memory.

Collective memory functions in three ways in this book. First, it provides the mechanism for explaining the confluence of Puritan ideology and older versions of racial theory into eugenic ideology in the twentieth century. This explains the direction of both intellectual thought and the receptiveness of the public for eugenic ideology. Second, collective memory provides for the perpetuation of eugenic ideology despite the discrediting of its most fundamental premise of the heritability of human behavior and ability. Third, collective memory speaks to the continued evidence of sorting and categorization that occurs in education in the present.

Authority and autonomy, reproduction, and reconstruction are all subjects inherently embedded within the concept of memory. These elements reveal the function of memory in society, both historically and in the present. Halbwachs (1952) argued that the notion of individual memory rests on meaningless assumptions and that instead, individuals acquire, locate, and recall their memories purely as a result of their membership in particular social groups. If we accept the basic premise of collective memory, then the implications of this research for all Americans are overwhelming in terms of how we think about race, ability, and equality.

Additionally, we must acknowledge that collective memory is not a constant. Collective memory constitutes a range of meanings (or various conduits) that are utterly dependent upon one's racial and economic vantage point. In other words, the past and present are inextricably intertwined, replete with a multiplicity of meanings, in ways that are constructed differently by different groups. Therefore, without a thorough examination of past assumptions any attempt in the present at, say, educational reform, can only lead to unintended replication, or worse, a population of well-meaning perpetuators.

My argument that social ideologies like eugenics are not historical relics but instead travel through generations by means of collective memory hinges on the idea that people create meaning by relying on external cues taken from cultural artifacts. As I demonstrated, these artifacts exist irrespective of public awareness and opinion and are capable of persisting within collective memory without the necessity of individual awareness. Furthermore, the establishment of a connection between individual, collective, and institutional memory relies on the notion that meaning is not created anew but is instead constructed from socially acquired memories which are residual within both ideology and the artifacts produced by culture.

By expanding our definition of what constitutes popular and media culture, and by distancing the theory's reliance on technological forms of transmission, we find that the ways in which people interact with their social environment are more constant than the seeming newness of experience in the present would lead us to believe. If we assume that meaning and identity are socially constructed, and that part of the human condition is to seek out sources that generate this meaning and identity, then it makes sense that the underlying cultural processes through which the formation of meaning and identity occur would have been present in society long before people began to theorize about them.

There is an ideological interdependence within social systems. An interdependence that connects identity, development, dissemination, and duration. In the case of racial constructs in the United States, ideological patterns of thought were developed within a miasma of fears around personal worth, safety, and prosperity. This combination reveals that Puritan conceptions of mission and morality have, in America, synergistically interacted with a capitalistic infrastructure and a positivistic verve for solving social maladies. Due to America's unique blend of contributing history and contextual influences, the conduit of race, as a social construction, has been particularly resilient. The challenge of identifying the form and function of racial memory in America is not, therefore, an act of re-framing, but of de-framing. This is achieved by expanding the scope of what we consider legitimate measures of historical reality.

We looked at the implications of the ubiquity of nostalgia, tradition, and revival in American culture for their ability to speak to the simultaneous depth of regard and degree of boundary with which the American public views history. The past then, is an artifact of the present. If, as Hutton (1993) asserted, history seeks to reconstruct the past through the very act of recollection, and if awareness of the past is founded on memory, then tracing the incarnations of a social construct like race becomes a personal as well as an intellectual pursuit.

Individualism in American society cannot help but run contrary to the principle of the greatest happiness for the greatest number of human beings espoused by eminent utilitarian John Stuart Mill (Degler, 1991). Human morality, on the other hand, exists at the bottom of conscious choice and indicated, to Darwin, an individualistic rather than a social basis of moral behavior. This distinction is important for understanding the connection between eugenics and education. The infusion of morality into the understanding of human nature, coupled with the move away from purely teleological explanations, provided a newly minted role for education in America—one that was comfortable because of its familiar Puritan inclinations. Gould (1996) argued that Darwin should not be castigated for repeating a standard assumption of his age. Although Darwin's belief in racial and sexual inequality was unquestioned and canonical among upper-class Victorian males, to justify their utterance and sanctification by pointing out that "everyone was doing it" fails to get at the issue.

This argument, as Gould (1996) noted, is an easy one and could be applied to any of the pivotal figures discussed in this work. What continues to be unacceptable is the blind perpetuation of such canons, brought about by an inability (or unwillingness) on the part of historians and educators alike. If we accept that inequality is part of the central dogma of Western culture, then what else remains but to dismantle the epistemological substrate that continues to govern education in this country? It is all well and good to *understand* why these men and women so easily and avidly perpetuated racist thinking, but until we understand that the fundamental underpinnings of society, especially education, continue to be governed by this thinking and that it is we who are the products of both, then change cannot occur.

As we have seen, education was not immune to the profound fear of the "Other" generated by eugenic ideology. The public and educators alike witnessed the massive immigration, burgeoning urban populations, and the effects of industrialization. Social activists were consumed by a defensive strategy that called for the eradication of the socially inferior and the preservation of "old stock" American values and genetic material. Eugenic ideology entered into the fundamental underpinnings of public education in America in a way that was contextually required, the argument goes, for the people of the time. Why then has the influence of eugenic ideology on education been left out of the literature? An understanding of the intertwining of memory, ideology, and culture allows us to speculate that there was no deliberate conspiracy, but instead that substantive oversight occurred because those who write the literature are themselves the products of the same culture that produced eugenics. It should be noted that despite reporting on many influential figures who were directly involved with the eugenics movement, namely G. Stanley Hall, Robert Thorndike, and John Bobbitt, nowhere does either Kliebard or Cremin mention eugenics in their seminal histories of education.

Additionally, this void is surprising given the fact that both Kliebard and Cremin reported on the considerable influence of the Herbartians, many of whom had studied in Germany during the rise of fascism and the ultimate manifestation of eugenics known as the Holocaust. Rather than suggesting any culpability on the part of these authors, I suggest that the absence of reference to eugenics in these histories of education represents the rule, rather than the exception, regarding this significant and, I contend, very much relevant portion of our historical legacy. The very tenacity of eugenic ideology compels us to recall Popkewitz' alert that we "consider reason as a cultural practice that orders the ways that problems are defined and possibilities and innovation sought" (2001, p. 46). Given the fact that virtually every individual educated in America has had their thinking "ordered" by policies that came directly out of a certain way of thinking about race, then it is no wonder that our collective vision is not focused on identifying our own roots.

Selden (1999) says "it is important that we do not use today's perspectives to freeze those eugenic actors into historical grotesques. Individuals reconsidered their positions and changed their minds" (p. 17). Be that as it may, we must also remember that for white America, the adage "there, but for the grace . . . go I" is wholly applicable, especially given the Progressive inclinations of many American educators and eugenic popularizers. Furthermore, we do need to be able to translate today's perspectives into an understanding of the historical past to the extent that models of understanding, instinct, and value are all dictated by collective memory which, like it or not, is deeply entrenched in racist ideology.

We have seen that for eugenicists, the great compromise when it came to the institution of education was that it direct students, according to their inherited lot, into the workplace. These end products, what have come to be known as curricular objectives, have proven to be one of the most enduring legacies of scientific curriculum as it was originally conceived. The initial working assumption by eugenicists was that human beings were born with whatever compliment of abilities their genetic heritage provided. Thus, the role of education was not an exercise in intellectual improvement but rather, the provision of a social role which depended on the lottery of birth. Education policy, therefore, was driven by inborn capacity. After all, as Wiggam pointed out, "many morons are most effective factory workers and enjoy the monotony of tending simple machines or carrying out simple industrial processes" (Wiggam, 1924, p. 355).

Among eugenicists there was wide acceptance of the idea that national and racial identities were equated and that behavioral characteristics were determined by race. Like heredity, the construct of race difference was so ubiquitous in eugenic thought that it is difficult to discuss eugenic beliefs about race separately from other programmatic imperatives championed by eugenicists. Furthermore, eugenicists believed in a hierarchical construct of *worth* that superceded race to include class, habit, and behavior. Educators and eugenicists' exclusion of environmental factors to explain axioms of behavioral and observable difference became a fundamental precept of early curriculum theory. The data show that despite protestations to the contrary, environmental factors were considered only to the extent that they identified a persons' origin. To that extent, our "at risk" students today were the "imbeciles" and "defectives" of yesterday.

We need only look to the persistence of the achievement gap, the disproportionate numbers of poor and non-white students represented in special education programs, drop-out rates, and suspensions for explication of the existence of institutionalized racism in American schools. To those who would argue that we take into account the highly charged, racially motivated social atmosphere that inevitably was reflected in the schools during their formation, before assigning any theory of continuation, I must respectfully disagree. The data require of us that we begin to acknowledge the fact that educational theory, philosophy, and practice were developed within the context of dominant eugenic ideology. To attempt educational reform in the present without this knowledge amounts to mere folly and perpetuation.

The implications of eugenic ideology's infiltration into education offer an intriguing platform for further study. The subject of testing alone deserves an exacting inquiry, especially given the increasing reliance of American schools on the sorting possibilities that testing offers. Tracking, special, vocational, and gifted education programs had their roots in eugenics and it would do their practitioners well to conduct a thorough investigation into the implication of the past for present policy and practice. However, the implications for further research extend far beyond education. Birth control, the law, family planning, social organizations of all varieties, immigration, marriage restriction, and psychology all have an enormous legacy of eugenic ideology to sort through as well. Not only are there similarities in the form and function of these social elements which are clearly visible through an examination of the events of each time period, but these are actually the same forces at work. Memory, driven by the use of words, well chosen and oft uttered, has ensured that eugenic ideology has continued to penetrate the American mind for the past 80 years.

In surveying this material from the vantage point of the present, it is clear that theorizing about curriculum has taken some highly intellectual turns, and has become infused with those difficult political questions that an appreciation for the complicated nature of any social institution require. Nevertheless, it is also clear that very little has changed in terms of what actually goes on in schools. It is not enough to simply criticize the education leaders from the early twentieth century, an age where "optimism about the power of science to solve a multitude of human and social problems was near its peak" (Kliebard, 1975/1997, p. 39). What is unforgivable, as Kliebard noted 30 years ago, is that in all this time, so little has changed. "To be critical of scientific curriculum making," he argued, "is not to be critical of science or even the importance of scientific inquiry into educational processes: it is to be critical of a simplistic and vulgar scientism. Its persistence is a source of embarrassment" (1975/1997, p. 39).

It is this persistence that begs the question, why? Why were these particular scholars so widely read, and their ideas so readily incorporated into what is now conceived as "the norm"? Common sense, appeal to memory, and Puritan forms of social discourse are part of the answer. To fully answer this question will require a sustained internal gaze on the part of many, but it is clear that language, along with appeals to "rationality" and "common-sense" are part of the language of reason, *as a cultural practice*, referred to by Popkewitz. Unless we can exact some kind of inexact definition, or a way of thinking about schools and education which would open a gap in the iron wall of *reason* as it is commonly understood, then surely we will be hard pressed to move beyond the state of affairs in which we currently find ourselves.

We have seen that eugenics was, as Ordover (2003) so aptly noted, "an extremely nimble ideology" (xxvii) so it should come as no surprise that it has morphed, dodged, and danced its way into the present in a number of creative, often elusive, ways. In addition to the workings of memory, eugenics

> [c]annot be isolated from the movements it bolstered and was conscripted by: nationalism, "reform-oriented" liberalism, out-and-out homophobia, white supremacy, misogyny, and racism. Its longevity relies on these confederacies for the simple reason that even as one falls into relative disrepute, others remain intact. (p. xxvii)

Clearly then, effective rebuttal to the current climate will require an integrated effort. What follows is a brief sampling of the legacy of institutionalized racism in the present. In no way will this be thorough; such an accounting will require a great many voices. What I hope to do, on the other hand, is to show that while eugenics may have been discredited, our newly realized enlightenment is in its infancy and, as such, is utterly dependant on the body of thought from whence it came. The legacy of the past is represented in, for example, education, reproduction, immigration, societal homophobia, and globalization. Within schools, we are still mired in the rut that was laid so long ago with recent reforms serving to solidify, rather than break out. Sorting, testing, tracking, "gifted" and vocational education, international test score comparisons, financial inequity, non-English speaking students, vouchers, privatization, "at risk" students, and new forms of "apartheid schooling" characterize the national dialogue about schooling today. So, how far have we come?

During the past few years, the press has found cause to report, however sporadically, on eugenics as it impacts the present. A number of states have issued apologies for forcibly sterilizing their citizens. This trend was sparked by a class action suit filed in 1984 by the American Civil Liberties Union on behalf of

Virginians sterilized by the state. Although a federal judge rejected the suit, citing the Supreme Court's 1927 ruling in *Buck v. Bell*, and effectively blocking any attempt at financial reparations, Virginia eventually apologized 22 years later. Thanks largely to the work of disability rights activists Phil Theisen and Keith Kessler, on May 2, 2002 at the dedication of a monument commemorating the 75th anniversary of the *Buck v. Bell* Supreme Court decision, Governor Mark Warner issued a formal apology saying "Today, I offer the Commonwealth's sincere apology for Virginia's participation in eugenics. The eugenics movement was a shameful effort in which state government never should have been involved. We must remember the Commonwealth's past mistakes in order to prevent them from recurring" (Reynolds, 2003). Apologies from Oregon, North and South Carolina, and California followed quickly prompting Theisen and Kessler to note with regret that no in-depth review of governmental involvement was forthcoming. Towards that end, they have since focused their efforts on the White House, calling for a formal investigation into the federal government's role in the eugenics movement—an effort that has so far gone unacknowledged.

One of the first efforts to document the stories of people (primarily African American women in this case) who actually experienced eugenic policies was achieved in 2003 by the *Winston-Salem Journal*. In an award-winning five-part series, the journal provided both personal testimony as well as an in-depth expose of those responsible for what can only be described as a gross misuse of state power, including the state's medical school, political, and philanthropic leaders. The newspaper itself acknowledged its own complicity, citing a 1948 article that warned readers that "The danger is in the moron group [who], among other things, breed like mink" (Begos et al., 2003).

During the writing of this book, I myself lived within one mile of both Dorthea Dix Hospital (opened in 1851 as the Insane Hospital of North Carolina) where those who were sentenced to sterilization by the North Carolina Eugenics Board until 1975 were sent, and, right across the street, Central Prison in Raleigh (where 27 people were executed between 2000 and 2005, within a mile of both downtown and North Carolina Sate University where I did my graduate work). I frequently walked the 300-acre Dix campus, which is being slated for closure and development within the next few years. What will happen, I wonder, to the over 900 graves of people who were buried there between 1859 and 1970? If I were a better person I would launch a campaign to make the site a national memorial for the victims of eugenics in the United States.

Another area of great concern are the technological advances in genetic engineering that make possible what eugenicists a century ago could only dream about. Almost on a daily basis there are news report of successful cloning, portents of parents being able to design their own "perfect" children, the identification of the genes responsible for certain forms of hearing loss, sexual preference, and a host of other supposedly "undesirable" attributes. Whatever excitement we might have felt at hearing definitive proof from the Human Genome Project that there is no genetic difference between people of different races has been buried under an avalanche of the moral and political quagmire that is genetic research today.

Our reasoning about the world, as Popkewitz (1997) noted, is never a "pure" philosophical question but is, by necessity, part of the larger context of social and power relations. Not only are notions of accountability, and the need for testing, social constructions but so too are media portrayals and the resulting intersection of public opinion. As has been the case since Ronald Reagan commissioned the *Nation at Risk* report in 1984, which warned Americans of a "rising tide of mediocrity," the media has been ready to discredit schools in ways that promote privatization. In January 2006, American Broadcasting Corporation reporter John Stossel hosted a program titled *Stupid in America: How Lack of Choice Cheats Our Kids Out of a Good Education* on the program 20/20. The show was a vicious, one-sided attack on the nation's public schools that claimed America's public schools waste money, are filled with failing students, and that choice and competition are the only hope for improvement. A great deal of fact checking has been done, by everyone from the American Association of School Administrators to Gerald Bracey and the Education Disinformation Detection and Reporting Agency. How far have we come, then from Bobbitt's efforts to purge society of the unfit? Bobbitt (1909) proposed the abolishment of the public school system, all charities, and any other public agency that went out of its way to "preserve the weak and incapable" (p. 393).

Bashing public education has become something of a national pastime, but to criticize the 2001 reauthorization of the Elementary and Secondary Education Act positions one as a person who advocates "leaving children behind" or, perhaps, one who does not wish to be "accountable" to the American public. Thorough exposure of the consequences of No Child Left Behind for children of color and children who are poor is available elsewhere—but clearly we are in an age that glorifies supposedly inherent cognitive ability as measured by standardized tests. Ordover (2003) explores a variety of governmental uses of eugenics to impose what she calls the "technofix" on the underclass at the same time as attention is diverted from meaningful correctives to the economic and political context in which inequity thrives. And so we find ourselves, 52 years after the *Brown v. Board of Education* decision in a state of what Kozol (2005) has called apartheid schooling. We are concerned about our international standing at the same time as we have the highest rate of poverty in the industrialized countries.

Maybe we are waiting for the children to revolt and refuse to take the test, but this is not their job, it is ours. Perhaps we are waiting for the inevitable alarming numbers of high school seniors who, it is predicted, will not graduate as testing becomes mandatory in state after state. It may be said that there are bigger fish to fry right now, we are at war, we were attacked, nothing else matters. I contend that if anything matters, it is this. The future of our response to terrorists, to our estimation of what they represent and of how things got to be the way they are lies in the hands of the millions of test takers sitting glazed and sweaty all over the country. We need to look back. Where did testing come from? What were the theories and societal influences that led us to where we are now? What would happen if we tried to look at the present and the past, simultaneously? Let us entertain the notion that we might be permitted a glimpse in a mirror, and then let us see what we think after that. Extricating cause from the innumerable influences of historical events is, perhaps, a nearly impossible task. Rather than attempt a binary cause–effect connection, this inquiry has sought to understand the context that created social efficiency, eugenics, and the commencement of the testing movement.

Cremin (1990) called for a much more extensive body of tested knowledge about the institutions and processes of education than is now available. This task is the charge of those members of society who are responsible for the development of education policy and the conduct of educational practice. I hope I have contributed to this call and extended it to the broader society. We are all the products of this society, and through whatever perspective we employ, change and progress can only come if the multitude of voices writing, thinking, teaching, and speaking about eugenics rises to a cacophony.

As a cultural heritage it is painful to gaze upon. As a story, it is torturous. As I have stated elsewhere, I approach this subject as a member of the dominant culture. I am a white American, I am privileged, and my ancestors were no doubt active participatory agents in the above tracing; this is my story, my reflected image. I cannot begin to imagine the stories of those who exist, and have existed, outside this dominance. Those are not my stories to tell. What I perceive to be painful comes to me as a matter of choice, but I deserve no accolades for looking. How does this pain compare to hundreds of years of ancestral pain, suffering, and humiliation carried daily in the memories of generations of oppressed peoples? Like an alcoholic, dominance requires frequent refreshment, is a master of manipulation, can be charming and seductive, and is dying internally. Children, dazzled by the promise of riches, adhere themselves to a societal framework that needs them to exist as workers and consumers but expresses its care inside a moral framework that, despite the best of intentions, cannot help but to care little for their welfare. If we fail to recognize racism as it exists in our social institutions, then there can be no hope of recognizing it within ourselves. Conversely, we must recognize racism within ourselves before we can begin the process of extricating it from our institutions. There is no question that I approach my subject from a particular stance. I have a mission to work towards the eradication of institutionalized racism, and I hope to see the demise of, among other things, mandatory high-stakes testing. I hope I have shown however, that my stake in this runs even deeper than political, social, or educational analysis alone. I acknowledge my personal investment in understanding how my own loved ones, and even I myself, might perpetuate that to which I am utterly opposed.

Notes

Chapter 1   Ideology, Tools, and Perspective

1. Throughout this book I refer to the United States of America by the shorter "America" for the following reason: My argument goes to the very core of identity in this country and citizens of the United States generally identify as "Americans" rather than some more complicated moniker. The construct of the identity American, I argue, is fundamentally formed by racial and class assumptions that have existed here since the first Europeans arrived on these shores.

2. For a complete treatment of the life and work of Galton see Derek William Forrest, *Francis Galton: The Life and Work of a Victorian Genius* (New York: Taplinger Pub. Co., 1974). as well as Mark Haller, *Eugenics: Hereditarian Attitudes in American Thought* (New York: Rutgers University Press, 1963), Daniel J. Kevles, *In the Name of Eugenics: Genetics and the Uses of Human Heredity* (Berkeley: University of California Press, 1985).

3. The Industrial Revolution is generally described as having occurred between 1760 and 1830 in England and between 1830 and 1900 in America. The term refers to the sharp increase in technology, particularly in textiles and manufacturing, the invention of the steam engine and a burgeoning worker class who filled the nation's factories. The Progressive movement in the 1920s and 1930s concerned itself in part with the plight of these workers and a number of reforms such as child labor laws, the implementation of an eight-hour work day, and various safety precautions resulted from their efforts. For further information on American history in general see Richard Hofstadter, *The Progressive Movement 1900–1915* (Englewood Cliffs, NJ: Prentice-Hall, 1963), Arthur Link and William B. Catton, *American Epoch: A History of the United States since the 1890s* (New York: Alfred A. Knopf, 1955), Howard Zinn, *A People's History of the United States* (New York: Harper Perennial, 1980). For further information about the role of Progressive activists see R. Hofstadter, *The Progressive Movement 1900–1915* (Englewood Cliffs, NJ: Prentice-Hall, 1963).

4. Social Darwinism was a philosophy popular in the late nineteenth century that sought to apply biological principles of survival and heredity to social problems.

5. Throughout this text, as throughout our history, references to the various "races" take many forms. While it is my preference to use the more geographically descriptive and non-color bound terms *European American, African American*, etc., I admit to having not fully reached a level of comfort with any of these terms. Therefore, for the most part I will use my preference. However, I reserve the right to occasionally include reference to white and black Americans whenever it seems that to do otherwise would detract from the spirit of what I am saying. Furthermore, although I regard the term *Negro* to be archaic and loaded, and would never use it myself, I will not include a [*sic*] whenever it appears in quotations. Were I to employ a standard that took to task every questionable use of words and grammar found throughout my data I fear the number of [*sic*]'s would tend to produce nausea. So then, only in the case of egregious grammatical errors will I employ [*sic*].

6. Many innovators worked on the developments of Intelligence Quotient (IQ) as a measure of intellectual capacity most notable among them Brigham, Stanford, Binet, and Terman. The IQ was said to measure intellectual age against chronological age. For a complete treatment of the history of testing in America see Nicholas Lemann, *The Big Test: The Secret History of the American Meritocracy* (New York: Farrar, Straus and Giroux, 1999).

Chapter 5   Eugenics: Content and Context

1. G. K. Chesterton was one of the most articulate and vocal critics of eugenics during the 1920s and 1930s. For contextual comments by editor Michael W. Perry and additional writings of the era see Chesterton, *Eugenics and Other Evils: An Argument Against the Scientifically Organized Society* (Seattle: Inkling Books, 1922/2000).

2. The stamp on the top of the document indicates that it was reproduced from the California Institute of Technology Archives. Other identifiers include the following header: "W23., USNC. 4M, MEDD., IPMEUZQF. (2nd Ed. 5M) (3rd Ed. 5M) (4th Ed. 4M) (5th Ed. 5M) (6th Ed. 4M)." The title is "Eugenics Pamphlets No. 16" followed by the sentence "Published occasionally by Eugenics Society of Northern California, Capitol National Bank Building, Sacramento, California, U. S. A." Hereafter this document will be referred to as CIT.

3. The Henry H. Laughlin collection is housed at the Pickler Memorial Library, Special Collections Department, Northeast Missouri State University, Kirksville, Missouri. The documents used here are from Section C, Shelf 2, Boxes 1–7, Section C, Shelf 4, Boxes 1–7. Documents from this collection will hereafter be referred to as HHL.

4. The American Philosophical Society documents, photos, and displays used here can be obtained from the online archival collection www.eugenicsarchive.org and will be hereafter referred to as APS.

Chapter 6   The Moral Solution

1. The Southern Historical Collection is housed at Wilson Library on the University of North Carolina Chapel Hill campus. Documents used here come exclusively from the collection identified as Human Betterment League of North Carolina and will hereafter be referred to as HBL-SHC.

2. One particularly poignant example of this is revealed in the Nell Battle Lewis papers found in the North Carolina State Archives. Lewis, a vivacious socialite, news columnist, and attorney took the case of a group of young women accused of burning down the institution in which they had been held involuntarily. Records of interviews with the young women, as well as hospital record show that many of them had been diagnosed "feebleminded" and were there because of "family issues," "insolence," and "running away." State Archives of North Carolina, S. Raleigh, NC.

3. Some American Philosophical Society documents were obtained from Alan Stoskopf. Hereafter, those documents will be referred to as APS-AS.

4. The State Archives of North Carolina contain a collection on eugenics that is two-fold. Public access to those documents that were published but the records produced by the Eugenics Board of North Carolina have been sealed because they contain names. For a discussion of the practice of sealing archival data concerning eugenics see Black (2003). The only person that I am aware of that was able to have access to the Eugenics Board data was Johanna Shoen which she used for her book cited in my references. That same data was used by the *Winston-Salem Journal* 2002 expose of eugenic practices in North Carolina. Hereafter, I will refer to documents retrieved from the State Archives of North Carolina as NCSA.

5. The Traveling Culture Series documents are available online through the Library of Congress. Source materials are housed at the University of Iowa libraries. According to the web site, "The digital collection presents 7,949 publicity brochures, promotional advertisements and talent circulars for some 4,546 performers who were part of the Chautauqua circuit. These talent brochures are drawn from the Records of the Redpath Lyceum Bureau, held by the University of Iowa Libraries. One of the largest booking agencies for the Chautauqua performers, the Redpath bureau managed a vast talent pool. Performers and lecturers were familiar names as popular entertainers or well known in the political, religious, and cultural worlds (http://memory.loc.gov/ammem/award98/iauhtml/tccchome.html)." These documents will hereafter be referred to as TCS-LOC. I will further identify individual documents by their Internet location tag line.

Chapter 7   Education—A New Frontier

1. See, for example, the writings of Galton, 1889, 1901, 1914; Thorndike 1903, 1931; Shannon, 1904/1915; Hall, 1906; Bobbitt, 1909; Pearson, 1909, 1919; Davenport, 1910, 1911, 1915; Davenport, Laughlin et al., 1911; Goddard, 1911, 1912, 1916,

1921; Hall, 1911; Grant, 1916; Stopes, 1918/1931; Stoddard, 1920, 1922; Sanger, 1922; Wiggam, 1924; Jefferis, 1925; Sumner, Keller et al., 1927; Davenport and Steggerda, 1929; Hollingworth, 1929; Bell, 1933; Holmes, 1936.

2. Documents from the State Archives of North Carolina fall in to three categories. As outlined in note 4, ch. 6 the eugenics data is restricted except for two files which were kept on the desk of the head archivist and not formally labeled. The other two primary sources are the Nell Battle Lewis Collection. Ms. Lewis was a columnist for the *Raleigh North Carolina News* and *Observer* and an attorney. Hereafter, documents from her collection will be referred to as NCSA-NBL. The other primary source are the Department of Public Instruction documents hereafter referred to as NCSA-DPI.

3. From the State Archives of North Carolina, Department of Public Instruction, Office of the Superintendent, Textbook Correspondence 1916–1921, Volume 1.

4. State Archives of North Carolina, Department of Public Instruction, Office of Superintendent, General Correspondence, January–March 1912, A–F, Box 8.

Chapter 8   Ability and Degeneracy in the Schools

1. State Archives of North Carolina, Department of Public Instruction, Office of the Superintendent, General Correspondence, January–March 1912, A–F, Box 8. Hereafter referred to as NCSA-DPI, n.d.

2. State Archives of North Carolina, Department of Public Instruction, Office of Superintendent, General Correspondence, 1934, N–T, Box 126, Folder: Public Opinion on Schools. Hereafter referred to as NCSA-DPI, 1934.

3. State Archives of North Carolina, Office of Superintendent, General Correspondence, 1935, A–G, Box 130, Folder: Education and Race Relations. Hereafter referred to as NCSA-DPI, 1035.

4. State Archives of North Carolina, Department of Public Instruction, Division of Publications, Mimeograph Materials, 1935, Volume 1, Volume 2, Volume 3. Hereafter referred to as NCSA-DPI, 1935v1 (2, or 3).

5. For a comprehensive history of the legal developments that led to the *Brown v. Board of Education* decision see R. Kluger, *Simple Justice: A History of "Brown v. Board of Education" and Black America's Struggle for Equality* (New York, Alfred A. Knopf., 1975).

6. State Archives of North Carolina, Nell Battle Lewis Collection, 1862: 1920–1056, Segregation, 1898: 1950–1956, Folder: Segregation. Hereafter referred to as NCSA-NBL, 1954.

7. As I have mentioned, this document is not paginated. For ease of reference I have assigned page numbers to the document.

8. The University of North Carolina numbers, based on the 1950 census, show that New Hanover County had a total of 63,272 students. Of those, 43,430 were white (68.6%) and 19,804 were African American (31.3%).

References

Books

Allen, Garland E., and Jeffrey J. W. Baker. *Biology: Scientific Process and Social Issues*. Bethesda, MD: Fitzgerald Science Press, 2001.

Apple, Michael. *Educating the "Right" Way*. New York: RoutledgeFalmer, 2001.

Bal, Mieke, Crewe, Jonathan, and Spitzer, Leo, ed. *Act of Memory: Cultural Recall in the Present*. Hanover: University Press of New England, 1999.

Baudrillard, Jean. *Simulacra and Simulation, the Body, in Theory*. Ann Arbor: University of Michigan Press, 1994.

Baudrillard, Jean, Paul Foss, and Julian Pefanis. *The Revenge of the Crystal: Selected Writings on the Modern Object and Its Destiny, 1968–1983*. London; Concord, Mass.: Pluto Press in association with the Power Institute of Fine Arts University of Sydney, 1990.

Bean, Robert Bennett M. D. *The Races of Man: Differentiation and Dispersal of Man*. New York: The University Society, 1932.

Becker, Carl L. *Everyman His Own Historian: Essays on History and Politics*. New York: Appleton-Century-Crofts, 1935.

Bell, Ralcy Halstead. *Some Aspects of Adultery*. New York: Eugenics Publishing Company, 1933.

Berger, Peter L., and Thomas Luckmann. *The Social Construction of Reality: A Treatise in the Sociology of Knowledge*. New York: Anchor Books, 1966.

Black, Edwin. *Ibm and the Holocaust: The Strategic Alliance between Nazi Germany and America's Most Powerful Corporation*. 1st ed. New York: Crown Publishers, 2001.

———. *War against the Weak: Eugenics and America's Campaign to Create a Master Race*. New York: Four Walls Eight Windows, 2003.

Blacker, C. P. *Eugenics: Galton and After*. London: Duckworth, 1952.

Bobbitt, John F. *The Curriculum*. Boston: Houghton Mifflin Company, 1918.

——. *How to Make a Curriculum*. Boston, New York etc.: Houghton Mifflin Company, 1924.

Bourdieu, Pierre, Calhoun, Craig J., LiPuma, Edward, and Postone, Moishe. *Bourdieu: Critical Perspectives*. Chicago: University of Chicago Press, 1993.

Brummett, B. *Rhetorical Dimensions of Popular Culture*. Tuscaloosa: University of Alabama Press, 1991.

California Institute of Technology Archives, CIT.

Callahan, Raymond E. *Education and the Cult of Efficiency: A Study of the Social Forces That Have Shaped the Administration of the Public Schools*. Chicago: The University of Chicago Press, 1962.

Carlson, Elof Axel. *The Unfit: A History of a Bad Idea*. Cold Spring Harbor: Cold Spring Harbor Laboratory Press, 2001.

Certeau, Michel de (1988). *The Writing of History*. New York: Columbia Press

Charters, W. W. *Curriculum Construction*. New York: The Macmillan Company, 1923.

Chase, Allan. *The Legacy of Malthus: The Social Costs of the New Scientific Racism*. New York: Alfred A. Knopf, 1975.

Chesterton, G. K. *Eugenics and Other Evils: An Argument against the Scientifically Organized Society*. Edited by Michael W. Perry. Seattle: Inkling Books, 1922/2000.

Coates, Albert, and Paul, James C. N. "A Report to the Governor of North Carolina on the Decision of the Supreme Court of the United States on the 17th of May, 1954." 206. Chapel Hill: Institute of Government, The University of North Carolina Chapel Hill, 1954.

Comte, Auguste. *A General View of Positivism*. London: Routledge and Sons, 1907.

Connerton, Paul. *How Societies Remember*. Edited by John Goody, Jack, Dunn; Eugene, Hammel; Geoffrey, Hawthorne, *Themes in the Social Sciences*. Cambridge: Cambridge University Press, 1989.

Coontz, Stephanie. *The Way We Never Were: American Families and the Nostalgia Trap*. New York: Basic Books, 1992.

Cremin, Lawrence A. *The Transformation of the School: Progressivism in American Education 1876–1957*. New York: Vintage Books, 1961.

——. *American Education, the Metropolitan Experience, 1876–1980*. 1st ed. New York: Harper & Row, 1988.

——. *The Genius of American Education, Horace Mann Lecture, 1965*. Pittsburgh: University of Pittsburgh Press, 1965.

——. *Popular Education and Its Discontents*. 1st ed. New York: Harper & Row, 1990.

Crotty, Michael. *The Foundations of Social Research: Meaning and Perspective in the Research Process*. London: Sage Publications, 1998.

Cubberley, Ellwood P. *Public Education in the United States: A Study and Interpretation of American Educational History*. Cambridge: Houghton Mifflin Company, 1934.

Curti, Merle. *The Social Ideas of American Educators*. Patterson, NJ: Pageant Books, Inc., 1935/1959.

Curtis, Bruce. *William Graham Sumner, Twayne's United States Authors Series; Tusas 391.* Boston: Twayne, 1981.

Darwin, Charles. *The Descent of Man.* London: John Murray, 1871.

Darwin, Erasmus. *Zoonomia, or, the Laws of Organic Life.* London: J. Johnson, 1801.

Daspit, Tony, and Weaver, John A., ed. *Popular Culture and Critical Pedagogy.* New York: Garland Publishing, 1999.

Davenport, Charles B. *Biographical Memoir.* Washington: Government Printing Office, 1926.

———. *The Biological Laboratory at Cold Spring Harbor, New York, U. S. A.* Leipzig: W. Klinkhardt, 1911.

———. *Eugenics.* n. p., 1910.

———. *The Feebly Inhibited.* New York: Cold Spring Harbor, 1915.

———. *Heredity in Relation to Eugenics.* New York: H. Holt and company, 1911.

Davenport, Charles B., Laughlin, Harry H., Weeks, David F., Johnstone, Edward R., and Goddard, Henry H., *The Study of Human Heredity.* New York: Cold Spring Harbor, 1911.

Degler, Carl N. *In Search of Human Nature: The Decline and Revival of Darwinism in American Social Thought.* New York: Oxford University Press, 1991.

Delbanco, Andrew. *The Puritan Ordeal.* Cambridge, Mass.: Harvard University Press, 1989.

———. *Writing New England: An Anthology from the Puritans to the Present.* Cambridge, Mass.: Belknap Press of Harvard University Press, 2001.

Dewey, John. *Experience and Education.* New York: Collier Books, 1936.

Eisner, Elliot. "Curriculum Ideologies." In *Handbook of Research on Curriculum,* Edited by Philip W. Jackson. New York: Macmillan Publishing Company, 1992.

Farber, Paul, Provenzo, Eugene F. Jr., and Holm, Gunilla, ed. *Schooling in the Light of Popular Culture.* New York: State University Press, 1994.

Forrest, Derek William. *Francis Galton: The Life and Work of a Victorian Genius.* New York: Taplinger Publishing Company, 1974.

Frank, Marc Henry. *Eugenics and Sex Relations for Men and Women.* New York: Books Inc., 1937.

Franklin, John Hope. *Race and History: Selected Essays 1938–1988.* Baton Rouge: Louisiana State University Press, 1989.

Fraser, Steven, ed. *The Bell Curve Wars: Race, Intelligence, and the Future of America.* New York: Basic Books, 1995.

Freeden, Michael (2003). *Ideology: A Very Short Introduction.* Oxford; New York: Oxford University Press

Galton, Francis. *Essays in Eugenics.* Washington DC: Scott-Townsend Publishers, 1909/1996.

———. *Hereditary Genius: An Inquiry into Its Laws and Consequences.* London: Macmillan, 1914.

———. *Natural Inheritance.* New York: AMS Press, 1889.

———. "The Possible Improvement of the Human Breed under the Existing Conditions of Law and Sentiment." *Nature* 64, no. 1670 (1901): 659–65.

Geertz, Clifford. *The Interpretation of Cultures*. New York: Basic Books, 1973.

Goddard, Henry H. *The Criminal Imbecile*. New York: The Macmillan Company, 1915.

——. *Feeble-Mindedness; Its Causes and Consequences, New Jersey Training School for Feeble-Minded Girls and Boys Vineland. [from Old Catalog]*. New York: The Macmillan Company, 1914.

——. *Heredity of Feeble-Mindedness*. New York: Cold Spring Harbor: 1911.

——. *Juvenile Delinquency*. New York: Dodd Mead & Company, 1921.

——. *The Kallikak Family: A Study in the Heredity of Feeblemindedness*. New York: Macmillan, 1912.

——. *Mental Deficiency from the Standpoint of Heredity*. Boston: Massachusetts Society for Mental Hygiene, 1916.

Gould, Steven Jay. *The Mismeasure of Man*. New York: W.W. Norton & Company, 1996.

Graham, Robert J. (1991). *Reading and Writing the Self: Autobiography in Education and the Curriculum*. New York: Teachers College, Columbia University.

Grant, Madison. *The Passing of the Great Race; or, the Racial Basis of European History*. New York: Charles Scribner & Sons, 1916.

Halbwachs, Maurice. *On Collective Memory*. Translated by Lewis A. Coser. Edited by Donald N. Levine, *The Heritage of Sociology*. Chicago: University of Chicago Press, 1952/1992.

Hall, G. Stanley. *Educational Problems*. New York, London: D. Appleton and Company, 1911.

——. *Life and Confessions of a Psychologist*. New York, London: D. Appleton and Company, 1923.

——. *Youth; Its Education, Regimen, and Hygiene*. New York: D. Appleton and Company, 1906.

Hall, G. Stanley, and Theodate L. Smith. *Aspects of Child Life and Education*. Boston: Ginn, 1907.

Haller, Mark. *Eugenics: Hereditarian Attitudes in American Thought*. New York: Rutgers University Press, 1963.

Hasian, Jr., Marouf Arif. *The Rhetoric of Eugenics in Anglo-American Thought*. Athens: University of Georgia Press, 1996.

Hofstadter, Richard. *The Progressive Movement 1900–1915*. Englewood Cliffs, NJ: Prentice-Hall, 1963.

——. *Social Darwinism in American Thought 1860–1915*. Philadelphia: University of Pennsylvania Press, 1944.

Hollingworth, Leta. *Functional Periodicity*. New York: Teachers College Columbia University, 1914.

Holmes, S.J. *Human Genetics and Its Social Import*. New York: McGraw-Hill Book Company, Inc., 1936.

Hooten, Earnest Albert. *Apes, Men, and Morons*. New York: G.P. Putnam's Sons, 1937.

——. *Crime and the Man*. Cambridge, Mass.: Harvard University Press, 1939.

Hutton, Patrick H. (1993). *History as an Art of Memory*. Hanover, NH: University Press of New England.

Kellner, D. *Media Culture: Cultural Studies, Identity and Politics between the Modern and the Postmodern.* London: Routledge, 1995.

Kevles, Daniel J. *In the Name of Eugenics: Genetics and the Uses of Human Heredity.* Berkeley: University of California Press, 1985.

Kliebard, Herbert M. *The Struggle for the American Curriculum 1893–1958.* 2nd ed. New York: Routledge, 1986/1995.

Kluger, Richard. *Simple Justice: A History of "Brown V. Board of Education" and Black America's Struggle for Equality.* New York: Alfred A. Knopf, 1975.

Lemann, Nicholas. *The Big Test: The Secret History of the American Meritocracy.* New York: Farrar, Straus and Giroux, 1999.

Link, Arthur, and Catton, William B. *American Epoch: A History of the United States since the 1890s.* New York: Alfred A. Knopf, 1955.

Low, W. Augustus, and Clift. Virgil A. *Encyclopedia of Black America.* New York: Da Capo Press, 1984.

Lowenthal, David. *The Past Is a Foreign Country.* Cambridge: Cambridge University Press, 1985.

———. *Possessed by the Past: The Heritage Crusade and the Spoils of History.* New York: The Free Press, 1996.

Ludmerer, Kenneth M. *Genetics and American Society: A Historical Appraisal.* Baltimore: Johns Hopkins University Press, 1972.

Lynn, Richard. (2001). *Eugenics: A Reassessment.* Westport, Conn: Praeger.

Macedo, Stephen. *Diversity and Mistrust: Civic Education in a Multicultural Society.* Cambridge, MA: Harvard University Press, 2000.

McCarthy, Cameron and Crichlow, Warren, ed. *Race Identity and Representation in Education.* New York: Routledge, 1993.

McKnight, Douglas. *Schooling, the Puritan Imperative, and the Molding of an American National Identity: Education's "Errand into the Wilderness."* Edited by William F. Pinar, *Studies in Curriculum Theory.* Mahwah, NJ: Lawrence Erlbaum Associates, 2003.

Montague, Ashley. *Man's Most Dangerous Myth.* New York: Oxford University Press, 1974.

Morris, Marla. *Curriculum and the Holocaust: Competing Sites of Memory and Representation.* Edited by William F. Pinar, *Studies in Curriculum Theory.* Mahwah, NJ: Lawrence Erlbaum Associates, 2003.

Numbers, Ronald L., and Stenhouse, John. *Disseminating Darwinism: The Role of Place, Race, Religion, and Gender.* Cambridge: Cambridge University Press, 1999.

Ordover, Nancy, American eugenics: race, queer anatomy, and the science of nationalism. Minneapolis, University of Minnesota Press, 2003.

Osofsky, Gilbert ed. *The Burden of Race: A Documentary History of Negro–White Relations in America.* New York: Harper and Row, 1967.

Paul, Diane B. *The Politics of Heredity: Essays on Eugenics, Biomedicine, and the Nature-Nurture Debate.* Edited by David Edward Shaner, *Philosophy and Biology.* Albany: State University of New York Press, 1998.

Pearson, Karl. *Francis Galton, 1822–1922; a Centenary Appreciation*. London: Cambridge University Press, 1922.

——. *The Groundwork of Eugenics*. London: Dulau and Co., 1909.

——. *The Life, Letters and Labours of Francis Galton*. Cambridge, Eng.: University Press, 1914.

——. *National Life from the Standpoint of Science; an Address Delivered at Newcastle, November 19, 1900*. London: A. and C. Black, 1901.

——. *Treasury of Human Inheritance*. London: Dulau, 1909.

Pearson, Karl, Napeolen, Louis, Filon, George, Alice Elizabeth, Lee, and Leslie. Bramley-Moore, *Contributions to the Mathematical Theory of Evolution*. London,: K. Paul Trench Trèubner and Co., 1894.

Phillips, Mark S. *History, Memory, and Historical Distance*. Edited by Peter, Seixas. *Theorizing Historical Consciousness*. Toronto: University of Toronto Press, 2004.

Pickens, Donald. *Eugenics and the Progressives*. Nashville, TN: Vanderbilt University Press, 1968.

Pinar, William F., Reynolds, William M., Slattery, Patrick, and Taubman, Peter M. *Understanding Curriculum: An Introduction to the Study of Historical and Contemporary Curriculum Discourses*. Edited by Joe L. Kincheloe and Shirley R. Steinberg Vol. 17, *Studies in the Postmodern Theory of Education*. New York: Peter Lang, 1995.

Popenoe, Paul, and Johnson, Roswell Hill. *Applied Eugenics*. New York: The Macmillan Company, 1918.

Prown, Jules David. *Art as Evidence: Writings on Art and Material Culture*. New Haven: Yale University Press, 2001.

Prown, Jules David, and Haltman, Kenneth. *American Artifacts: Essays in Material Culture*. East Lansing: Michigan State University Press, 2000.

Rabinow, Paul. *Essays on the Anthropology of Reason*. Edited by B. Sherry, Dirks Ortner, B. Nicholas, and Geoff, Eley, *Princeton Studies in Culture/Power/History*. Princeton: Princeton University Press, 1996.

Roberts-Miller, Patricia. *Voices in the Wilderness: Public Discourse and the Paradox of Puritan Rhetoric*. Tuscaloosa: University of Alabama Press, 1999.

Robinson, William J. *Birth Control or the Limitation of Offspring*. New York: Eugenics Publishing Company, 1916.

Saleeby, C. W. *The Progress of Eugenics*. New York, London: Funk & Wagnalls Company, 1914.

Sanger, Margaret. *The Pivot of Civilization*. New York: Brentanos, 1922.

Scheinfeld, Aram. *You and Heredity*. New York: Frederick A. Stokes Company, 1939.

Schlereth, Thomas J. *Artifacts and the American Past*. Nashville: American Association for State and Local History, 1980.

Schlereth, Thomas J., and American Association for State and Local History. *Material Culture Studies in America, American Association for State and Local History Book Series*. Walnut Creek, Calif.: AltaMira Press, 1999.

Seixas, Peter, ed. *Theorizing Historical Consciousness*. Toronto: University of Toronto Press, 2004.

Selden, Steven. *Inheriting Shame: The Story of Eugenics and Racism in America.* Edited by Jonas F. Soltis. Vol. 23, *Advances in Contemporary Educational Thought.* New York: Teachers College Press, 1999.

Shannon, T. W., and Truitt, W. J. *Eugenics: Scientific Knowledge of the Laws of Sex Life and Heredity.* Marietta, Ohio: S.A. Mullikin Company, 1904/1915.

Simon, Roger J., Rosenburg, Sharon, and Eppert, Claudia, ed. *Between Hope and Despair: Pedagogy and the Remembrance of Historical Trauma.* Edited by Henry A. Giroux and Joe L., Kincheloe. *Culture and Education Series.* Lanham, Boulder, New York, Oxford: Rowman & Littlefield, 2000.

Sinclair, Samuel, and Tracy, Frederick. *Introductory Educational Psychology: A Book for Teachers in Training.* Toronto: The Macmillan Company of Canada, 1912.

Smith, David G. (2003) *Teaching in Global Times.* Edmonton, Alberta: Pedagon Press.

Starr, Harris E. *William Graham Sumner.* New York: H. Holt and Company, 1925.

Stoddard, Lothrop. *The Revolt against Civilization: The Menace of the Underman.* New York: Scribners, 1922.

———. *The Rising Tide of Color: Against White World Supremacy.* New York: Charles Scribner's Sons, 1920.

Stone, Marie Kirchner. "Ralph W. Tyler's Principles of Curriculum, Instruction and Evaluation: Past Influences and Present Effects." Book, Loyola University of Chicago, 1985.

Stopes, Marie Carmichael. *Married Love.* New York: Eugenics Publishing Company, 1918/1931.

Stoskopf, Alan. *The Forgotten History of Eugenics* Rethinking Schools Online, 1999 [cited 2/23/02 2002]. Available from www.rethinkingschools.org/Archives/13_03/eugenics.htm.

Strinati, Dominic. *An Introduction to Theories of Popular Culture.* New York: Routledge, 1995.

Sturken, Marita. *Tangled Memories: The Vietnam War, the Aids Epidemic, and the Politics of Remembering.* Berkeley: University of California Press, 1997.

Sumner, William Graham. *Social Darwinism; Selected Essays.* Englewood Cliffs, NJ,: Prentice-Hall, 1963.

Sumner, William Graham, and Albert Galloway Keller. *The Challenge of Facts, and Other Essays.* New Haven: Yale University Press, 1914.

Sumner, William Graham, Keller, Albert Galloway, Davie, Maurice R., William Graham Sumner Club, and Philip Hamilton McMillan Memorial Publication Fund. *The Science of Society.* New Haven, London: Yale University Press; H. Milford Oxford University Press, 1927.

Thorndike, Edward L. *Educational Psychology.* New York: Lemcke and Buechner, 1903.

———. *Educational Psychology.* 2nd ed. New York: Teachers college Columbia University, 1910.

———. *The Elimination of Pupils from School.* Washington,: Government Print Office, 1908.

———. *Heredity, Correlation and Sex Differences in School Abilities; Studies from the Department of Educational Psychology at Teachers College, Columbia University.* New York: Macmillan, 1903.

———. *Human Learning*. New York, London: The Century Co., 1931.

———. *Thorndike Intelligence Examination for High School Graduates; Instructions for Giving, Scoring and Interpreting Scores*. New York: Bureau of Publications Teachers College Columbia University, 1924.

Thorndike, Edward L., and Columbia University Teachers College. Institute of Psychological Research. *The Measurement of Intelligence*. New York: Bureau of Publications Teacher's College Columbia University, 1927.

Thorndike, Edward L., and Arthur Irving Gates. *Elementary Principles of Education*. New York: The Macmillan Company, 1929.

Tucker, William H. *The Science and Politics of Racial Research*. Urbana: University of Illinois Press, 1994.

Tyack, David B. *The One Best System: A History of American Urban Education*. Cambridge, Mass.: Harvard University Press, 1974.

Tyack, David B. and Hansot, Elisabeth. *Managers of Virtue: Public School Leadership in America, 1820–1890*: Basic Books, 1982.

Tyler, Ralph W. *Basic Principles of Curriculum and Instruction*. Chicago: The University of Chicago Press, 1949.

White, Dana F. *The Urbanists, 1865–1915*. Edited by Robert H. Walker, *Contributions in American Studies*. New York: Greenwood Press, 1989.

Wiggam, Albert Edward. *The Fruit of the Family Tree*. Indianapolis: The Bobbs-Merrill Company Publishers, 1924.

Zerubavel, Eviatar. (2003) *Time Maps: Collective Memory and the Social Shape of the Past*. Chicago, Ill.: University of Chicago Press.

Zinn, Howard. *A People's History of the United States*. New York: Harper Perennial, 1980.

Book Chapters

Apple, Michael. "Is There a Curriculum Voice to Reclaim?" In *The Curriculum Studies Reader*, edited by J. David Flinders and Stephen J. Thornton, 342-49. New York: Routledge, 1997.

Eisner, Elliot. "Educational Objectives—Help or Hindrance?" In *The Curriculum Studies Reader*, edited by David J. Flinders and Stephen J. Thornton, 69–75. New York: Routledge, 1997.

Dillabough, Jo-Anne. "Degrees of Freedom and Deliberations of "Self": The Gendering of Identity in Teaching." In *Revolutionary Pedagogies: Cultural Politics, Instituting Education, and the Discourse of Theory*, edited by Peter Pericles Trifonas, 312–51. New York: RoutledgeFalmer, 2000.

Frisch, Michael H. "American History and the Structures of Collective Memory: A Modest Exercise in Empirical Iconography." In *Memory and History: Essays on Recalling and*

Interpreting Experience, edited by Jaclyn Jeffrey and Glenace Edwall Lanham: University Press of America, Inc., 1994.

Kliebard, Herbert M. "The Rise of Scientific Curriculum Making and Its Aftermath." In *The Curriculum Studies Reader*, edited by David J. Flinders and Stephen J. Thornton, 31–44. New York: Routledge, 1975/1997.

Laughlin, H. "Model Eugenical Sterilization Law." In *Eugenics Then and Now*, edited by Carl Jay Bajema. Stroudsburg, Pennsylvania: Dowden, Hutchinson & Ross, Inc., 1922.

Popkewitz, Thomas. "The Production of Reason and Power: Curriculum History and Intellectual Traditions." In *Cultural History and Education: Critical Essays on Knowledge and Schooling*, edited by Thomas S. Popkewitz, Barry M. Franklin, and Miguel A. Pereyra, 151–83. New York: Routledge Falmer, 2001.

Journal Articles

Bix, Amy Sue. "Experiences and Voices of Eugenics Field-Workers: 'Women's Work' in Biology." *Social Studies of Science* 27, no. 4 (1997): 625–68.

Bobbitt, John F. "Practical Eugenics." *Pedagogical Seminary* (1909): 385–94.

Call, San Francisco. "The White Man's Burden." *The San Francisco Call*, February 7, 1899.

Dewey, John. "Mediocrity and Individuality." *The New Republic*, no. December 6, 1922, 35–37.

Gould, Steven Jay. "Carrie Buck's Daughter." *Natural History* 93, no. 17 (1984).

Hollingworth, Leta. "The Production of Gifted Children from the Parental Point of View." *Eugenics* II, no. 10 (1929): 3–7.

Keller, Diana. "The Text of Educational Ideologies: Toward the Characterization of a Genre." *Educational Theory* 44, no. 1 (1994): 27–42.

Lanzar-Carpio, Maria. "The Anti-Imperialist League." *Philippine Social Science Review* 3 (1930).

Loeb, Joseph. "Motives of Municipalization." *Municipality* 1, no. 2 (1900): 28–29.

Nora, Pierre. "Between Memory and History: Lex Lieux De Memoire." *Representations* 0, no. 26 (1989): 7–24.

Spencer, Herbert. "Progress: Its Law and Causes." *Westminster Review* 67, no. April (1857): 445–65.

Court Cases

Brown V. Board of Education, 347 U.S. 483 (1954).

Buck V. Bell, 274 United States Reporter 200 (1927).

Archival Resources

American Philosophical Society (APS)

California Institute of Technology Archives (CIT)

Harry H. Laughlin Archives, Truman State University, Lantern Slides, Black Case, Section 7, 1708. "Relative Social Inadequacy of the Several Nativity Groups and Immigrant Groups of the U.S.: Crime, Dependency." www.eugenicarchives.org, circa 1921.

Harry H. Laughlin Collection Northeast Missouri State University (HHC) Pickler Memorial Library, Special Collections Department.

North Carolina State Archives Raleigh, North Carolina (NCSA) NCSA-DPI North Carolina Department of Public Instruction Papers NCSA-NBL Nell Battle Lewis Papers

Southern Historical Collection University of North Carolina-Chapel Hill (SHC) SHC-HBL Papers of the Human Betterment League of North Carolina.

Online Resources

Allen, Garland E. *Social Origins of Eugenics* [Web site]. Dolan DNA Learning Center, 2000 [cited 2/5/02 2002]. Available from http://www.eugenicsarchive.org/eugenics/.

American Philosophical Society. www.eugenicarchives.org Dolan DNA Learning Center.

Darwin, Charles. *The Voyage of the Beagle* Project Gutenburg, 1845 [cited February 6 2004]. Available from http://www.literature.org/authors/darwin-charles/the-voyage-of-the-beagle/index.html.

Kipling, Rudyard. *The White Man's Burden* Jim Zwick: "The White Man's Burden" and Its Critics in Anti-Imperialism in the United States, 1898-1935, 1899 [cited 2004]. Available from http://www.boondocksnet.com/ai/kipling/.

Tillman, Benjamin. "Are We to Spread the Christian Religion with the Bayonet Point as Mahomet Spread Islam with a Scimitar?" In *Republic or Empire? The Phillipine Question*, edited by William Jennings Bryan, et al. Chicago: The Independence Co., 1899. Reprint, http://www.boondocksnet.com/ai/kipling/ In Jim Zwick, ed., Anti-Imperialism in the United States, 1898–1935. http://www.boondocksnet.com/ai/ (February 11, 2004).

Traveling Culture Series, Library of Congress. "University of Iowa Libraries." http://memory.loc.gov/ammem/award98/iauhtml/tcchome.html.

Zwick, Jim, ed. *"The White Man's Burden" and Its Critics in Anti-Imperialism in the United States, 1898–1935.* 1995 [cited February 5, 2004]. Available from http://www.boondocksnet.com/ai/kipling/.

Books and Theses

Marks, Russell. "Testers, Trackers, and Trustees: The Ideology of the Intelligence Testing Movement in America 1900–1954." Book, University of Illinois at Urbana-Champaign, 1972.

Schoen, Johanna. " "A Great Thing for Poor Folks": Birth Control, Sterilization, and Abortion in Public Health and Welfare in the Twentieth Century." Book, University of North Carolina at Chapel Hill, 1995,

Winfield, Ann Gibson. "Cultural Resistance, Change and Continuity among the Hopi." Theses, University of California—Santa Cruz, 1988.

Index

OMPLICATED

A BOOK SERIES OF CURRICULUM STUDIES

Reframing the curricular challenge educators face after a decade of school deform, the books published in Peter Lang's Complicated Conversation Series testify to the ethical demands of our time, our place, our profession. What does it mean for us to teach now, in an era structured by political polarization, economic destabilization, and the prospect of climate catastrophe? Each of the books in the Complicated Conversation Series provides provocative paths, theoretical and practical, to a very different future. In this resounding series of scholarly and pedagogical interventions into the nightmare that is the present, we hear once again the sound of silence breaking, supporting us to rearticulate our pedagogical convictions in this time of terrorism, reframing curriculum as committed to the complicated conversation that is intercultural communication, self-understanding, and global justice.

The series editor is

Dr. William F. Pinar
Department of Curriculum Studies
2125 Main Mall
Faculty of Education
University of British Columbia
Vancouver, British Columbia V6T 1Z4
CANADA

To order other books in this series, please contact our Customer Service Department:

(800) 770-LANG (within the U.S.)
(212) 647-7706 (outside the U.S.)
(212) 647-7707 FAX

Or browse online by series:

www.peterlang.com